RETURN TO BASE

Memoirs of a B-17 Co-pilot
Kimbolton, England, 1943-1944

RETURN TO BASE

Memoirs of a B-17 Co-pilot
Kimbolton, England, 1943-1944

JESSE RICHARD PITTS

First published 2004
Howell Press, Charlottesville, Virginia, USA

This edition 2006

Tempus Publishing Limited
The Mill, Brimscombe Port,
Stroud, Gloucestershire, GL5 2QG
www.tempus-publishing.com

British Library Cataloguing in Publication Data.
A catalogue record for this book is available from the British Library.

ISBN 0 7524 4025 X
978 0 7524 4025 5

Typesetting and origination by Tempus Publishing Limited
Printed and bound in Great Britain

CONTENTS

FOREWORD

In the winter of 1943–44, Jesse Pitts and I flew together as pilot and copilot for twenty-five missions. During approximately 260 hours, his actions as copilot were a determining factor in our survival. Decisions had to be made in seconds and had to be very correct. For every second flown, our lives depended upon each other.

He was recognized by his peers as a very 'eager beaver'. We were trained for lead crew in anticipation of D-Day, and it was Jesse's idea that we should use extra space in the ship's radio room to increase our bomb load when we went over the targets. We discussed many times what would happen in the event we had to parachute out over France or Germany. His speaking French would greatly assist in our escape and, speaking for myself, this is one pilot who would have been right on his coattails. Toward the end of his tour, Jesse encouraged the crew to consider flying an extra twenty-five missions with him as pilot.

Like everyone, Jesse made some errors, but it was our good fortune that there were no problems. On more than one occasion, his quick actions saved our lives and the lives of our eight other crew members. What do you say about someone like that? It was a pleasure to have this outstanding copilot to put his life on the line with me.

Thank God for this great favor.

Lt. Col. Hershell Streit

To the crew of *Penny Ante*

ACKNOWLEDGMENTS

Throughout the writing of this book, I have been often encouraged by my friend William Barrett, copilot in my squadron at Kimbolton. He read every word, made helpful remarks and corrections, and remembered details I had forgotten. It is my great regret that Bill passed away before I could send him the finished manuscript. He remained a friend to the end.

I am also indebted to Hershell Streit, our 'naturally brave' pilot, who discussed with me some finer points of the missions we flew together, side by side. I am particularly grateful to him for giving me the chance to fly the *Penny Ante* so often.

I consulted many times the computerized database for the 379th, created by Arlo Bartsh. This was an invaluable assistance to me in checking names, missions, and who was doing what and when. He graciously authorized reproducing parts of this data.

Many thanks to Frank Betz, John Sanda, and Robert Watkins of the 379th Bombardment Group (H) WWII Association, who provided me with countless documents, mission reports, and statistics.

Thanks also to the Turner Publishing Company and the 379th Bombardment Group (H) WWII Association for allowing me to reproduce several photographs from the 379th *Anthology*.

I am deeply grateful to my son Christopher. He not only wrote the 'Introduction' but spent time scanning and printing about thirty photographs from my personal album. I am also grateful to my daughter Florence for her advice about style and structure.

Elizabeth Porter has been an enthusiastic editor, who put some order in an otherwise chaotic manuscript. She consulted me many times on passages that were not clear, and it is thanks to her that many mistakes have been avoided.

My wife, Monique, deserves very special thanks for her relentless help in preparing the manuscript, for reading my handwriting and typing it to computer, for discussing passages where I was carried away by imagination, and, most of all, for her tireless efforts in seeing this book come to light.

Jesse Richard Pitts

INTRODUCTION

I was privy to reading early drafts of *Return to Base*, and in doing so, I was taken aback at how little I knew about this segment of my father's life. And I realized that if this book had been merely a 'we bombed this, then we bombed that, narrowly escaped this, etc.' recitation, rather than the more personal point of view it offers, I would have never seen the connections between the father I grew up with, and the young man of 1943–44 serving aboard the Flying Fortress of the Second World War, and I would never have learned the source of my father's American patriotism.

While I feel this book is a real gift to me for the personal discoveries, I also believe it is a gift to all of us. It comes at a time when we need answers about our future, when together we are looking for ways to get things back on track. And it is applicable because it is about ordinary people placed into extraordinary circumstances. *How*, we wonder, *would we behave under life and death situations?* In war, men and women have the chance to find out rather quickly what they are made of. Will one suddenly freeze under duress and perhaps cost others their lives, or will one rise to the occasion, meet the challenge, and behave with honor and with grace? In peacetime, however, one can live an entire life without getting a real answer.

While I knew my father had been a B-17 copilot, he did not speak much about his exploits during the Second World War. For me, the war was an event recounted in films and on television, but the courage required by my father was not something that I in my youth could grasp.

I'm not sure at what age courage becomes tangible, but I began having inklings of it from several memorable events with my father. From them I learned not only about courage, but more importantly, I learned something about my father, about the kind of man he is. And I relate these incidents here because, in the end, you too will see as I now see how my father's character, built by a time of war, translated into times of peace.

Dad was not much of a sports fan, and the only sport he ever engaged in was sailing. This he did with gusto. I spent quite a few summers sailing with him in various sloops up and down the coast of France.

In the Mediterranean, there is a well-known phenomenon called *le mistral*, which is a cold wind that can blow up very quickly, gusting sixty miles an hour or more and which can trap unprepared sailors with disastrous results.

My father and I, along with a student, had embarked for a night sail. I was all of nine years old at this time, and as things got rough, it was up to them to handle the boat. Sure enough, *le mistral* decided to drop in, and we soon found ourselves in some nasty seas around the Cap de Creus, known for some bad shoals, in full darkness. It started to rain pretty hard, and I remember cowering inside the boat with only the view of my father at the helm, a soaked towel around his neck, peeking from his foul-weather gear, while he and the student shouted back and forth as they tried to make our way to harbor. I knew from the bits of conversation I could hear that this was not a good situation, and yet my father never let fear show on his face. He did what a captain is supposed to do: keep his wits no matter how bad the situation.

A couple of years later, my father at the tiller, we were running the with the wind from the Bahamas back to Florida after Hurricane Camille had been through. We were 'bare poles' – meaning no sails – the wind being strong enough against the mast of the boat to bring us to full speed. It was daylight, and I watched the horizon change from gray skies to nothing but water as the boat rode up and down the large seas. When each wave lifted up the stern, the boat would pick up speed as it began the descent down the watery slope. Eventually the wave would overtake the boat, allowing us to slowly ride down the other side, then the whole process would start over again.

This time I could see concern on my father's face as he scanned the following seas for waves large enough to cause the boat to broach. If a wave was too large, the boat could surf down till it could go no faster then either lose control and turn sideways to be engulfed by the waves usually flipping over and demasting, or more dramatically, it could go end over end. In any case, a lot of damage can happen, and people can get hurt. When a large wave was spotted, we would turn around and ride over it, crashing down as we crested the top. While we made the 100-mile crossing, the danger of broaching was constant and wearing, but my father kept his 'stiff upper lip' which, of course, helped everyone else, my brother and my mother, keep their wits.

In reading those first drafts and thinking about the events in my life that showed me something about the man who wrote this book, there was a night I awoke remembering an incident that was handled so subtly that it could easily have been forgotten. While I was staying in Nice, the French coastal town bordering Italy, with my grandmother, I developed a fascination for Jacques Cousteau and underwater exploration. I was given the opportunity to learn how to scuba dive and went out dozens of times with a local diving boat.

One morning, my father decided he wanted to come along, and he was given a crash course in diving. Geared up for his maiden dive, my father must have felt some of the same excitement and apprehension everyone does on their first dive.

Any diver will tell you that little mistakes can cost a life, and unfortunately, the divers had misjudged how much lead my father needed, and plunging into the water, he found himself rapidly descending into the depths – far too rapidly. Two divers launched themselves after him and brought him back to the surface. Now, my father, rather than being justifiably angry, frightened, or overwhelmed, was actually more concerned about the possibility of having embarrassed me in some way.

It may be possible that the examples I cite really have nothing to do with my father's war years, but to come to that conclusion would require me to dismiss all the events that transpired during his young adulthood He handled these situations with such cool that, in retrospect, I suspect his war experiences must have played a part in his ability to deal with such circumstances. Not only can I not dismiss these events, but I would go one step further and suggest these pages offer a deeper understanding of all those individuals who endured and survived the astonishing elements of that war. And that is truly a gift.

Christopher Bonnier Pitts

1. Jesse Pitts, cadet training, after graduation, June 1943.

EVE OF BATTLE

Here I am,
Spreadeagled on the rocks of fear,
A man, promised to the sky.
Tomorrow
Sweet tomorrow, smile of women tomorrow,
Tomorrow of dew, of tulip closed, of rooster cry,
Of manly shake, of breath exhaled, of voices in the room.

I make myself heavy to the push of time,
Somewhere in Germany they plot my destruction.
I, the murderer,
Spreadeagled on the rocks of fear.

Tomorrow my men will break my bonds and I will fly
With them
Into the wall of fate.

Tomorrow: a door that opens so slowly
Into the dark.

Jesse Richard Pitts
Kimbolton, 1943

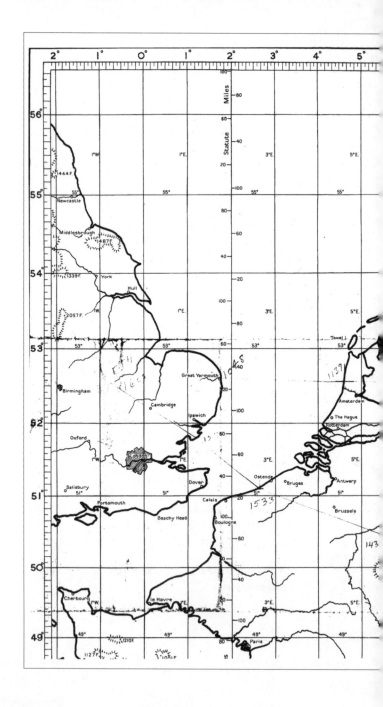

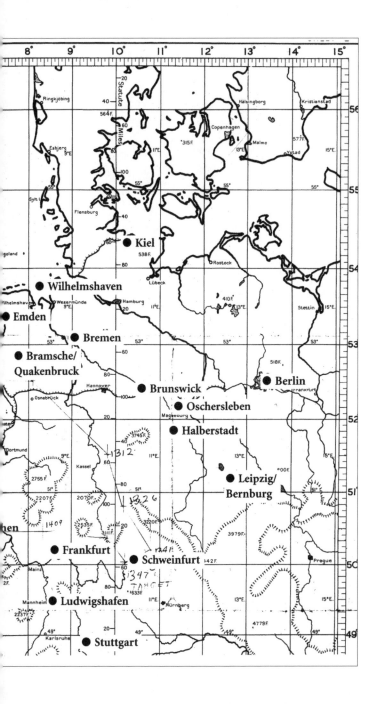

1

THE 'NIGHT BEFORE'

IT'S NOT SO MUCH THE MISSION AS THE NIGHT BEFORE

Leave was over, and we all stumbled off the last train from London onto the platform at the Bedford station where trucks waited to take us back to our airbase in Kimbolton. We loaded in the dark, some with folding baggage, some with musette bags full of dirty linen, soap, toothbrushes, and unopened chocolate bars.

We sat silent in the trucks, even those who recognized each other, each of us lost in his own thoughts, all of us trying to prolong the leave through daydreaming. Back to the grind, my second month of operations, and we were already thinking about the next pass, normally three weeks away. If we were not shot down first.

Some lit up, and in the dark, the red dots of their cigarettes punctuated our unspoken reveries.

My own were of the hotel in London, of a warm room, of warm sheets and a good bed, and the woman with whom I had spent the previous night. She was a Red Cross girl and prettier than the ones stationed at Kimbolton. She had been sitting alone at the club near St James Court, apparently waiting for someone. That someone was not, to my surprise, making an appearance, and when she gave signs of having given up on him, I made my move. We bantered for an hour over gin and tonic, about the colleges from which we had graduated, the places in Manhattan we knew (*You know the Amanda? You know the Maisonnette? You know so-and-so?*). I gathered from her questions that, though she may have been stood up, she was not about to end the evening with a social inferior.

I passed this initial social confrontation okay, and afterwards we wound up in my hotel room (some lie about having to wait there for a phone call from base). We gave each other, for that night, whatever the other needed, but I could not give her any chance for a relationship. Tonight, on my way back to the base, I thought of her. I had not even asked her for a telephone number. To tell the truth, though the memory of the night was pleasant, I felt a bit of a cad.

When we arrived at the base, the driver of the truck lowered the gate, and we jumped to the ground, splashing the mud with our boots. The mud. We were back home all right! I set out on the long walk to my squadron's barracks at a far end of the field.

I was back; the pass was over. It was like the feelings I had when, at the age of twelve or thirteen, I returned on Sunday nights to the French *lycée* where I was a boarder, coming back from weekends with my French mother. Divorced and hard-working, she was rarely able to visit me at school. Classmates who had seen her said she was pretty and looked young enough to be my sister. Riding in the subway on the way back to school, half my mind would be basking in thoughts of the weekend, now over, while the other half would be mobilizing for the week to come: dodging the *pions*, or proctors; enduring the math classes; doing the homework, always at the last minute; hunting down the one friend with whom I argued French politics and the other friend with whom I exchanged fantasies about planes, ships, and gangsters. (Having an American father, I was granted expertise in these matters.)

But it was still essentially a lonely week without my mother, and I thought about her now as I walked, hands in the pockets of my coat, and my boots making 'pfuee pfuee' in the thin layer of mud that covered the road.

I kept on walking, more slowly, towards the barracks. As they loomed into view, I had two questions on my mind: were we alerted for tomorrow, and was there any mail?

As far as the alert was concerned, I could have asked any of the personnel whom I passed. In my early days in the squadron, I was eager to go out on missions. I looked forward to being alerted, rather than 'stood down.' No more. Now when the alerts came, they softened my insides, reminding me of my vulnerability, and I would have to toughen myself to get ready for tomorrow's ordeal. I did not wish anymore for an alert, and I delayed finding out about it. I preferred to be informed by friends or even by our operations officer, Brownlow.

The more danger we had incurred in previous raids, the more fragile we felt. Frazer, our lead group bombardier, had lived through a lot and when an alert came, he would get drunk and try to start brawls with whoever crossed him. When nobody would fight with him, Frazer would once more feel omnipotent. Once in a while he would get a bloody nose out of his challenges to the whole world, but he kept on flying the missions.

Remained the mail. A day with mail had more consistency, more density. I used to do a lot of letter writing when I first came to the squadron, partly to entice replies. Now it had become practically impossible to fill a page. And yet this was the time when the letters from home, from friends still in a world where time and place had their accustomed meanings, were most needed. Without these ties to the past, a past of only a few months ago, I often felt I had been cast off on some desert island. A day without mail became a day of doubt. A day without mail left only the ties between the crew and the squadron, a fraternity with high intensity but low intimacy. It was what our fathers, at least the few who had seen combat in World War I, might describe as the 'fraternity of the trenches,' where each soldier in the squad, platoon or company was crucially important to the survival of the whole; each soldier's welfare was the concern of everyone. But when he was killed, somewhere down the line, he was gone, and that was that. It was said that the intimacy of friendship could not be afforded because friends might die the next day, and the need to mourn could not be spared.

A tempting and feasible explanation, but Americans of my generation did not unveil their souls easily to one another. Beyond an initial cordiality, they chose solitude. But they would trust beyond any European comprehension, because the Europeans trusted only their families and their friends and perhaps the leaders they loved. Americans took for granted that you were a straight fellow, working 'in the vineyard' as they were, a fellow worker with the same problems and the same interests. In other days it would have been said that you were all working to 'build the city of God'. And because of this you deserved a hand when you needed it, even if you were too proud to ask. The burden for refusing trust was upon those who refused it.

I finally arrived at the squadron's dayroom. When I opened the door, I found the room empty. We were alerted all right, otherwise the room would have been full of officers, some of them playing bridge or poker or solitaire, some writing letters or just bantering about with each other. The lights were on, and decks of cards were strewn upon the tables, good hands and bad equally abandoned. A cigarette was burning itself out, and my opening the door had transformed its feather of smoke into a writhing snake. The fire was out, and the room was cold. The radio, which no one had dared switch off, was playing to itself. I checked the mail that was sitting on a table against the right wall. Nothing for me. There were three letters and a package for Fowler, one letter and a package for Mueller, and a letter from Brazil for Davis. Tomorrow, Operations would return them to their senders with the mention 'Missing in Action.'

I turned from the table to look instead at the painting on the wall behind me, a fresco of a knockout blonde dressed only in a diamond bracelet. I was not ready, that night, to find the dayroom empty, and she offered some consolation. But I felt guilty, as if I had tried to dodge the alert. The squadron had received the challenge without me, and I felt left out of an intimate ritual, deprived of sharing with the others that same interior look that meant we were all so uniformly vulnerable. Within these four walls there remained nothing, neither warmth nor smell nor memory of movement; the air had lost that faint stir that lingers after the voices have stifled. I left the lights on; I did not shut off the radio. And as I closed the door, the cigarette from its tray threw out an angry coil of smoke.

Outside, the soft hands of a breeze pressed against my face; the dusty light of the moon dissolved the opacity of the blackout. So many stars the sky glowed like a woman's skin. In peacetime, one would stop to remark what a beautiful night it was. But that night's beauty was a threat... anything unusual was a threat.

Now began my ritual, my own personal contract with Fate. I walked to my barracks, my flesh more sensitive with each step, my body hollow. If for the next ten seconds I did not see a light, I would get through. I waited those ten seconds for a door to open, a curtain to drop, a spark to fly out a chimney. And though I wanted to hurry it through and the count, I stretched to eleven to make sure.

No lights, I would come back. At that moment I had never doubted the outcome. Yet I was leery of such confidence, fearful that any arrogance might bring vengeance from that too perfect sky.

I needed now to let Operations know that I was back; it would simplify their planning. The building was nearby, and the fluorescent light inside, escaping through cracks, gave it an eerie glow. Brownlow was inside shuffling papers and greeted me with, 'Hi, Pitts. I was wondering if you made the last train. Did you have a good time in London?'

'I'm not sure how good the pass was,' I replied, 'but I'm here any way, ready to go if you need me.'

'If I need you, eh? I seem to remember a time when you were a bit more eager than that.'

'Perhaps I was more eager because I was also dumber. But I'm still available.'

'That's good enough for me. By the way, your navigator, Kundin, stayed on base while the rest of you were on pass.' He gave me a look and went on. 'He wound up putting in two missions with McCall because their navigator was down with a bad cold.'

'I'll be damned! Did he have to go, or did you give him the option?'

'Oh, he had a forty-eight-hour pass just like you, but when I asked him if he could stay and replace McCall's navigator, he seemed to jump at the chance. You know we're very short of navigators.'

Kundin was always an uncertain factor. He flew scared, unable to find a way to deal effectively with the fear that kept at him and showed itself with every alert. A more arrogant part of me condemned him for that fear. And yet I also had to admire Kundin, because in spite of every thing, he kept on going out on the missions.

Brownlow continued, 'I thought it was a good sign. He must have done all right, otherwise I would have heard about it.'

'I'll go and see McCall before I turn in,' I said, 'and hear what he has to say.'

'Do that, but get to bed early, because I think I'll probably be calling you around 3.00a.m.'

'Thanks for the warning. Will you be going with us, per chance?'

He paused and then replied, 'No, not this time.'

'I'm sorry to hear that' I said and quickly added, 'You know I don't mean that sarcastically.' Although I did, somewhat. My admiration for Brownlow vied with the resentment I couldn't help feeling. I was going, and he was staying behind, safe. Brownlow knew all that.

'I know,' he said. 'I'm sorry too.'

The squadron lived in a Quonset hut that had been divided into double rooms and singles. Out of my usual need for privacy, I had chosen a single but soon discovered that it was impossible to keep it heated. However, the room that McCall and his copilot, Gurney, shared was always warm, McCall being a patient, methodical fellow who knew how to keep a furnace going. I knocked at their door now, sure of my welcome. The two of them were there, as were Tex, Simons's copilot, and O'Neil, one of our lead bombardiers and chief rumor monger. We sat, not saying much, while McCall wrote to his father, all of us just pleased at being together, friends beyond the factitious, on that night of common concern, of a shared and uncertain tomorrow.

After a bit, I ventured, 'Tell me, McCall, how did Kundin do on yesterday's mission?'

McCall paused in his letter writing to answer. 'Okay, you know. He did his job, said very little over the intercom. He gave everyone in the nose miniature maps of the mission with accurate headings and all the distances and minutes of flying time. We weren't attacked by fighters this time, so I can't say anything as to his handling of a machine gun. But he answered promptly the oxygen checks, and when I asked him for our ETA in getting back to base, he gave me a correct answer within three minutes.'

I thanked him and thought, *Well, that's more than we usually get out of Kundin. McCall and I will have to discuss it some more when there are fewer listeners.*

Outside, we could hear the ground crews marching to the planes to start their night-long labor, and though their activity gave finality to our alert, their voices passing under our windows had the reassuring quality of neighbors walking by our house on a winter night. One by one the generators started purring and, as the crew chiefs taxied the ships toward the bomb-storage areas, we heard the shrieks and whines of the brakes.

For later, the loneliness, the anxious self-questioning, the sleeplessness. For now, it is warm here in McCall's room, sheltered against the morrow, against our skin raw with the wear of danger. Once in a while someone speaks, giving voice to a sort of collective euphoria, dreaming, half not thinking at all, so relaxed words come out automatically. It is an awareness that here we are imbibing strength for tomorrow's battle, making ourselves heavier against the merciless push time, a time that continually and relentlessly increases the odds against us. McCall's pen scratches on the paper. Gurney taps his pipe against his shoe. Wood puffs and hisses in the fire.

These were the last moments when we still existed as distinct personalities, each with his virtues and vices. In McCall and Gurney's room we still had names. In the air, we no longer had names. We were ship 828: pilot, copilot, bombardier, navigator, engineer, tail gunner, radio man, right waist gunner, left waist gunner, ball turret gunner. We abdicated our individuality for our combat role. We belonged to no one but the squadron and our group. And we belonged, also, to our country, but we never spoke of that; it was part of the sacred, the unsaid. Discipline took over our lives; we existed only for the mission, we surrendered our right to live.

And what about our wives and sweethearts, or our children? What about our mothers? We would never talk about that either. A soldier is always betraying his mother; it is the supreme act of cutting the umbilical cord. If his mother had done her job right, he was ready to leave her for the good fight with his peers against the enemy, at the risk that she would never see him again.

And into this room came not only the living – McCall and Gurney and Tex and O'Neil and others who came to partake of this time spent together – but also, slowly, the room filled with those who had never returned, their presence more real as we spoke of them. It didn't happen frequently. Usually we left the 'scrags' where they belonged; the present was too demanding for us to pay much attention to the past. And often, if we mentioned them at all, it was with reproach. They had made fatal errors, and we considered each failure to return a failure of judgment: *Davis gave up too easily when the gauges got in the red, Schuenemann and Ratcliff did not collaborate, Morse did not get out of the way quickly enough.* We performed our dissection of the dead so that we, the living, would not repeat the same mistakes and die of the same disease.

Yet why was their presence on this night so demanding? Was it because from the corner of my eye I was seeing dead Ratcliff entering the room? It was the same paleness, the same height. It was not Ratcliff, of course, just Barrett coming in to chat with us. Sitting at a bridge table, I leaned down to pick up a card that had fallen on the floor, and Davis walked by my side stirring some cool air behind him. But Davis had been killed a week ago, and facing quickly about, I saw it was only Ralston who shared with Davis the same lock of dark hair, the same stoop. Only Ralston, unlike Davis, was definitely alive.

Still, I looked at Ralston queerly, for why should he be carrying Davis's ghost with him? Why should the movement of his head suddenly give blood to a body otherwise reduced to ashes?

And if at that moment, in that room of the living, we uttered their names – Ratcliff, Davis, Mueller, Schuenemann – we were not speaking as judges, not speaking with the smugness of those who had come back, whose mistakes had not been seized upon by fate. In that moment the dead were no longer cadavers but brothers, above judgment, who had taken the rap for us, the living. They might not always, when alive, have been our friends, but they were part of the 'band of brothers.' That night we felt humble, while minutes formed, swelled, and dropped one by one into a quiet pool. That was how we buried our dead, without formal ceremonies. Our joint and silent prayer was, 'Forgive us, we the lucky survivors. But allow us to bury you, for your ghosts make it more difficult for us to do our job.'

Our existence would be as strong as the weave that night. For when many had fallen, when the fight had been long and hard, and capability could be maintained only by a constant effort against fatigue, there arose, fleeting but strong, the temptation to surrender. Surrender to mistake, to movement too late begun, to exhaustion or despair, surrender so that we too could gain the rest of death. Alone, each of us was but one man, flying in an aircraft whose metal cohesion might be any moment overwhelmed by the superior force of flak, of rockets, of machine-gun fire or cannon fire. With the cloth woven of many hands pressed against our skin, we were strong of many arms, attentive with many eyes – and responsible to the smile of companions who had acknowledged us to be one of their breed and of their own resolve. If we surrendered to fatigue and despair, we were deserting them.

This was a combat in which the only way to help our brothers-in-arms was to keep on flying. No putting a comrade on your back to bring him to the dressing station. No crawling to fetch him out of no-man's land. Forget *Paths of Glory* and *All Quiet on the Western Front*. And neither could we leave the formation to stay with a friend who had lost two engines, to give him the cover of our twelve machine guns and then share in his final misfortune when the Me-109s caught up with the both of us. Our crew came first; salvation meant sticking with the format, come what may.

Without ever having gained the comforting dullness of habit, alert happened that night as it had happened many nights before: Brownlow would arrive and stand a moment in the dark of the vestibule, listening to the conversation and laughter surging intermittently from the other side of the door. Hearing these last moments of the band of brothers, of men tied to other men by the slap of hands on forearms, the contraction of shoulders, the squinting of eyes. Security of animal understanding; of the gestures; of the words, the said and the unsaid, each one weaving an imaginary cloth to carry as his shield into battle. Each one weaving with the fierceness of too little time, with gratefulness for the giving of others. And in the growing cloth, eyelash added to eyelash, the blue iris, the roots of blood upon the cornea spreading with the strain, the tiredness – to become the eye of Ralston. The angles of the cheeks, scars of shaving with cold water – the skeleton of Ralston's head, always clear beneath the flesh. Ralston, who never spoke ill of any man. A white line, circuitous, would round out the hands of Simons, always carving, drawing, repairing. Violet splotches revealing the ever renewed fragility in the log of Tex's body.

And Brownlow would push the door, the word 'alert' would fall, and nothing could be added. He would enter with the announcement as casually as possible, knowing he was not going – the flesh rejoicing but the soul lonely, and every rope he tossed to the others would fall short. He would resolve the dilemma by scheduling himself for as many missions as possible – Brownlow shared our risks rather than merely sending us out on them. Although he had already fulfilled his quota of twenty missions, he kept on flying combat, as copilot to the squadron lead crew or even as an observer, armed with a fancy movie camera.

This night he tried bellowing jovially, 'Big deal tomorrow; everybody takes the buggy ride.' Nobody laughed and embarrassment replaced our former ease. Brownlow awkward and alone, sensitive and aware, tiptoeing on creaky stairs in a costume full of bells. And as if he had said something outrageous, as if a smell had become suddenly overwhelming, one by one we would get up and bid goodnight. And Brownlow would watch us go as casually as we had come in, each being careful not to slam the door or crush his cigarette or shut off the radio.

And the work would be accomplished; the band of brothers would have gathered itself together. Now the parting began. Now there was nothing left to be done except to go back to our rooms and get as much sleep as possible for the coming day.

2

REMINISCENCE:
SOLO FLIGHT IN TEXAS

I watched my instructor getting out of the rear cockpit of the PT-19, our primary trainer, in which I now occupied the front cockpit. A tall, spare man from Oklahoma, he stood blinking in the face of the morning sun and told me, 'Well, take her up and shoot a couple of landings. I'll be watching you from the wind tee. Come and see me after your second landing.'

And I thought, *He is letting me fly solo after only seven hours! Yahoo! Even though I just muffed the last landing, I guess he believes that I can make it! I'm not so sure myself but if he is, enough to let me solo, I ought to make it. I must make it! I will make it!*

I gunned the ship toward the beginning of the cinder and gravel path, which served as a runway at this auxiliary field, took a forty-five-degree position at the beginning of it, checked the traffic (there was none), checked my magnetos, and, after waving to my instructor, I pushed the throttle forward.

Soon I had the tail up, and giving the plane some right rudder, I brought the leftward torque under control, something I was not always readily able to catch. I understood all about action and reaction, and Newton's law of motion, but I could not always think as well with my hands and feet as I could with pen and tongue.

I lifted the plane off the ground into a shallow climb. I kept the nose above the horizon, checked my airspeed – seventy to seventy-five miles an hour if I remember correctly – turned to the left into my crosswind leg, and leveled off at 500 feet. And I exulted: *Now I am not a 'dodo bird' anymore; now I am a pilot!*

I reduced the throttle. The morning air was clear and snappy, the sunlight yellow and sharp. I noticed cars on a road nearby and the control tower on our field. I turned into my downwind leg and saw Mr Hinds, my instructor, by the wind tee. He spat in the grass, disturbing a couple of fat birds sitting near him.

I had to turn into my base leg soon. I could see by the limp windsock that there was very little wind, and what there was came from hither and yon. I was now at forty-five degrees of the point where I needed to land. I cut my throttle, lowered half flaps, and kept the nose up to bring my airspeed down. I turned left into my final approach, aiming my glide a bit below my landing spot, because when I rounded out close to the ground, I was going to float a bit past it. I chided myself for not putting my base leg out a little further.

There still seemed to be no wind, and I was gliding to my landing. And then I cursed as I began to climb – too much speed in my round out. I lowered the nose, pulled back on the throttle (which might have crept up on me), pulled back on the stick, and – clunk! – my front wheels hit the ground. I kept the stick back until I had slowed enough to be able to taxi. Did I bounce? Maybe it was just a little bounce. Had I muffed it again? As I passed the wind tee Mr Hinds gave me the high sign. I was elated; I made it!

I taxied back to the beginning of the take-off area. I took a forty-five-degree position to it, checked incoming traffic, and ran up the engine to check the magnetos. All was well. I waved to Mr Hinds, who waved back, and I took off again. This time I was nearly caught by the torque but managed to kick the rudder in time and straighten out my take-off. No more problems until the downwind leg where I spotted another PT-19 ahead of me. I would have to wait until he turned into his base leg and then lengthen my downwind leg to make sure of a safe separation between us.

There was more wind on this second circuit. I put down half flaps and, as I turned into final approach, gave it a little bit of throttle, partly to clear my engine and partly to give me a couple of miles of extra speed. I saw the plane in front of me make two bounces before settling down. I had a good glide path, and I rounded out smoothly, bringing the stick back toward my gut. I made a three-point landing, stalling about one or two inches above the ground, and 'greased' her in. Hinds gave me the high sign with both hands.

My elation reached a new peak. It had been a long time since I had such sheer pleasure. I shall remember those two landings all my life. The second one, as a matter of fact was one of the best I ever made, granted landings were not my strong suit. The fact was I had lousy depth perception, and each time I had a major physical exam, it cost me a fiver for the 'help' I got from the enlisted man in charge of the eye-sight check up.

I taxied to the wind tee to pick up my instructor. He shook my hand and congratulated me with, 'You showed good judgment on that last landing. Keep it up and you'll live to be a hundred. Well, take us home.'

Another take-off, another landing, but this time it was on the hard runway of the main field. And this time, instead of stalling the plane two inches above the ground, it was more like two feet. So much for 'greasing her in'. It was more like I 'clunked' her in. Not really the sort of landing one would hope for with one's recently and perhaps now formerly impressed instructor sitting in the rear cockpit.

Back home, the other members of my flight (there were five per instructor) were ready for me with their welcome, and I received the contents of two pails of water upon my face and chest, substitute for the dunking I would have been treated to if a pond or river had been readily available. The two cadets who threw them at me had, I believe, already soloed. I have never more enjoyed having cold water thrown at me, although on this winter morning in Texas, with the breeze already up, I was quickly a mass of shivering flesh. Mr Hinds dismissed me from the flight line and took another member of the flight out for an hour of instruction.

I went back to the deserted barracks to dry off and change, celebrating my 'baptism of fire'. I had died as a dodo bird and was reborn as a pilot, and I must never make again the mistakes that could be forgiven a dodo. The chances were now very good that I would graduate from 'Primary School' to go on in ten weeks to 'Basic' and, ten weeks after that, to 'Advanced'. And at the end of Advanced, I would receive my silver wings, my second lieutenant bars, and, after additional training, I would fly a plane in combat.

Back at the barracks, a cadet I had known in preflight at Randolph Field was packing up to leave: he had washed out. I felt sorry for him, in a 'there-but-for-the-grace-of-God' sort of way, but those were just words. I would not tempt fate by denying that it could have been me packing up instead of him, but I really did not believe it. Good fortune should riot be triumphant, but henceforward he and I belonged to different worlds, and I was indifferent to his. He came over, and we shook hands. He congratulated me on my soloing, and I was embarrassed. What was I to say to him? 'Sorry you didn't make it' sounded condescending to me. So I asked, 'Do you know what you are going to do?'

He answered, 'No. But I am not going to volunteer...'

How could I reply? He was already talking like an enlisted man. The eager young cadet had vanished.

'Well, at least you are going to leave this forsaken hole of a dry county,' I joked. 'No more bad bootleg liquor at ten dollars a pint!'

'You're right there.' He had finished his packing and gathered up his belongings. 'Well good luck to you, Frenchy. Don't go catching the clap!'

'No, thanks, I'll do my best.'

'And keep them flying!'

'I will. Sorry to see you go...'

'Couldn't be helped. Well so long!'

'So long.'

I was glad when he was gone. It had been awkward, and I felt that the continued presence of the defeated, the failed, only served to remind us of our own fragility. With relief, I lay down on my bunk and slept until lunchtime.

When medical students begin their five- to eight-year apprenticeship, the first experience they undergo that is definitely medical is the dissection of the cadaver, and a certain percentage of the students quit right there. They have taken their pre-med courses and are fully capable of assimilating the curriculum, but what they find they cannot take is the treatment of a dead body as carrion rather than the sacred envelope of somebody's loved one. Dissection of a frog or of a cow's eye is what they remember from high school days, but this is different: this is a person that is lying under their scalpels, and they suddenly feel the need to apologize for the forthcoming violation of that person's body. A physician must abstract everything about that body except the information it can provide him or her. For some this will prove too difficult. It will seem a betrayal. Unlike their fellow students who are able to get past this feeling – some so well that they will gleefully partake in the traditional medical-student joke of putting body parts in each other's lockers – they cannot go through this necessary rite of passage.

For aviation students, apprenticed to the air, the equivalent lay in learning the skills of recovering from stalls or, even more crucially, from spins. Within the first twelve hours of instruction – seven or eight if you were gifted or lucky – your instructor would suddenly reduce the plane's engine to an idle and ask you to prepare for a forced landing, letting you test your judgment until you were about ten feet above the ground. Then he would shove the throttle forward and resume his lesson. What was indispensable to the cadet was that he must learn to repress the fear of falling and to take for granted that he belonged in the air. This fear was something no one ever mentioned, but it was there all the same, an invisible part of learning the procedures, of being in the air. This was our rite of passage.

The student pilot is dealing with a vehicle that is at once a land vehicle, a rather awkward contraption on the ground, and also a bird in the sky, fast and supple, at home in the air. It is the pilot who must manage the shift between these two identities, the transition from land vehicle to air vehicle. Feeling the strain of the engine, the noise of the plane's power, the pilot guides it through the take-off. Achieving a certain speed, it lifts from the ground, no more a land-bound bird but a flying bird, having found its preferred element and requiring less power, less noise, less tension.

Now, if the plane loses forward speed, it will become the awkward bird again. The student pilot has to learn the signs that it is on its way to reverting back to a land vehicle – meaning that it is coming closer to a stall. It is as if Cinderella is hearing the chimes of midnight; there is a growing mushiness of the controls, sometimes vibrations on the control surfaces that transmit to the stick and to the foot controls in the cockpit, all telling the pilot that the wings are in the process of losing their lifting power.

Beneath him, the ground: fields neatly plowed; forest that makes a green ocean, some of its trees erupting with their branches and leaves above the rest; roads on which cars move leisurely, while his plane moves two to four times their speed. In his gut, he feels the growing fragility of his ship and knows that he has to lower the nose and come closer to the ground. He must pay out some of his altitude by expanding the power of his engines. All this is counterintuitive; to fight the forthcoming stall he must accommodate it. The plane wants to go down, let it go down – let it fall! Keep the wings straight, and let it ride on its own kinetic energy, until flying speed can been recovered. But then, get out of there!

The plane cannot remain in the air forever. The gas tank, which furnishes the energy for our bird, is getting low. Time to go home; time to return the plane to its identity as a land vehicle.

The plane is moving at about two miles a minute, coming closer toward the spot of ground on which the pilot has chosen to land, making that choice when he was some five or six miles from the spot and a thousand feet above it. The problem here is to dissipate the energy implicit in the plane's altitude, return it to the ground in a power-on glide, and stall it a foot – or better still, a few inches – above the runway. For that purpose the plane has air brakes called flaps, which dissipate the forward speed as they also lower the speed at which the wings will stall. With his engines running softly and smoothly, the gliding capacity of his aircraft will permit the pilot to alter the plane's altitude by five or six times its forward distance.

This is truer of light planes, like our primary trainer, than it is of heavy planes such as the B-17. Power off, you can glide a light plane to a very satisfactory landing. You must fly a heavy plane to its landing using the engines to the very end of your final approach and keeping them responsive to the throttles. All sorts of things can go wrong in the last ten minutes of flight: a change in the direction and speed of the facing wind slowing your descent; priority to land given by the tower to a severely damaged plane, compelling you to go around and try a new landing approach; one of your engines running out of gas. The worst thing that could happen is that, during combat, one wing will stall out before the other because it has been damaged by fighters or flak, forcing you to glide at a higher speed to cover the possible discrepancy and to maintain control of the wings until the very last second of flight.

Recovering from an incoming stall, or even from a full stall, is no problem if you have some altitude to spend in the recovery, or some reserve engine power, and if both wings stall at about the same time. It is when one wing stalls before the other that trouble begins. The wing that stalls first pulls the plane into a vertical bank, and the plane does not respond to your controls. It pivots around the 'dead' wing without gaining any airspeed; the propellers still bite the air but do not pull the plane. You are spinning, not flying. The French pioneers of flight had beautiful expressions for these situations: *partir en vrille* – going into a spin (a 'vrille' is the coiling tendril of a vine), and *tomber en feuille morte* – falling like a dead leaf.

Part of our training involved purposely transforming a stall into a spin. 'The Spin' was the maneuver most fraught with rumors and wild stories and which cadets thought the most dangerous. Many students believed that the more turns in a spin, the more difficult it was to get out of, especially if the spin became 'flat', the nose of the airplane becoming parallel to the horizon. Not too many cadets spent much time practicing spins. Our instructors would sometimes tell of situations where a cadet froze at the stick during a supervised practice spin or made a failed recovery and stalled again as he pulled back on the stick with insufficient airspeed, precipitating the airplane into another spin from which it did not recover. (My instructor had lost a student in such a situation. Since he was not with the student when he crashed, he could only surmise what had happened; he had kicked his student out of the nest too soon.)

I had the opposite tendency: I would keep the stick against the dashboard until the plane was in an eighty- or even ninety-degree dive, but doing this I lost excessive altitude, and when I recovered from my dive I had gained a lot of unnecessary airspeed. It at least showed I had no fear of falling, and I did recuperate from all my practice spins, much to the relief of my instructor, no doubt.

Recuperation from a real accidental spin would ordinarily take place much closer to the ground, and if you did not want to crash, you could not afford to keep the stick forward for more than a minimum amount of time, after you had pushed the rudder pedals in the direction opposite to that of your spin. How long should you keep the stick forward? I was never told. It was one of those procedures you had to figure out for yourself.

It was not until Basic that certain things became apparent to me. Here I began doing spins under the hood, a training procedure in which the student-pilot's head and seat are covered, cutting him off from the outside world and creating artificial flying conditions in which he must fly by instruments alone. Sitting at the controls of the BT-13 – with the instructor or a fellow cadet monitoring the landscape to prevent me from running into any tall buildings, mountains, or other planes – I had only the altimeter, the airspeed, and the needle and ball to guide me. It was doing spins under the hood that I discovered there was no need to go into a steep dive in order to recuperate enough airspeed for control of my plane. It was something I taught myself, and that kind of learning will last a lifetime.

By letting you solo, your instructor certifies that you have reached a level of skill and judgment that will permit you to cope with the situations that are likely to occur in the entry into and out of the air traffic pattern, in the landings and running take-offs with a trainer plane, and generally in flying within sight of the field. He also certifies that the cadet is sufficiently rid of the fear of falling, that he will not panic in the air. Often enough the student pilot is less sure of his competence than his instructor seems to be, but that is precisely the point. The instructor's trust in the student's capacity is usually an effective self-fulfilling prophecy.

What then replaces the solo is the 'check-out'. An instructor or an experienced pilot will certify that you possess the basic elements of a given technique: check-out on cross-country flying, which presupposes that ground school has taught you how to read an aerial map; check-out on acrobatics to ascertain that you have repressed the fear of falling to the point that you can purposely put yourself in all sorts of odd positions in relation to the ground and the horizon; check-out that you will not lose your head in a spin – that you will recognize the difference between an intentional 'snap roll' (a quick 180-degree turn on your wing) as opposed to an unintentional 'high-speed stall' if somebody's prop wash should ever put you in one. In the Basic and Advanced stages of your cadet career you will go through check-outs on night cross-country flights, on flying in formation, and on piloting more powerful airplanes. Many times in the next six months you will be asked to 'die' as a student and to be reborn as a more skillful pilot, capable of teaching yourself and of monitoring your own progress. If you don't 'check-out' you will get the 'check ride', prelude to elimination from the program.

Teaching oneself was certainly one of the strengths of our training, but it was also one of its weaknesses. We were taught the basic maneuvers, the procedures, as if they were ends in themselves instead of having it explained to us their role in solving flying problems.

It reminded me of the way we were taught mathematics, especially geometry. You draw a line from here to there, and hop: the problem is solved. Now, why did you draw the line from here to there? You are supposed to know. If you don't know, you just haven't got 'it'.

Those who were gifted understood right away. Those who were not just followed along or, like me, became convinced that they were impermeable to math and adjusted to it. I wonder how cadets are taught now.

Learning how to take-off; how to turn, power on and power off; how to glide; learning how to round out and how to stall, first a foot, then half a foot, then an inch above the ground; learning how to stall it at 3,000 feet in the air; how to recover from a spin and from so many simulated forced landings – these were all part of the overt learning experience, all part of the skills your instructor attempted to impart to you.

Just as important was the invisible learning experience, when you are not conscious of the lessons being offered, but nevertheless you internalize them and act accordingly. For example, your mother might not ever have told you, 'Don't play doctor with your sister,' but somehow you got the message. Or as in learning language, grammar is not always explained to a child, yet he still learns to speak.

With us, the 'language' we were learning took the form of a cockiness of flying – of breaking the rules, in buzzing, in hedge-hopping, in dog-fighting. Whether we were risking our cadet's wings or our lives, we were learning to see ourselves as invulnerable, learning to repress our fears, especially that most elemental fear of falling. All our experiences reinforced this basic attitude.

Our training was not biased toward obedience, it was biased toward audacity tempered by the knowledge that nine people were riding in the airplane with you; it was biased toward relying on one's own assessment of a situation, rather than mechanically applying a procedure. The latter will be both the safest and simplest way of solving a flying problem in most circumstances, but there will be times that it will be neither. It would be our duty to override the procedure whenever our judgment told us that right now was one of those times.

In solo practice with the PT-19, I had noticed that I would come out of a spin with enough airspeed to complete a loop, and I decided to attempt one at the first chance I had. As it was 'the first chance' turned out to be the last hour of solo practice that I was scheduled for at my Primary field. So, once in the plane, I climbed to 4,000 feet. I 'cleared my area' (made reasonably sure that I was not likely to spin into any planes flying below), idled the engine, put the nose up, and stalled the plane. Holding the stick back, I kicked the rudder to the right and took the plane into a spin: one revolution, two revolutions, three, four, and I decided to recover. I reversed the foot controls and pushed the stick forward. The revolutions stopped. I went into my usual dive and pulled the stick back to go into a loop. All went well until I was flat on my back at the top of my loop. At that time the propeller came to a dead stop, the carburetor must have flooded. But the plane did not stall. It simply finished the loop without restarting the propeller.

I put the plane into a regular glide at about seventy to seventy-five miles an hour. I was at 3,500 feet. If the PT-19 gave me a forward glide of about seven times my altitude, I could go about four and a half miles – more than enough to reach the field, enter traffic, do both my base leg and final approach, and make a 'dead-stick' landing.

I did not follow the usual procedure for entering traffic, of coming at a forty-five-degree angle to the downwind leg; I just let down into traffic altitude plus 400 feet. There was little traffic, and I stayed to the left of the usual downwind leg. I did not want to drop on someone's head, but neither did I want to stray farther from the field than I had to. I turned into my base leg and, once I was sure I could make it into the field, slowly continued to turn into my final approach at higher-than-usual altitude. I used full flaps for my landing, rounded out and greased her in.

The tower sent a truck to me. After the driver restarted my engine, I taxied over to the flight line to park my plane. My instructor, Mr Hinds, met me, and I told him my story. He congratulated me on using good judgment; I had met the unexpected and had mastered it. My Primary Training ended on a high note.

In my time, flying was an experience that had only a forty-year history. We knew as much about the air as medieval seamen knew about the sea and winds – probably less, for humans had been sailing for thousands of years, although the basics of storms had been scientifically understood only since the 1820s. In the beginnings of flight, turbulence was often misunderstood as being caused by 'air pockets.' (The French were the first to name them: *trous d'air* – holes in the air.)

Such deadly phenomena as flying through clouds and becoming coated with 'clear ice' were dreaded but not very well understood – why at some times one could fly through undamaged and at other times find one's plane covered with an unbearable load of ice. At the end of the war, the P-47 would sometimes, in a dive, come within reach of the sound barrier and be buffeted by it. Test pilots knew that in their trials with a new plane they would often meet the frontiers of flight and would sometimes pay, with their lives, the price of exploration.

Many stories floated. Older pilots, instructors, sometimes described in bull sessions experiences that had left the storyteller with white hair. We would listen attentively, especially when we were convinced that the speaker was not solely on a vanity trip and was describing a real experience from which we could all learn. Then we might go as far or even farther than he had. By avoiding his errors and imitating his innovations, or simply his good judgment, we might come back safely.

3

KIMBOLTON

When we arrived at Kimbolton as fresh replacements in November of 1943, we had classes in aircraft identification, radio procedure, engine operation, and first aid. We were briefed on what to do if shot down in occupied territory and on the different strains of British gonorrhea (some of which were said to resist sulfa treatment). We were rehearsed repeatedly as to where to apply tourniquets and how to ask a radio station for a bearing home if our navigator was lost over Great Britain and us with him. We could not just come up and over the air and say, 'I'm lost; give me a course to steer home?' Instead there were key phrases, giving our Masonic sign of Allied allegiance. Our name in the brotherhood might be *Crystal Q for Queen, Rosebud G for George, Enamel C for Charlie*. Once the proper 'sesame' was uttered, searchlights might point the way in long sweeps or make a cupola of lights over our field. A woman's voice would shimmer through the darkness or the thick British haze, offering us magic numbers, spinning an Ariadne thread to lead us out of the chaos, giving substance where there had been the blank face, the nowhere of too many choices. Sometimes before dawn, when the RAF had been out and clouds obscured the ground, one might hear all the flowers of the British garden – *Petunia, Rosebush, Peony* – or all the different names of sails of a full-masted galleon and be led home by the genteel voice of a WAAF. It gave the whole mechanical show a touch of chivalry with tender rites: King Arthur and his knights coming out of the night, wounded, harried, but proud of a ransacking well done.

Americans, too, brought the words of their mythology – *Cowboy blue, Fatgal white* – names that gave humor and impertinence to these dialogues of the air.

Veteran copilots, like Tex, took us up and checked us out on combat formation and evasive action. Navigators had their classes in the 'Gee' box, an electronic device pioneered by the British, which permitted an accurate pin-pointing of one's position over the sea of clouds, even 150 miles out. Bombardiers were taught new techniques; gunners were lectured and given movie camera demonstrations on sighting systems. We had ground school in the afternoon and took off on our first assignments the morning after. Some of us were rather eager and carried notebooks to class. Others skipped out after roll-call. Since I had been a good student in college, I thought it might pay off to be a good student here; war could in part be reduced to a difficulty with which I had some familiarity.

Some never lived long enough to find out what good grades they had made in the weekly quizzes.

Early one morning, Operations needed an extra crew in a hurry to complete the squadron. They called out Mueller who took off on his first mission before he knew what was happening. He never came back. Up in the air, he suddenly started to crowd his element leader, backed away, went into a dive, tried a loop, stalled out. He dove again, this time completing a full loop, fell into a spin, and was soon swallowed by the thick clouds underneath. No chutes came out.

Nobody could understand it. There had been no enemy fighters and little flak. Was it that the controls froze? Was it lack of oxygen? We were puzzled by the strange sequence of events; why would he try to loop a B-17? We had not trained with Mueller, so we hardly knew him. We finally decided that lack of oxygen was responsible.

It was said that lack of oxygen at high altitudes could drive men to act drunk or go plain berserk. An anoxic man would feel full of pep, on top of the world, as boastful as drunks frequently are. So perhaps Mueller, in his delirium, grinning ear to ear, had decided to loop the loop to celebrate an easy initiation to combat. Had the rest of the crew participated in this drunkenness, we wondered, or had they tried to fight a pilot gone mad? Could this ever happen to us?

Afterwards, we were repeatedly briefed on oxygen discipline, with orders to give frequent oxygen checks to the crew during the flight. Yet, as one veteran said, oxygen might not have had anything to do with Mueller's not coming back; no one would ever really know. In the air, as in the sea, there are events that defy rational explanation.

A couple of days later, Brownlow got us up at 2.00a.m. and received our curses with an apologetic grin. Daylight in this November night came late, and there would be plenty of dark left for a cross-country from one end of England to the other. Even though we had been declared operational, we were still new crews with a training schedule to fulfill, and that training schedule called for a night cross-country at the first break in the weather.

We were only required to take skeleton crews on each plane: pilot, copilot, navigator, engineer, radio man. Bombardiers could come if they wanted to. Ours could not be expected to do the normal thing and stay in the sack – on the contrary, Marcott was eager to go, wanting to 'see it through with the buddies.' During crew training in the States, he had tried to get himself washed out by consistently making lousy bombing scores… at least that's what he said. However, once in England, he determined that he should become lead bombardier and went doggedly about the process of apple-polishing and 'buddy-buddying' in order to secure that chance.

There were lots of bombardiers, and because in a squadron you had only two or three who knew how to set the complicated Norden bomb sight under fire, only one out of seven bombardiers ever got the chance to use a sight in combat. These became our lead bombardiers; the rest were glorified gunners who salvoed upon the leader's signal. This secondary role did not appeal to Marcott. One would have thought his lousy training scores would have disqualified him, but no, he managed to ingratiate himself with the leadership (he would finally be taken off our crew to be given special training). While we went out on missions, Marcott trained for the day when he would lead, when he would be the one to make decisions for others.

Meanwhile, he was running around like an officer in a training film, busily engaged in promoting himself as informal leader of our crew and stepping on toes in the process, mine included, and I did not appreciate it.

Marcott had enlisted into the regular Army when he was seventeen – something about running away from home for obscure but romantic reasons. Shooting craps, he would recite his life story while warming and blowing on the dice. 'Come on seven, come on seven' he would plead. 'Be nice to me; be nice to me like Mary was. Oh Mary… she was the only woman who ever loved me. Come on seven.'

The others, intent on the money and the numbers, would pay no attention. I was fascinated, and when Marcott went broke, I would lend him money just to hear him confess his failures, his hopes, exposing the taut, frayed rope of his self. But I was a bit ashamed, as if I had been peeking at the intimate through a keyhole.

A crap game in which he lost his entire pay enabled me to discover that his father was a professor in Syracuse, New York, who had remarried a social worker. Mary was a girl Marcott had picked up in Odessa, Texas, who was eight years older than he. She had befriended him, besexed him, and believed in him.

Tucker, another bombardier, was normal and, as such, reluctant to do anymore than the strict necessary. In the early morning we left him in bed, his yellow sheets wrapped around him, his cheek marked by a button of the coat he used for a pillow.

Schu's copilot, Ratcliff, who was required to go, was rather hard to arouse. Curled up, with clenched fists against his face, he lingered in bed while we made ready. It was hard for Schu to prompt him, as they both knew this was to be their last ride together, Ratcliff having requested to change crews. To help out, Borowski, a copilot whose enormous frame entitled him to the dealing out of both kindness and justice, ran over and pulled his sheets off. Ratcliff arose, squealing like an enraged puppy. But the clammy coldness had him dressed in no time. He skipped washing up and instead ran outside and claimed the coveted warm seat in the truck next to the driver.

In the truck, after the initial groaning, everyone fell silent. We could hear Ratcliff in the front seat, bragging to the driver how he had just become a father three days before of, yes, a baby boy. Hearing him tell the story for the hundredth time renewed the groaning and prompted a lot of sarcastic snickering as well. Barely twenty and already a father. A kid with a kid; what a silly situation. We prolonged our laughter and remarks for even longer than the matter was worth, just to let Schu know we were with him and sympathized with him for having to put up with such a character. Schu remained silent, feeling that his side was not the whole story, too honest to believe their failure to get along entirely his copilot's fault.

It was hard to see how anybody could fail to get along with Schu, who never got mad and apologized for everything he did well, like playing base-ball or poker – or flying. But anything Schu asked Ratcliff to do, Ratcliff would argue with or do the opposite. And Ratcliff was not that competent a formation flyer. He was very neat in his person, but we thought that rather superfluous in a theater of operations where a tight formation was more important to survival than clean boots. Schuenemann's crew had become operational two weeks before our crew, and on their second raid, over Bremen, Ratcliff kept weaving in and out of the squadron formation and then tried to make a joke of what was really an incapability of staying in position. Schu had taken over the controls in disgust and flown the rest of the way. As it happened, some of the boys got badly shot up that day; they did not appreciate Ratcliff's 'joke'.

Two days after that, Davis needed a copilot, and Ratcliff went out with him, Schu's crew not being scheduled that day. On the way back home, Davis saw the oil pressure drop on his #3 engine and feathered immediately. A while later, his #4 did the same thing, and again Davis feathered. On two engines he flew back to England and crash-landed in a beet field, barely missing a clump of trees.

At the base, when we failed to see them return, we thought they had been done for. But late at night Davis and Ratcliff got back in an RAF truck, the heroes of the day, Ratcliff very patronizing to us who had yet to have such a close encounter with death. While we were still JBs, 'Junior Birdmen', he was now a veteran.

Some weeks later, when the reports came in, we learned that Davis had feathered his engines needlessly. By not taking the time to cross check the oil pressure with the oil temperature, he had mistaken an instrument failure for engine failure and washed out a good plane for no good reason.

We did not yet know these details; here in the truck, we were somewhat jealous of Ratcliff and failed to give him his share of compliments. That crash in the beet field, plus being a father, trumpeted proof of his virility. The kid was rather unbearable.

Schuenemann was the first to take-off for the cross-country. Our engines were turning over, warming up, and we waited permission to taxi out to take-off position for our turn. On the radio I could hear the Control towers shaking the sleep out of their ears and calling each other, mixing good mornings with technical criticism of their transmissions.

Suddenly Schuenemann's voice broke through: 'Hello, Eartone, hello, Eartone. This is *Enamel L for Love*. Request permission for emergency landing, #4 engine feathered.'

And to *L for Love* permission to land was immediately given, all other planes being told to hold off the runway.

I suspected Schu of pulling a fast one, trying to get out of this chore and go back to the sack. Soon a few lights swept over the runway; we could vaguely guess at the form of a plane, subdued like a dimmed-out Christmas tree. Some tents and parked planes prevented us from following his landing. We gave up watching and buried ourselves in our cockpit, busy with our own affairs. A few lights in the nose were seeping through to the cockpit; electric motors purred as we checked the inverters. We were sleepy, but the ship felt like home with its familiar sounds and crew.

A dancing glow reflected in the window made us look up. We saw a rolling cloud of fire shooting up, breaking itself into spears of clear flame.

For a few seconds we tried to fool ourselves; perhaps a ground crew's tent was burning, what with the fancy oil stoves and loose rags about. But then we saw the flares going off, red and green lights above the fire, and there could be no doubt: *L for Love* had crashed and exploded.

Some fool called up and asked whether those red flares were meant to cancel our cross-country. (But why call him a fool? He probably had just switched on his radio and could not see the runway.) From the tower, the message came back: 'You are to disregard those flares and stand by.'

Schu, Ratcliff, and three other men had died. We were callous then, sitting in our good solid plane, ready to taxi out and take off, alive and very desirous of showing the world we were not afraid, that nothing could dent our confidence in our invulnerability.

But the cross-country was canceled without a word being spoken over the air about the crash. At breakfast, Brownlow fielded our tremulous questions with an air of official grief. We remained indifferent, glad to be indifferent. Too bad; Schuenemann had been a good man, Ratcliff had been a rather immature boy. We ate breakfast heartily.

After breakfast we went to the scene of the crash, moved by the kind of morbid curiosity that makes people rush to view an accident, officially relieved but secretly disappointed if no one is killed.

The ammunition belts had stopped exploding, and the fire had burned itself out. Among the twisted propellers, the torn wings, we could vaguely distinguish the blackened forms of those who had died there. The smell of burnt flesh was rather sickening. I did not dare come too close: the less my imagination had to feed upon the better.

Two of Schuenemann's regular crew had gone down a few days before with Mueller, Mueller's own radio man and engineer being ill that day. So Mueller's men had been assigned to Schuenemann, and now they were dead, as if fate had just been waiting for them to catch up. It seemed that if fate once attached itself to a crew, there was little you could do.

Against so much metal, so many jagged edges, so much fire and crushing weight, how fragile a construction of bones and cells, veins and nerves, our bodies turned out to be. We walked back in silence, our shoulders hunched against the cold.

Schuenemann's crash could be explained. He overshot the runway on his first approach, tried to go around on three engines, which would have been easy enough if the flaps and wheels could have been raised quickly. But those flaps and those wheels were still down when he hit a target embankment at the insufficiently lit end of the runway. Three more feet of altitude and he would have made it. If Ratcliff had obeyed orders and raised the wheels and flaps instead of riling Schu on his missed approach, they would have been all right.

Perhaps that's not what really happened, but given Ratcliff's past history with Schu, it's what some of us guessed.

We went through our first missions in a daze. We were eager; we were unafraid. The risk of death inebriated us like a sparkling wine. We slept soundly and were somewhat surprised at and contemptuous of the veterans, who would stay up all night playing cards because they couldn't sleep, soundly or otherwise. We didn't mix very much. The old timers knew we still had not 'had it' yet. We still had to learn the password to their fraternity, which was controlled fear.

In those days, our main worries were getting our laundry and dry cleaning done. Keeping warm and getting mail.

The showers and baths were at a place called the Latrine. True, that was one of its functions; all the same, Latrine was not an auspicious name. The water was rarely hot, and it was recommended that we not bathe on freezing days so as to avoid chances of catching pneumonia. The weather was cold and damp, and unless there was a deep fog, we would all be up, either on missions or practice flights.

Fog broke down the organic unity of living things. Sounds faded quickly, as if absorbed by cotton. Normally one could encompass in a single glance the airfield: the ships, the mechanics' tents, the control tower. Each object had its immediate meaning in relation to other objects; it stood as part of a whole. In fog, our sight dissolved into blank nothingness. Each object stood alone, without substance, a freak. On the road, a shadow would surge in front of you and be gone before you could tell whether it was a friend, almost before you could tell it was a man.

Anyway, we had no desire to catch pneumonia. Getting a shower was an expedition, and when we were not flying, we were too tired, too frozen, and too restless to do anything. We might get a truck and go down to the Red Cross in Bedford where they had hot showers in a warm environment, but for the most part we quickly resigned ourselves to being dirty. The oil from our skin was supposed to keep us warm. We shaved though – that was part of everyday morale. It also made for a tighter fit of the oxygen mask. And that was important.

After a month of lectures, demonstrations and formation practice, we were ready for our first mission.

4

THE FIRST MISSION: EMDEN

First mission. We had been looking forward to the moment for a long time. Fifteen months we had been preparing ourselves; all the movements of our youth, all of our minds and hearts, trained for a new life. This was to be the test of our manhood. This boy of peacetime, of the paper route, of the soda fountain, of first dates, of college, of easy living, was to become tomorrow a warrior.

My first alert. Full of excitement now. Joy more than anything else. Fear also, perhaps, but not enough to pierce through my defenses. Afraid of being afraid, but that has been with me for some time. I write 'last letters' to be sent to my best friends and family. Frankly I don't know very much what to say. It seems superfluous, and I can't succeed in taking a serious tone. How can you tell your people you were overjoyed to go on that mission from which you didn't return? But I have always heard that you must write letters to your dear ones before you go over the top, and I want to do this right. I shall have my baptism of fire with all the trimmings. So, last letters I write, saying so sorry I was shot down.

Early rise. Wake up; wash your face, brush your teeth, get something to eat. Go to briefing. Our target: Emden. It doesn't seem too bad. Still not too anxious. I walk to the tent where the crew is readying the guns and pass around some Mars bars. For all of us it is the first mission. Owens, our ball turret gunner, takes a stick of gum in trembling hands. That decides it for me I am as calm, as free of fear as I could ever expect to be. Even more so. I am responsible for these boys. If their hands quiver, mine mustn't.

Everything is finally ready. I am in the cockpit, tied to the airplane by all kinds of wire connections. I've got earphones, throat mike, and oxygen tank; I've got a steel helmet at my feet – I am as overloaded as a new boy scout. When our turn comes, we take off and assume our position.

For some reason I am not flying formation very well. I am not scared, at least not in any conscious way. If I am not flying a good formation, it is probably not by accident, but I am not then asking any questions. I think of a girl's body; I think of nothing. Before I know it, I am lagging behind. The supercharger on one of the engines is acting up.

And now, ahead, the enemy coast. On the interphone, our first pilot Streit and I listen to the crew, who are keeping an incessant high-pitched chatter that I find somewhat exasperating. Our tail gunner, Boyovitch, usually has a good deep voice, but today he reaches the high 'C.' Not that he has much to do. No enemy fighters dare come close – our P-47s are there to change their minds. Some of them, in fact, are dog fighting among themselves for fun. We can only see their vapor trails – sky writers on a drunk.

Okay. Let's get it over with. I shout, 'Bomb bay doors open!' Ahead, little black clouds appear. Flak![1] Anti-aircraft fire meant for us. The formation in front goes through without casualties; the flak doesn't seem too bad.

'Bombs Away!' Away, it is to be hoped, somewhere over our target.

'Okay, let's close those bomb bay doors!' No response. 'What's the matter? Can't you get them up? Bombardier, let's get those doors up; they are slowing us down!'

Somebody cuts in, 'The bombs didn't go out.'

'God damn it! What's the use of coming here if we can't even get rid of our bombs! Eh, bombardier, do something. We can't keep formation this way; we are getting left behind.'

Marcott replies, 'I know it, I know it!'

The flak seems to be getting more personal, caught as we are with our bomb bay doors down. I curse the bombardier over the interphone. The curses come back. The navigator talks too much; I could slay him. I am not scared, I'm angry. Suddenly the ship lurches as if it had been punched in the bottom. A dull ache seizes my arm. *A cramp or a piece of flak?* I check. It's a cramp, and I am thinking, *Now you are no more than a ham actor, just when you were near to greatness. Damn!*

The bomb bay doors finally go up. We have given up on getting rid of our bombs and head for home. Soon we are out of danger. We were over enemy territory for only fifty-two minutes roundtrip. I take off my 'flak suit' armor, like a knight of old, and my steel helmet, a regular GI helmet in which I have cut spaces for the earphones. (It would be a couple of months before we were finally issued special helmets that would make such handiwork unnecessary.) We start letting down into lower altitudes, from 21,000 feet down to 10,000. The bombardier and I are friendly again. The navigator wants to urinate and is dancing up and down like a kid.

I fly it back. The boys are still chattering over the interphone but more in the baritone manner. Except Boyovitch. We must make a decision about the bombs. If the shackles are frozen, the only way to jettison the bombs will be to reopen the bomb bay doors and send Finicle, the engineer, or Snell, the waist gunner, to unlatch the shackles with a screwdriver. With the North Sea 10,000 feet below, slipping on the catwalk would spell curtains. Personally, I would prefer that Boyovitch do it, but Finicle outranks him, and it is normally Finicle's job. But Streit and I prefer to have him in the top turret, keeping an eye on things and available to help us if something should go wrong with the propellers or the engines. *What about the bombardier?* But sending him will look like we are holding him responsible for the malfunction.

Finally Streit says, 'I'll land the ship with the bombs. It's a cinch.'

It is not exactly proper procedure, and if I insist, he will jettison the bombs. When we get down to 3,000 feet, the bomb latches should unfreeze, and we can do it in less than ten seconds. But if it is not a case of frozen shackles, then what? Half an hour on the catwalk for whomever we decide to send.

This is an opportunity to show how much we trust Streit's flying. I would not have done it because of my tendency to land two feet (sometimes three) above the runway, instead of greasing her in as Streit does. My way is okay but not something to do with 5,000 pounds of bombs still in the bomb bay.

And so Streit brings the ship in and makes a perfect landing. We shake hands on it, and I wave to the ground crew. On the ground, we count five holes in the ship. No, wait; we have to add a rather large hole close to the tail gunner's station.

'Ha, ha, Sergeant Boyovitch,' we are all laughing. 'Is that why you fell so silent for a while? Everybody was talking but you.'

'You bet your life, sir! I don't like that stuff coming close to me like that.'

'You and just about everybody else.'

Marcott has an excuse for the bombs not coming out, but we don't bother to question whether it really was the malfunction he claims or him forgetting to hit his rack switch to release the bombs. Right now we are just proud as hell. Six holes! We climb in a truck. Coffee, sandwiches, interrogation by intelligence officers, and home. Our first raid is over. Of course, it wasn't much. We had expected a lot, you know, just like a first date with a girl you've been chasing for a long time. It was all over before we knew it. We're a bit silly now, making a lot of noise about nothing.

'I wasn't scared,' I volunteer. 'But I wasn't very calm either.'

'Ah, that's all right, Pitts, you'll learn. A first raid is a first raid. You'll never forget it though.'

I agree. 'You bet your life I won't. Sure was glad to see those bomb bay doors up.'

'Okay. You guys better get some sleep. You are alerted for tomorrow.'

'Swell.'

'Listen, fellows, he says "swell".'

'Sure, what do you want me to say?'

'Ah, gowon, Pitts. You're all right.'

'Goodnight, fellows.'

'Goodnight, Pitts. Sweet dreams.'

5

THE SECOND MISSION

TOP BRASS AND THE 'BIG B'

We did not fly a mission that next morning after all, the alert having been scrubbed during the night. I just slept in and went to ground school in the afternoon, a chore the veterans didn't have to put up with. One more reason for becoming a veteran as quickly as possible.

Our topic that afternoon was 'Proper Procedures for Ditching a B-17 in the North Sea'. To raise our level of attention, the instructor, a senior pilot, told us we would be lucky if half the crew survived a ditching, especially now in December. Did anyone dare ask if landing instead in Switzerland or Sweden would be considered 'a suitable alternative'? No; no one raised this iffy question to which the answer might have been, 'If you ditch, the Air Corps will recuperate an average of five people for further combat duty.' Meaning, of course, that half the crew left alive and recyclable was preferable to a whole crew alive but out of reach.

The instructor told us of a navigator from the 687th Squadron, a veteran who had been to both raids on Schweinfurt, who had just left the base to return to the States after his twenty-fifth mission. Returning from a raid to Stuttgart, the ship on which he was flying had been forced to ditch. Of the 151 ships, including our wing, which made up the First Division that was carrying out that raid, about twelve others had found themselves in the same predicament.

'Why?' our instructor continued.

Because General Travis, who had led the First Division that day, had been told by the bombardier in the last two minutes of the bomb run that the target, a high-priority ball-bearing factory, was covered by one of the intermittent clouds drifting over the city. Consequently, the General decided to make a complete circle over the target, come back, and hope that his bombardier could then find a clear sighting. Throughout the entire twenty minutes of circling, he kept his bomb bay doors open. Was this to signal to the groups who followed him that he was going around for another go at the target, even though it increased the drag on the plane and raised the gas consumption, or had he simply forgotten to close his doors?

'Strict radio silence,' our instructor went on, 'prevented us from finding out whether this was an oversight or the result of some greater wisdom. So, everyone left their bomb bay doors open. Can you imagine someone calling up the General and asking, 'Sir, have you forgotten your bomb bay doors?' It would be like saying to him, 'Sir, you have left your fly opened?'' (Or, as the French would have said, 'It is high noon at the zipper factory.') By now our instructor had us in stitches, though I had never been so attentive to a lecture in all my life.

The trouble with the General's plan, he explained, was that the 360-degree turn threw the formation into disarray. In formation flying, it was very difficult for the leader, the hub, to make a turn fast enough to evade all the flak guns that were pounding away and, at the same time, slow enough to not cause those who were further back in the formation, the rim, to be whiplashed all over the sky. The high and low squadrons, and especially their second elements, were covering thirty miles more than the leader's wing men, often at full throttle. The margin had forced ten percent of the ships into the sea.

Luckily, it was early September, and all those who had ditched had been plucked alive by Air-Sea Rescue, but they cursed the name of Brigadier General Travis.

In addition to this mishap, the bombing pattern had been mediocre, and the losses to enemy action substantial, sixteen percent failing to return. A wasted mission.

I felt our instructor was trying to seduce us into joining the consensus of opinion against General Travis. It was an attitude that would find no disfavor on our base, where it was rumored that our Colonel Preston had little sympathy for the General, who was his immediate superior. I did not say anything, but I resolved at that time to keep an open mind – were we not expected to make a circle over the target if the first bomb run misfired? Was General Travis responsible for the fact that our division had been spread out and disordered by the 360-degree turn? Was he supposed to waste a mission in order to preclude casualties, instead of making every effort to accomplish the goal?

For him, the individual risks and sufferings were overridden by the mission. And in the end, a demanding general might get credit when it was all over. In the meantime, he would have to bear the brunt of our fears and frustrations, while the 'nice guy' who showed understanding of our weaknesses, who in the last analysis would subordinate the mission to the survival of his men, would be popular.

But who would pay the price for a sloppy and ragged formation? At what point would 'battle fatigue' proliferate, AWOLs and sick calls multiply, and crews get 'lost' on their way to the rendezvous point?

Our instructor had opened a window for us, the new crews, the junior birdmen, on the inconsistencies and dissensions of war. What had been a 'correct' command decision was decried by the veterans, revealing to us their real feelings toward some of our top Brass. How much of our eagerness would we lose as we shed our naïveté?

Two days afterwards, on the evening of December 13, 1943, we were alerted for what promised to be a long mission. The ground crews told us that the 'Tokyo' tanks in the B-17 Gs' wing tips had been filled, tanks so named because they would supposedly get you all the way to Tokyo if need be. In addition, the older B-17 Fs had had half the space in their bomb bays preempted by bomb bay tanks. None of this impressed me, because I was still in a state of elation from my initiation to combat. I was glad to be going on a long raid; Emden had been only a 'milk run' really. At last I would be going on a 'serious' mission.

On the evening of the alert, we met in McCall and Gurney's room to chat. O'Neil, our squadron's lead bombardier and our pipeline to the Brass, had little to say and seemed a bit concerned. There had been no leaks about this mission.

At briefing the next morning, we waited expectantly for the curtain covering the map of Western Europe to be pulled up, clueing us in on our destination. When the curtain was finally removed, and we saw where the ingoing lines of red wool and the outgoing lines of blue wool were converging, the audience was stunned. There were none of the usual cat calls or mild heckling or terrified clowning that occurred when the division was being sent out into 'deep penetration', which in these last two or three months had meant Augsburg, Schweinfurt, Frankfurt, Anklam, Munster. The lines ran to none of these places. This was BERLIN.

I looked at the faces of some of the Schweinfurt veterans, and they were all incredulous, growing even more so as the briefing continued. In the presentations made by Intelligence and Weather, we were told that we could not expect much fighter protection over Germany, the number of flak guns over Berlin was very high – we were probably going over the ball-bearing plants of Erkner, a suburb of Berlin – and we could expect a high number of German fighters. Also the weather would be excellent.

At the end of the briefing, General Travis got up and made a speech. He said that the B-17 was originally designed for deep penetration without fighter escort. Nevertheless, we would have escorts until about halfway to Berlin and would be picked up at about the same spot on our way back. This was a crucial mission; it would be an enormous blow to the German ball-bearing industry and the German morale. It would be a historic mission, a triumph of American technology and fortitude.

Marcott nudged me and whispered, 'Eh, Pitts, what's "fortitude?"'

'It's like Flying Fortress, stupid. *Fort*ress, *fort*itude. It's what comes from flying these planes...'

General Travis was continuing. He would be flying with our group, flying in the very lead of the 41st Combat Wing of the First Division, followed by three other wings and by the Second and Third Divisions, which made up the rest of the Eighth Air Force. He warned us that he would accept no excuse for aborts. 'If you lose an engine you will go over the target on three engines.' Some audible murmuring met this statement.

Much later I was to realize that we were being 'invited' by the General to charge the enemy in the style of Tennyson's 'Charge of the Light Brigade.' For General Travis this would be the apex of his career. Whether he came back or not, he would go down in history.

The veterans, who comprised a quarter of the audience, had yet to accept junior birdmen like me into their ranks. If we came back from this one, there would be no question of being accepted into their fraternity – we would have been together in the Balaclava of the air.

Colonel Preston closed the briefing with a few words. He told us that we 'had a job to do,' that we should 'keep a tight formation,' and 'get those bombs in there'. To his ritual inquiry, 'Any questions?' came no reply. Nobody would ask the question, 'Had not Schweinfurt proved that the theory of deep penetration without fighter escort was not tenable?' Even I, still an eager neophyte, had heard something of this sort. But I was still in the excited haze of a 'combat virgin', and I was not about to ask such an irreverent question. Like most of us, I could be brave facing the enemy, and still remain cowardly in front of our own bureaucracy.

This would be my second mission. What I remember of my feelings is that I was closed up tight as an oyster. I was not consciously afraid, although I thought that there was only an even chance of surviving this mission. But since I had joined the Air Corps I had always accepted an even chance as quite sufficient for me to make it. I had accepted the odds, one of the invisible functions of the briefing. Indeed I was eager to go, but I was also aware that my enthusiasm cut me off from the feelings of others. It was obvious to me that if they knew how I felt, they would think I was nuts. They would think I was of the same ilk as the General, except he at least was a great poker player. He was considered an 'iron ass'. I would be considered 'bonkers'.

Briefing broke up. I went in line with the other copilots to pick up the ten pocket-sized, waterproof escape kits containing silk maps of Northern Europe, French money, rations, and compasses that were handed out to each crew, along with ten Mars bars for the crew. Even the chocolate admonished us to live up to the war-like virtues. Nobody spoke. The line was usually full of pats on the back and jocularity – at least it was that way after the briefing for Emden. This time, silence.

We had been instructed to start engines at 7.00a.m. When we arrived at the ground crew's tent, we found it had been postponed until 8.00. The gunners looked at me, questioning silently, and I said, 'It's okay. It's a very important mission. The General will be flying just ahead of us; we'll make it.' As if his rank were a guarantee of our safety. I passed around the escape kits and the candy bars.

Marcott was silent, as was Streit, who remained by himself, sitting pensive in a corner of the tent. Kundin came in from the navigators' briefing obviously shaken but still committed. To Streit and me he gave miniature maps of the mission with compass headings and distances. Another delay was phoned in. Start-engine time was now 9.00a.m., which meant that it might be dusk when we came back to base... another problem.

The grass was still wet with the morning dew, so we lay down on the tarmac, trying to relax. Our major concern was to find something on which we could rest our heads – coats, rolled-up blankets, jackets, anything the ground crew could spare.

I remember it was unseasonably warm that day. I saw General Travis, wearing his flight suit with the star of his rank embroidered on each shoulder, walking aimlessly through our dispersal area. He was here because we were the squadron that, with the rest of our group, would be flying immediately on his wing. Lead group: a pretty good position I'd been told, and we would be in the lead squadron, second element. The second 'V' of mechanical geese. We couldn't complain.

The General seemed pensive, and I wondered if it was because no one was yelling, 'Atten – TION!' as he passed the clumps of airmen lying on the taxi strips. Or perhaps it was that he was worried that these delays might portend an order from Wycombe Abbey to scrub the mission. For him this was probably the dream of a lifetime, leading the Eighth Air Force on its first raid to Berlin. Another star on his shoulder when he replaced the commanding officer of the First Division. And if we really clobbered the target, and sustained losses below the percent ages of those at Schweinfurt, perhaps even the Congressional Medal of Honor.

Lying on the tarmac, waiting for our mission to begin, I began conjecturing what might be going through the General's mind. I was aware that he was known as a stickler for military etiquette; how would he interpret the present silence? Would he see it as a feeling that in sweating out the mission together, differences in rank were suspended? Or, in view of the disgruntled murmuring that had occurred during I speech, would he interpret it as the beginning of rebellion?

And how was anyone to recognize him anyway? After all, once we had put on the blue electric suits and the flight suits over them, the only apparel that identified our rank were the officers' hats and the fact that, naked or fully dressed, the crews knew us, and they never saluted us one way or the other. The General probably did not have his service cap on and nobody was expecting embroidered stars on the shoulders of flight overalls, hence most crewmen did not see them.

Was he going to order us to stand at attention and salute him? If he demanded his pound of respect and started chewing ass, anything might happen. Boyovitch might say something irreparable. Fowler, Davis's copilot and our ex-juvenile delinquent, was capable of open rebellion and would have no qualms about chewing the General's ass in return. What did they risk? Immediate arrest and being locked up while preparations went on for their general court martial in two weeks? Nobody in the American Air Corps was going to be put against the wall and shot for 'disrespect toward a superior officer.' On the contrary, they would be taken off the mission to Berlin and become famous on the base for their nerve in telling the General to stick it. Brigadier General Travis had little left standing after ordering us to 'go over Berlin on three engines, if necessary.' It showed he did not trust our judgment, that he did not trust that, if it were at all possible, we would, on our own initiative, go over the target on three engines. His order was a slap in the face, very much resented by those pilot-copilot teams who were closest to the temptation of flying to Switzerland to give up, to bail out. They could transform guilt into self-righteousness – a chance not to be missed.

The General would, of course, I continued fantasizing, send for the MPs to arrest the culprits. During the time it took for them to arrive, the ground crews would lose no time in calling the other squadrons to tell them what was happening. By the time the news reached the flying crews, it would be well amplified, and with what consequences? There were other Boyovitches and Fowlers on the base, eager to get arrested. And our Colonel Preston would probably arrive on the scene before the MPs; having to reinforce the General's authority, what would be the cost to his own?

I wondered where our Major was – our handsome blonde and mustachioed squadron CO had apparently not scheduled himself for this mission. Was he needed on the ground? But Brownlow, I was sure, would be sweating it out with the crew he had chosen to accompany, armed with his movie camera. Brownlow came from a social class equal or superior to that of the General and had friends in Washington as well. If the General, in his anger, went too far out of bounds, William G. Brownlow III would not hesitate to tell him so, couching it in terms such as, 'Please, sir, remember who you are,' or perhaps, more gently, 'I am sure the Brigadier General did not mean that; it is only the tension of a complex day.' Brownlow would be fully aware that a difficult mission augmented the moral position of the troops destined to pay its costs. Nobody was going to step on the toes of a Schweinfurt veteran scheduled for the first raid on Berlin – or even on the toes of a junior birdman like myself.

As it turned out, the General kept his mouth shut and nothing happened. As usual, my seditious imagination had gone far beyond the actual situation.

Suddenly, shortly before 9.00a.m., red flares shot up from our tower. The mission was scrubbed.

Were we glad? We had gone through a rough psychological workout in committing ourselves to the undertaking, come what may – half the mission was over. And now the workout had been in vain. I got up. Here and there someone cheered, but most were silent. I saw General Travis, his face white and drawn. He seemed at a loss. I felt I should say something, that I knew what a great disappointment it must be for him, that I was sorry. It would have been only half a lie. But I realized how idiotically patronizing my condolences would sound, coming from a mere second lieutenant. For once, I thought the better of it and, instead, gave him a Class A salute, trying to convey, as I realized years later, the message, 'I have really thought it over, General, and I'm still with you. See you next time.'[1]

After replacing his service cap, he returned my salute.

I picked up the escape kits from the crew and walked back to my barracks with my B-4 bag, a bulky two handled, zippered cloth bag. I was not going to wait for the truck to take us back to our dressing room at Headquarters. I did not want to change with all the others, have to listen to the angry comments and curses concerning General Travis. I was a traitor: I admired the son of a bitch. I didn't have the excuse of belonging to his retinue, to his court. If my voice rose to defend the General, it would not help my standing with the band of brothers.

General Travis was what we called an eager beaver, and that quality in a crew member or in the higher staff aroused our suspicions. Like Patton, he belonged to a culture that was too military, too feudal for us to share. We were essentially civilians in uniform. General Travis was a general after the fashion of my old Napoleonic War books – in my mind's eye I saw him astride a great horse, sword in his hand, charging the enemy as fiery steam poured from the nostrils of his mount.

Our Colonel Preston was much more in tune with the problems of the air crews. When at the end of briefing he spoke a few words to us, he spoke only in terms of 'a job to be done.' That we understood. He spoke to us like our fathers had spoken when we had to help with the uprooting of a big stump, or with putting a new roofing on the house, or with staying all weekend to take inventory of the family store. No heroics, just hard work. If death came, it would carry no lyrical meaning as it did for the French or the Germans; it would only be a work accident, and work did not frighten us.

Our barracks were quite close to the dispersal area. When I reached my room, I fell on my bed and slept from 9.00a.m. until 1.00p.m. When I arose, I ate a few sandwiches, wrote some letters, and returned the escape kits to Intelligence. My friends and I never discussed the briefing, or our feelings when the mission was scrubbed.

Many years later, I learned through the grapevine that the mission had been planned as a phony, permitting Intelligence to ensnare those persons who had been feeding the Germans and Axis Sally details about the targets of our mission. I was not convinced, however. Perhaps this story was a cover for the incredible stupidity of intending to send us on a raid to Berlin with little or no fighter escort, when the first long-range P-51s with Rolls-Royce engines were just trickling onto our fighter bases, before flooding them in the winter of 1944. As it was, we went to Erkner three months later, when our escort outnumbered the German fighters.

On December 16, 1943, three days after the mission to Berlin was scrubbed, we went to Bremen. It was a step up in difficulty compared to our first mission; Emden had been only ten miles inside German territory, whereas Bremen was fifty. Bremen, a naval and manufacturing center, was also a more important target. It was on this raid that I first saw a B-17 go down, falling from the formation just ahead of us in a spasmodic slow roll, its right wing torn off by a direct flak hit on the bomb run. No one took evasive action, no one budged, except for a 'Tail-end Charlie' who took the place of the fallen ship. The formation remained as tight as if it were on parade. It was magnificent, and I was part of it.

Back at the base, after debriefing, I went back to the squadron dispersal area to look at our planes. Except for the loss of the one shot down, our group of twenty ships had sustained damage to only seven planes. Ours, the *Penny Ante*, had thirty-five holes. The one next to it seemed to have suffered more, and as I inspected it, I was suddenly transfixed by the sight of the ball turret. Two inches of blood covered its bottom. The gunner must have bled to death. It had been his last raid. Not quite a milk run.

Nevertheless, compared to the 'Big B', the intended raid on Berlin, Bremen remained 'Little B'.

6

OUR LEADER, COLONEL PRESTON

OUR LEADER IN BATTLE

In November of 1943, as we arrived at the base, we were greeted, not by the squadron commander, but by a sergeant who showed us to our quarters. I remember we were able to exercise some choice, and I opted for my single room. Then we went out to eat dinner.

Here we were on our new base. We belonged to the 379th Bomb Group and, more immediately, to the 524th Squadron. We were tremulously curious and were met by a couple of 'old timers' who were eager to enlighten us. One was a bombardier with a face full of acne scars who had been to Schweinfurt. Not knowing what to ask, we inquired, 'Was it tough?'

'What do you mean 'tough'? Of course it was tough!'

What we meant, I think, was, 'Can one contain his fears and still do his job?' So the bombardier, enjoying the attention given to him by pilots, tried to frighten us by giving us graphic stories of planes exploding or falling into spins, of missions where twenty-five percent of the crews failed to return. At the same time, he was implicitly offering himself as a role model. He had survived. He had done his job, and we should do the same. It did not quite satisfy our hunger for 'the lowdown dope', 'the real thing'. I hoped that one day, when other crews would ask us for the lowdown, that we would not try to frighten them.

The day after, we went to ground school, morning and afternoon. We did not meet the squadron leader, Major Culpepper, in any formal way, nor our operations officer, Captain Brownlow. After classes, we, the junior birdmen, showed up at the squadron dayroom timidly, to write our mail or play cards. The regular members of the squadron, the 'veterans', tended to meet at the Officers' Club. Each group preferred to stay by itself.

Some of us went to the Control tower to watch the aircraft returning from a mission. I believe Bremen had been the target. That is when we had the first glimpse of our group leader, Col. Maurice Preston. He was tall, with the build of the successful football player he had been at West Point. Some of the crewmen, the 'Subway Alumni' knew him by his grid-iron exploits, and it gave him a certain charisma. I would not say he was handsome; personable would have been a better term for the Colonel. No one spoke badly of him, and that included our self-designated 'initiators' who had met us with the charge-of-quarters. During my whole five-month stay with the 379th, the only complaints I heard about the Colonel were about his aloofness and his favoring the members of the old cadre who came overseas with him.

Normally the Colonel ate with his staff in a room behind the large Operations Room. Here, on blackboard walls, the names and organizational references of all the crews sent on a mission were displayed in chalk, as was also a permanent white drawing of our base with its runways, buildings, and taxi strips. Ground personnel, perched on tall ladders, armed with chalk and sponges, would bring the blackboards up to date. After a mission, but before dinner, the Colonel could take in at a glance the situation: how many crews were missing in action, and what squadrons had been hit hard. How many crewmen had been brought back from the mission killed or wounded? How many aircraft might be in working order for tomorrow's duties, practice flights, or some more war?

The Colonel would have a pretty good idea of the situation already because he would be at the tower when our planes returned from a mission. However, it was not rare for planes to land on different bases or crash onto British beet fields for lack of gas or because of faltering engines. It might be a while before they were reported in by phone, so sometimes the blackboard and the stepladder would know it before the Colonel did. If the group was alerted for the following day and the Colonel wanted to discuss our potential for the next mission, he wanted to talk to his closest associates – Lieutenant Colonel Kittle and Lieutenant Colonel Rohr, the four squadrons' COs, the heads of engineering and armament, and the chief flight surgeon – without having the troops eavesdropping.

The first and only time I sat at the same dinner table with him was when we attended the Thanksgiving Dinner of 1943. I had not been on my first mission as yet. We were all in our Class A uniforms, except for a navigator who sat next to me and who wore, in lieu of a jacket, a rather messy and torn khaki sweater. I felt embarrassed by such a raunchy display and thought that the Colonel was not overly pleased by the presence of the navigator. Seated next to Colonel Preston was Lieutenant Colonel Kittle. They did not speak to us, and we were not about to break the ice. Mutual embarrassment was the tone.

We were in the officers' mess. There were no flags hanging on the walls, no pictures of past commanders, no high table; it was just a cafeteria, and the food usually was not much more varied or better cooked than in the enlisted air crews' mess.

Today the fare was uncommonly good, and I wondered if, besides the holiday, the presence of the Colonel at our table had something to do with it. We had a white tablecloth; we were being served (which was a change), and the waiter asked us, 'White or dark or both?' We ignored the Colonel, as he ignored us, and ate with gusto the turkey, the stuffing, the cranberry sauce, the sweet potatoes, the gravy, the hot biscuits, the apple pie with ice cream. (Some had cheddar cheese on top of their pie, an American custom that made me blink.) Between mouthfuls we would congratulate each other on our good fortune or use an expression made famous by a banjo-playing Texas governor: 'Pass the biscuits, Pappy.'

My companions, who sat further down the table, out of reach of the Colonel's silence, ate with visible pleasure, once in a while mumbling to one another with lines from the popular radio show *Amos 'n' Andy*: 'This is very good chow; have a cigar, Mr Jones!' 'YOU have a cigar, Mr Kingfish!'[1] Needless to say, there were no cigars, but the boys did enjoy their meal.

On ordinary days the food was quite acceptable, even though many of the officers and most of the enlisted men complained systematically and reminisced about mother's apple pie.

For drink we had ice water and black coffee, unlimited. I had never been a big coffee drinker, certainly not with my meals, but here I became used to it. As a child I had been a big milk drinker. When my parents' marriage broke up and my French mother took me with her to France, I was six and a half years old and drank at my grandmother's table either light beer or watered wine, because that was the custom at Dunkirk where she lived, and it made me feel very grown up.

In the French boarding school watered wine was the rule. But when I returned to the States nine years later to visit my father during the summer vacations in 1936 and 1937 (before I entered college as a sophomore in 1938), I went back to milk as if I had never left it.

At the airbase, we had milk reconstituted from milk powder – not the same thing. Then I found out that our Colonel, who was probably a milk addict as I was, had bought a cow from one of the local farmers and had delegated an enlisted man with a farming background to look after her, seeing to it that she was milked and fed regularly. One of our medical officers was, in fact, a veterinarian, so that the Colonel's cow was really given the VIP treatment and checked for TB, hence her raw milk was safe, something not to be taken for granted with a French, Italian, or Spanish cow at that time.[2]

And so the Colonel and his staff, flying or non-flying, had fresh milk every morning, milk so unctuous that its top surface in the glass made a convex curve.

Meanwhile, we, the troops, had reconstituted milk we splashed on our cereal. I would also make myself a tepid *café au lait* in which I dunked a piece of toast. It was not bourgeois manners, but I preferred it that way. Early morning, in a Paris café I would have dunked a piece of thin baguette sliced lengthwise and buttered or, better still, a croissant. But compared to the infantry in Italy or in the Pacific, I had it very good.

'Hey, Jesse, you damned frog, what do you do that for?'

'To wash down these pancakes and the watery syrup, you damned dago!'

'I wish I could do that with a glass of milk from the Colonel's cow! It's not fair!'

'He can't transform the base into a dairy farm!'

'The problem with you, Frenchy, is that you always have a different idea. I should be able to get pissed off without your forcing me to look at 'the big picture.' So, I get angry at you!'

'I know, I should keep my mouth shut. Anger cleans the soul!'

And listening from the end of the table, Barrett, our good Catholic boy, with whom I had many inconclusive discussions on the existence of God, added, 'But it also shrinks it!'

When I first heard the story of the Colonel's cow, toward the end of my tour, I was a bit put out but pleased to discover a fissure in our fearless leader. That was the only story I heard about the Colonel during my stay at Kimbolton. There was little gossip about the Brass in our squadron, even when we met in small groups at night as we did in McCall and Gurney's room. The poker players made up another group, mainly veterans of Schweinfurt, Anklam, Munster, Stuttgart; but we were not privy to their gossip. We were only junior birdmen. They were seasoned veterans.

The great gossip mongers were the enlisted men who worked in Group Operations, and they would speak to their counterparts in each squadron. O'Neil, one of the group lead bombardiers, was the recipient of many of their rumors, even though he was an officer, perhaps because he always seemed to be on the verge of sharing a good joke. Aside from O'Neil, officers were restrained in their gossip mongering. Although having 'hot poop' to share was a claim to prestige, it was, as the Brits would say, 'not quite cricket.'

There was very little spit and polish on our base. Every month or so, on a Saturday morning, we had an inspection by the Colonel. We had our canteen opened for his inspection, each pair of socks neatly folded into a ball, our toilet articles arranged in something like military order. We met the Colonel in some semblance of ranks and gave him a Class A salute. He inspected us perfunctorily. I seem to remember our squadron executive officer, an old fighter of the First World War nicknamed 'Pinky' following him around with a notebook in which he would inscribe the observations that fell from the lips of the Colonel. Within the air crew there was no saluting. During my tour on the base, the only parades I remember were the ones for the giving of decorations. I slept in my bunk for all of them, as the majority of the recipients did, and there were no complaints from any of the squadron Brass.

Curiously enough, it was military life that taught me the modicum of order of which I am capable, not family life – of which I had little experience past the age of six and a half – nor French boarding school, nor American college. The major difference was the fact that I admired military order, even though I had some problems adapting to it.

What Colonel Preston (and his superiors) did care about were the statistics that compared the Eighth Air Force groups, which were pitted against one another every month. Headquarters in Wycombe Abbey, or 'Pinetree' as its code name described it, would let our group headquarters know our comparative scores for best bombing results (greatest percentage of hits on a target), greatest tonnage of bombs dropped on targets, greatest number of aircraft attacking targets, lowest numbers of aircraft lost, lowest abortive rate of aircraft sent out. The 379th led all the other groups in most measurements, but I and many others did not hear of it until we had left the group. Nevertheless, we knew that when the Eighth Air Force wanted to impress honored visitors, it was usually our group that was chosen to demonstrate what a heavy bombardment group looked like.

Preston saw the 379th as a sort of rebellious orphan, who had to rely on its own resources – a self-sufficient, autonomous creature that, by hard work, triumphed over all the obstacles fate threw its way. It is a view that reminds me of John Bunyan's *The Pilgrim's Progress*. Even if Preston had not read it, by the osmosis of the milieu in which he was raised, he had many of its basic attitudes: self reliance, suspicion of the ties of the flesh, devotion to the pursuit of right regardless of the consequences. And the spirit of the 379th: '… Probably it grew out of rebellion against the fact that the 379th was not given a chance from the start … From its activation at Wendover right on through combat it was 'on its own' and received no help from anyone … Discouragement bred resentment, resentment bred anger, anger bred resolution and a do-or-die attitude, and the latter resulted in a mighty fine outfit.'[3]

In October, November, and December of 1943, the experienced cadre on our base, depleted by the missions flown in the fall, had a hard time coping with the influx of new crews, who were coming in from a thicker pipeline and through a method of piecemeal initiations. It was a situation that Colonel Preston knew well, from the early days of the 379th's formation; somehow they had managed, lifting themselves by their own bootstraps. In that spirit, the Colonel sent all of his junior birdmen on an Air-Sea Rescue mission off the coast of Holland.

Under the command of one of our lieutenant colonels and one of our squadron commanders, we flew for several hours in a very loose formation, sweeping the North Sea at an altitude of 500 feet, just below the cloud bank, looking for dinghies that might contain living or dead RAF crews who had ditched or bailed out on the way back from a mission to Germany.

We also kept a tense lookout for German fighters, who had a golden opportunity to shoot down B-17s while the gunners had their eyes fixed on the sea rather than on the clouds and could not cover each other by a wall of formation fire. If they came, each B-17 would move up into the cloud bank and head for home. But perhaps the ceiling was lower over the airfields than it was thirty or forty miles from their shores, or perhaps they suspected a trap or diversion, and the Germans did not come.

We did not sight any RAF crewmen, just a floating mine and an empty dinghy with water covering its floor. With Streit's agreement, I told our gunners that we would circle the mine and the dinghy, and they could sink them, which they did, the mine sinking without exploding.

At that point, few sights had been more poignant than that empty dinghy, moving up and down in a choppy sea before our gunners put so many holes in it that it sank. Yes, that too, we realized, was a part of combat – dying in the cold sea or in a dinghy, of exposure or exhaustion, alone at night. But we would make it. Ever since cadet days, we had been threatened with fifty-percent odds of survival, and we had made it. No reason why we should not survive another fifty-percent screening that from now on the enemy fighters would be administering most of the check rides.

Such as it was, our Air-Sea Rescue mission would have to serve as our initiation into combat. From the indices kept by our top headquarters, it must have been sufficient, for the 379th remained ahead in performance. I don't know whether or not we were more skillful after this flight than before, but our judgment from now on would incorporate the presence of the enemy and, also, a certain awareness of fear as to what that presence might mean for our lives. We had challenged him and he had not come; we might not be so lucky next time. I would never forget the dinghy, empty but for the water sloshing in its bottom.

Higher headquarters – Wing, Division, or Eighth Air Force – were always full of good ideas that we thought came from Colonel Preston and his staff, and sometimes did. For instance, at the end of November, they picked up our forty-five automatics under the pretext that they did not want to facilitate suicides. Sounded a bit strange to us, since if you wanted to kill yourself you could just walk into a moving propeller.

In reality, what our staff was trying to do, if we were shot down, was to make us less vulnerable to the German civilians with shotguns and pitchforks. Pulling your pistol out and, even worse, starting to shoot, ensured your death at the hands of the frightened and angry civilians. With no pistol, you knew that your task was to surrender quietly while preserving as much as possible of your dignity, a dignity that, you hoped, would not offend them. Woe to you if a militant Nazi was present to rally his neighbors and them on you. A Nazi who was not fighting at the front had probably many reasons for transforming your capture into a warlike episode. If they were going to kill you, better die like a man, if possible silently. No question of begging for mercy.

It was better to fall into the hands of the regular armed forces. They were professionals, you were a professional; there was nothing personal in the destruction you brought. The German soldiers and the veterans of the First World War understood that. The German women did not, and there was no fury like that of a German woman who had lost a child to our bombing. If you stood up with no weapon, you certified your personal innocence, and it might impress your captors, because bravery in face of terrible odds often reminds the enemy of the human condition and throws it up to them to equal your virtue.

Explaining to green replacements what might await a bailed-out crewman on German ground might create additional fears that higher headquarters had not yet thought about. So they lied to us: 'We want to prevent suicides...'

There were consequences to landing by parachute in enemy territory both with a gun and without a gun, and it was better for you to learn them with your friends in a bull session. We discussed once the women of Hamburg who, as the rumor went, would tear you limb from limb if they found you before the soldiers did. Conclusion: try to hide until you see some soldiers and keep a couple of packs of cigarettes to promote some good will. If they want your wrist watch, don't argue. If you are in the hands of vigilantes, ask at least for the right to smoke a last cigarette and pass the pack around. Anything can happen before you have taken your last puff, including the arrival of regular soldiers (who always moved more quickly when they picked up the smell of American tobacco).

During the hard summer and fall of 1943 when losses were high, friendly fighters stymied by the lack of long-range droppable tanks, and the strength of the Luftwaffe was at its peak, the high Brass at Wycombe Abbey was searching for ways to bolster the morale of flying personnel. Somehow the word must have come from 'above' to try a procedure inspired by the Japanese. Colonel Preston is reported to have told his airmen: 'Is anyone scared? If not, there is something wrong with you. I'll give you a little clue about how to fight this war: make believe that you are dead already.'

I checked this with a couple of veterans who had participated in the Schweinfurt raids, and they had no recollection of hearing the Colonel ever use words to that effect. That doesn't mean he never did, but they were not his usual style. They did not fit his personality, and after the passage of time, the crews would not remember the words that did not fit what they knew of him.

The idea behind that pessimistic injunction was to cut the links that the airman had to his past, especially to his family, sweetheart, and friends – to make him psychologically more identified with his group and more emotionally dependent on it. I can see General Travis using that language but not Colonel Preston. Acceptance of death is not an attitude that could come easily to American crews, who have resolved to fight and defend their lives against all trespassers.

Colonel Preston detested speeches to the troops as much as General Travis loved them. When he felt he had to say something at the end of a briefing, it would be in the nature of last recommendations: to keep a tight formation, to not waste ammunition, or other useful details. He would end with, 'Any questions?' As usual, there were none, so he would dismiss us with 'Good luck'. Some wags in the back would yell, 'And goodbye!' And that was that.

He was considered one of the best commanders of the Eighth Air Force, but like most of his fellow group leaders, he was not inclined to write. We shall never know how he felt and what his torments were. Very rarely did he allow 'the troops' to look into the recesses of his personality; all we know of him was that he knew his business and was unflappable. What else would we need to know about our leader? That he liked fresh milk and was partial to his cronies? Who cared?

I never heard any negative comments about our Colonel's qualities as a combat leader. In my early combat days, I must have gone on a couple missions that he led, but I don't remember any incident about them. I took his courage for granted. After all, he was a West Pointer and a hotshot pilot. Furthermore, like all men who are thrown into circumstances full of uncertainty and danger, I needed a leader who seemed to have the magic touch, who would 'keep his head though all others might lose theirs.' I projected upon him the greatness that was required by those circumstances and saw in him what we call 'charisma', the gift of grace. Colonel Preston fulfilled the needed role well, because, aside from our projections and needs, he brought something of his own to the situation. He was naturally brave, while many of us were not. If asked to give our opinion, I would venture to say that most of us preferred having a colonel who might be distant but who delivered the goods; essentially that was what our experience with Colonel Preston proved to be.

I've discovered in the last few years that he was also a West Point snob. Apparently on April 6, 1944 (I was gone by then), in a seminar held on base for all bombardiers, '… the CO told them that bombardiers were nothing more than glorified bomb togglers who should be enlisted men, not officers. No wonder the officers seemed agitated.'[4]

Our Colonel was quite right, but it was a mistake to say it publicly. To his closest staff members, he also confided that the great bulk of us should have been made sergeant pilots instead of being commissioned. Luckily the Headquarters staff kept their mouths shut, and no one ever heard of this 'anti-democratic bias'. I don't think it affected his performance as a group commander, and all of us got our promotions in due course, although it must have grated Colonel Preston to hand out so many first lieutenancies and captaincies.

Such is a less hagiographic concept of Colonel Preston. All I can say is that even if I had known of all his warts and the intemperate talk of which he was capable, I would still have been willing to follow him, if not into the 'jaws of hell' as the expression goes, at least into a repeat version of the second Schweinfurt.

Of course, I say that now, when I am too old to fight, when I know that perfect leaders do not exist and that at least one out of three of the difficult decisions they make turn out to be, if not the wrong ones, at least the less desirable ones.

7

THIRD MISSION

BEAUVOIR: A RETURN TO FRANCE

Coming up from the Channel, I recognized the coast of Northern France, how it makes a wide angle from Calais to Dunkirk, and from Calais to Abbeville, the estuary of the Somme River. It was December 24, and I was on my way to Beauvoir, my third mission.

Beauvoir was the location of one of the dozens of concrete ramps built by the Germans in Northern France and Normandy for the launching of the VI rockets that were to fall on London from the middle of June to the middle of August in 1944. These launchings would have been far more deadly had they been directed in May or June against the ships, trucks and arms depots assembled for the invasion.

It was not our bombing that delayed the launchings. The damage we inflicted on the ramps could be repaired in a couple of days at most, so the Germans did not bother to send their fighters up to cope with these raids. Their only defenses were a few flak guns, which did, however, shoot with greater accuracy since we flew at 12,000 feet instead of 21,000 feet. This altitude permitted a better view of the French countryside, with its convoluted property lines and tens of thousands of tiny plots, which made it a far more complicated landscape than the straighter boundary lines and larger plots of Germany.

When I was a school boy, I would use a cardboard reproduction of France, perhaps a millimeter thick, not much larger than my open hand, to draw its outline, and then I would fill the inside of the map with the rivers, canals, mountains, and industrial centers of France. Geography was a serious matter in the French equivalent of junior and senior high school. In our books, the average annual production of wheat, coal, iron ore and wine was symbolized by drawings of sacks of various sizes; or barrels in the case of wine. This was to show that, with the exception of the USSR and the United States, France was second to none. Students felt they lived in a rich and powerful country with no real competition in Europe.

What a comedown when, on May 10, 1940, the war began in earnest, and the French Army, the 'best in the world' was defeated in ten days. At the end of this time, Louis XV could have sued for peace, but a democratic army must fight until most of its soldiers are convinced that the war is lost. All the professional soldiers realized that it was, but the Army continued to fight a rear-guard action for another thirty days before the government and the people would consent to surrender.

The spectacle of those last thirty days of the war was a horrible one. Soldiers, unkempt and unshaven, lurched along the roads half drunk, the traces of rivulets of wine on both sides of their dirty mouths. Dressed in pieces of uniform, many with no rifles but carrying bayonets they used mostly to open cans, they marched in disorder on roads already packed with civilians running away from the dreaded *Boche*. The bourgeois and the officers rode in cars with mattresses strapped to the roof, and the family silverware sharing space in the trunk with containers full of gasoline. The common people rode in horsedrawn carts or fled on foot, pushing baby carriages full of crying babies or, more often, full of copper pots and pans, bread, butter, and boxes of camembert. Peasants on the side of the road were selling water by the glass to customers who paid them angrily.

The soldiers would ask, 'Where are our officers? They have vanished.' Or they would say their officers had ordered them to meet them in Limoges or Clermont Ferrand. This was their excuse for fleeing, but it often was an accurate statement. In a few cases, they had shot in the back officers who demanded they make a stand against the German troops. In other instances, *adjudants*, master-sergeants, had managed take over; they kept some semblance of order, preventing the worst by looting and raping.

The whole society seemed to have liquefied. There were no orders, no directive idea around which to rally except to run south. All towns with a population over 25,000 had been declared 'open' by the government. Any troops who remained under the leadership of a lieutenant or a captain, who was *dur de dur*, tougher than tough, and wanted to build barricades and fight it out in the cellars, were begged by the mayor and his council of that town to go elsewhere. Rather than being impressed by those officers and men who wanted to do their duty in heroic circumstances, these town fathers thought them mad and would tell them so to their faces. 'You will get us all killed, and for what?' they would implore. 'You will delay them for a couple of hours, if that! You're going to get this town destroyed; for that you will get women and children killed? Show us your orders! We won't give you any food if you stay here!'

The officers, well aware that they couldn't obtain a written order for anything anymore, would often walk away, under the relieved eyes of their troops, who had been nonetheless willing to give it a go, for the *patrie, pour l'honneur*, they would now join *l'exode*, the exodus. It was as if all of France could find its collective soul only in running away together. At least in running away they knew they still existed as a nation. And Pétain, the great patriot, the victor of Verdun, had become the only authority unsullied by lies and errors. He was the first of the nation and would tell them what to do. Whatever he decided was bound to be the best thing for the country. Pétain, the great patriot, who nevertheless asked for an armistice.

For a while, a great number of the French population rallied behind his government in Vichy, while others, even before the armistice, were already searching for ways to continue the fight and go to England.

Meanwhile, the inhabitants of the villages who remained behind would often loot the houses of those who had left, using the excuse that it was 'one thing that *boches* will not take.' When those who had left trickled back home two months later, they would go door to door to reclaim their furniture, their sheets, their coffee pots, their clocks. And often their neighbors would lend a hand, perfectly willing to squeal on their fellow robbers.

To the divisions of the classical French village or small town (and France was a nation of villages and small towns) – divisions between the right and the left, between the church goers and the 'free thinkers' – were added now the divisions between those who had left and those who stayed, between the collaborators and the resisters. And in the middle, the enormous mass of the *attentistes*, waiting to join the victor.

The surprise to the French population was that the German soldiers, far from being the Huns described in story books about the First World War – monsters who 'cut off the hands of Belgian babies' or 'boiled corpses for fat' – actually turned out to be the best behaved occupiers in the history of modern warfare, and that included the British and the Americans. Stories were told of French girls who had been raped by German soldiers being taken in front of assembled troops standing at attention and asked to point out the culprits, who were then put against the wall and shot within the hour. Looters as well received the same treatment. That kind of quick reprisal, with its potential errors, discouraged most from engaging in the sort of activities that might bring such retribution. And after all, there were the local bordellos, which graced every town in France and where German soldiers were welcomed.

Officers as well had their own bordellos, in larger towns, more exclusive and refined, where they might meet the local notables, including the local doctor who came once a month to check on the health of the 'ladies'. There, also, procurement officers might arrange with the local wholesalers in meat, beer, potatoes, yard goods, and so forth, deals that would be mutually beneficial. Bank notes would be exchanged, sometimes counted on the backs or the hefty derrières of their lady companions, where they would pick up the heavy scent of their perfumes.

Until 1943, the near-unanimous opinion of the French people was that the soldiers and officers of Wehrmacht behaved 'correctly'. Then, after Stalingrad, the Germans started rounding up in earnest young men for paid labor in the German factories that were being bombed by our Air Force. Faced with the prospect of getting bombed in Germany or remaining in their home districts, where they could still see families and supplement their military diet with goodies from the family larder, young men volunteered for the Résistance in substantial numbers for the first time. They drilled under the direction of officers of the *Forces Françaises de l'Intérieur* (the Army of Interior France, as opposed to the French Army serving in Africa and England) and, once in a while, would blow up some railroad junctions, kill a collaborator, or even ambush a German squad, waiting for D-Day.

The communists belonging to the Résistance, who were easily one-third of it and who kept their own army, the *Franc-Tireurs et Partisans*, would push for more assassinations, for more frequent and ambitious ambushes. Their theory was that German reprisals would inevitably embitter the families and friends of those who were shot or deported to the concentration camps. Mutual suspicion and fear would break up the easy relations that many of their countrymen, especially the peasants and tradesmen, had established with the 'correct' Germans, broadening the recruitment pool. Many of the communists came from the big French cities and did not know the populations surrounding them; they did not know those who were taken hostage and who paid with their lives for the sabotage and killings.

The non-communists were more often locals and more closely concerned about the population on whom German reprisals fell. They preferred a strategy of training, accumulation of weapons, and just enough combat to weed out the frightened and tighten discipline; they wanted to engage in enough fighting to remind everyone that they were not playing a game of hide-and-seek and yet not trigger massive German retaliation.

Linked to the Résistance, but separate in organization from it, were the escape networks, *Les Réseaux d'Evasion*, which would pick up crewmen who bailed out over France and convoy them to the Channel harbors in the north, or more commonly, all the way to the Pyrénées Mountains. There the men would be passed on to guides who would cross over the mountains with them to Spain, where the American consuls would arrange air passage to Great Britain. There were, of course, some guides who killed their charges and robbed them or who delivered them to the German patrols and split the loot. The Jewish families who hid their fortunes on their bodies – thousand dollar bills, diamonds, gold coins – were especially vulnerable.

I used to have fantasies about bailing out over France, fantasies that were rather romantically inclined, but the boys would tell me, 'Listen, your problems will not be with the mademoiselles but with the fact that your French is too good. Furthermore, you know nothing of baseball and little of football. You will flunk the little tests London has given the French locals to administer to determine if you are a genuine American flyer or one of the stooges the Germans are trying to pass off.'

'But –'

'Who won the World Series in 1941?'

'Um –'

'What year did Babe Ruth retire?'

'Well … uh –'

'Right. The French may just execute you on the spot rather than wait for London to confirm that, yes, indeed, Jesse Pitts speaks French like a native and English with a French accent, and that, yes, he was a copilot on B-17 8202 when it was shot down on such-and-such a date, and that, no, he knows nothing about baseball, but he does indeed make great crêpes Suzette.'

I could see my rescuers turned captors in the countryside, handing me a frying pan with the flour, butter, eggs and sugar, orange rind and Cointreau, saying, '*Allez-y*, go to it – the crêpes!' with a sten gun at my back. We all laughed about this, but it made me aware of some of the problems I might face.

Right now, on the landscape below, there were few physical traces of the war except for some craters made by our bombing. I saw flames, seven or eight feet long, coming up from the ground, and it took me a second or two to realize that they were from flak guns shooting at us. These flames would herald, by about four or five seconds, the shells that would burst, but not too closely, at our level. Somehow these tongues of fire, coming out of the mouths of guns, reminded me of the tongues of toads flicking the insects that would become their meals, tongues that made meals too, sometimes, of smaller toads.

There were no German fighters, and the flak, although comparatively accurate, was light. The mission was a milk run. Normally we should not have been selected by Brownlow for such a treat, a treat by priority reserved for crews that had had it rough on previous missions or for individual crew members who were on their twenty-fifth and last mission. But there were too few of these at present to make up a squadron or even an element of three. We, instead, had been the beneficiaries; it would help fill out our quota of twenty-five and make up for later slaughterhouse raids.

The morning after this mission was Christmas Day. Not much of a date for a soldier, at least not a date that we could afford to truly celebrate. Christmas meant home, and we were far away from home; it meant children, and we were the killers of children. We had been told of course, that we were bombing only strategic targets: factories, docks, submarine pens. But after three raids we already knew that, with few exceptions, our bombing held a large percentage of error, and than twelve percent of our bombs ever fell on the target proper. The remaining eighty-eight percent fell on French or German civilians or onto fallow fields. No one ever spoke of the fact, but it must have lain somewhere in the back of all our minds.

Christmas and war had little to do with each other. We might have had a better dinner that day, but I am not sure. I don't remember any special ceremonies given by the chaplains; at least, they made no efforts to reach the unbelievers like myself. On Christmas Eve, I went to bed early, but Gurney came in thoroughly drunk, and I became rather depressed at the prospect of having to listen, the partition being rather thin, to his noisy efforts to get into bed. Jennkowitz offered to help him, as he was so drunk he couldn't stand up and was overwhelmed with nausea. Gurney was luckily very cooperative and apologetic. He also let out some vigorous farts in the process, all the while mumbling, 'Christmas comes but once a year, yes, Christmas comes but once a year.' At that I found myself in fits of laughter.

The morning found us warm and secure in the knowledge that the day could be one of rest. No ground school, no flying, and rumors that we could go to Bedford for the evening if we wished (which I did not). So the day went by, in bed, at the dinner table, listening to the radio and getting slightly tight on gin and orange juice. And so passed Christmas.

8

FOURTH MISSION

LUDWIGSHAFEN: RETURN TO SCHOOL

On the thirtieth of December we went to Ludwigshafen, a name that aroused some memories in me. When I was a young school boy in France, I remembered our math teacher telling us that during the 'Great War', French bombers had attacked the chemical complex at Ludwigshafen. Now, twenty-five years later we were about to do the same thing.

I don't know how the math teacher got from explaining equations with two unknown variables onto the subject of bombing. I did know he had been a wartime pilot, was still slim and agile, and had a good deal of presence. That presence, in addition to his war record, preserved him from being *chahuté*, the object of heckling by the students, as were twenty-five to thirty percent of his colleagues.

French school boys systematically tested their teachers at the beginning of the term, and those instructors who did not know how to crack the whip or who did not have the gift of *répartie* would see their classes erupt into permanent revolution. It left many a teacher in the throes of depression and unable to teach, except to the four or five students who sat in front and actually listened to him. Meanwhile the 'revolutionaries', which excluded these *pollars*, the 'goody two shoes' were fighting one another with paper airplanes, tossing cherry bombs from their desks (and, on occasion, stink bombs), covering the blackboard with insults and caricatures, and making loud bird and hen-house noises to one another.

It was not the American 'blackboard jungle', because the *chahuteurs* were often brilliant students. Although they pretended not to study, they would

be willing to stop their rioting and listen if the teacher could come up
with a witticism that would leave their leader completely disarmed. If the
teacher knew how to prove himself the 'Master of Words', he could recover
his authority and silence the class. That was rare once he had already been
boxed into the role of *chahuté*. He had to assert himself in the very first
classes, or it was over for him for the whole school year. That is how the
French learn to disobey and how their leaders learn to command. Anyway,
I admired our teacher-pilot, although I remained impermeable to math.

I had been daydreaming on our return from Ludwigshafen, a raid that had
been a long milk run so far, with little flak over the target and no fighters. I
had been wondering if my math teacher had survived the defeat of France
in 1940, and suddenly a Me-109 went right through our formation, not
firing, and disappeared from sight.

Most everybody was awake now. He had not fired; neither had our
gunners. But Boyovitch, from his tail gunner's position, was reconstructing
what had happened and was happening now.

'Do you see him, Snell, and you, top turret and ball turret? He's rejoined
three Me-109s at six o'clock high who were waiting for him out of range
of our guns. Now he's lining them up, and they're going to make an attack,
four abreast. It's a school for fresh fighter replacements. The guy who went
through must be teaching them how to do it. That's why he didn't fire at
us; he was showing off how invulnerable he is. Here they come! Let's give
teacher and his students some lead! Come on, wake up you guys!'

And he started shooting at the enemy fighters. His insight left me
speechless. That's what I should have said to the crew (granted I could
not see behind my head), and Boyovitch was covering up his own surprise
by his great gift of gab.

They came through the formation all right, but everyone was firing now,
140 machine guns against these four German fighters. They got through
unscathed, except for their leader, the teacher. I saw him as he passed by my
window, his engine trailing smoke, his speed reduced practically to our own.
His rudder was covered with symbols of victories over Allied airmen with
two or three chevrons on his fuselage indicating his rank. He would now be
facing the fire of the navigators and bombardiers (though less well-aimed
than the fire of our gunners); even the top turret might get a whack at him.
I felt like yelling to him, 'Get your nose down, get some speed and get
away, professor!'

Meanwhile I raised my left hand in a form of salute, which he could
not acknowledge because he was probably dead already, although at that
moment I was sure that he saluted me back. Poor bastard, poor professor,
poor enemy.

That was all very nice and chivalrous, but on that second pass, 20mm cannon shells had exploded just in front of our nose and below. From our cockpit I couldn't see much, but I could feel a draft of cold air coming in from the nose of the plane. Marcott called up and said he had been hit.

'Where?' I asked.

'Oh nothing,' he replied. 'There's just a hole in our nose, and some thing hit me in the eye.' I felt bad for him, and yet, Marcott being Marcott, I also suspected something phony. But I played the game.

'Are you badly hurt?'

'Well, I can't see with my left eye.'

'Does it bleed?'

'Why don't you lie down and get Kundin to put a compress on it?'

'Oh, that's all right. I can manage.'

'Marcott how big is the hole in the nose? Can you cover it with a flak suit and stop the draft?'

'Yes, I'll try that.'

Marcott must have done some good, because in the cockpit we did not feel the cold air coming in anymore.

So, these German students did not miss us by much after all, less than three feet very likely. It must have been a deflection shot, otherwise Boyovitch would have ordered us to 'jump it', a maneuver where pilot and copilot both pull the wheel to their stomachs and cause the plane to rear like a horse, neatly avoiding the shells exploding where the ship had been a half second before. Boyovitch had probably thought the Germans had been aiming at the low group on his right; next time he would not take any chances. It was better to make us jump unnecessarily than be misled by a deflection shot. The Germans had been close enough to the formation that they started shooting while turning in to attack us. They had sprayed the group and, in fact, had hit a ship. Losing gas, and with the trailing edge of his right wing on fire, the pilot left formation, and we saw the chutes starting to come out. I think all ten got out, was a rarity.

With their leader gone, the three Me-109s disappeared, and we returned to our home base undisturbed. Except that the lead navigator took us over the five flak guns of Dunkirk, and the German gunners there were 'post graduates'. So we had another little ration of danger before letting down over the Channel.

Back at barracks, I retold Boyovitch's account of the German fighter school and related my own story of their schoolmaster's death. Nobody would listen except for McCall and Tex, who said I was probably right but told me, 'You are an incorrigible romantic. Someday it is going to do you in.'

New Year's Eve wasn't much different from Christmas. The boys organized a party, and a truck full of English girls from Bedford had been brought in for entertainment. The good-looking girls were cornered by the Brass, our Major having first dibs, of course. The liquor was lousy. I thought, *Why should everybody pretend so hard to be having fun, when actually they were bored stiff?* Instead, I stayed in the dayroom, listening to some very good music on the radio – Marcott and I alone there with Wagner, Weber and Mozart coming through without any voice commentary whatsoever.

Marcott and I had never been very friendly. I had no illusions as to his bombing, and he would moan mockingly if my landing was rough. He was also engaged in his campaign to become squadron bombardier, and too overt an ambition was rather frowned upon in this man's army. This was not only because it may have set up too high a standard of performance, but because ambition also meant competition, and competition meant a strain on our fraternity, which we all felt, more or less clearly, to be the best thing we had going for us.

But that night, since Marcott and I both were standing aside, proud freaks refusing to mix in the orgy, we decided to like each other. All I had to do, perhaps, was to see myself mirrored in his failings and, from this, to see at once and to understand the source of my own weaknesses. Two freaks. How much of wisdom, how much of conceit, how much of loneliness?

A pause in the music, followed by a brief comment, identified the station as German, but we didn't give a damn. I thought of German pilots who must have been listening as we were, enemies no more, just young men with a job to do who were now enjoying some time off. It was hard to imagine that among them might be the one who would kill us or who might be killed by our gunners. That realization was, perhaps, as close as we would come to the Christmas spirit.

Somebody on the radio began giving a pep talk to the German people. We couldn't understand German, but pep talks are always made in an unmistakable tone of voice, whatever the language. After that, there was no more Mozart, no more Wagner, their music replaced instead by some rather brassy band music. The charm was broken. German bells tolled in 1944, and we went to bed.

I always hated being wakened. Sleep was a precious commodity, the time when the organism tried to repair during the night the nervous fatigue of the day. I slept with a frenzy and was vocal in my crankiness at being disturbed. Tex, when drunk, would come and wake me up just for the pleasure of it. Since he weighed 200 pounds to my 140, there wasn't much I could do about it, and suspicions of cowardice would leave me limp.

And now came Chruby, Williams, and Boyovitch in the middle of the night to wake me up and wish me a happy new year. My first impulse was to protest the disturbance, as well as their beery breath, but fortunately I checked it. Instead, eyes sticky, tongue heavy, limbs wrapped in sleep, I returned their wish before falling into a slumber of utter oblivion.

9

MANAGING THE
GROUND TROOPS

In order to win the contests set up by Pinetree (the code name for Wycombe Abbey) between the different group commanders of the three divisions, or, more simply, in order to do his job, there were two categories of personnel that Colonel Preston had to treat very carefully. One, about whom he knew a lot, was the pilots and copilots, the navigators and the bombardiers. The second group, about whom he knew comparatively little and who made up ninety to ninety-five percent of his command, were the ground personnel. When I first arrived; there were about thirty air crews on the whole base. When I left at the end of March 1944 to return to the States, we were more than seventy air crews serviced by some four thousand ground personnel that included cooks, drivers, medics, typists, guards, radio repairmen, radar specialists, parachute riggers, weathermen, armorers, and mechanics. The last two categories, the armorers and the mechanics, made up the group we thought of when we referred to 'ground crews'.

The ground crews, especially the mechanics, kept the planes in flyable condition. They would work their normal shift in the daytime repairing the damage done to the ships by the last raid, changing wings and engines, replacing brakes, patching the aluminum skin, or replacing whole panels that had been torn or shredded by flak. Sometimes they would recuperate one or two 20mm shells that had come to rest in the gas tanks without exploding. (After disarming them, they would give the shells to the pilot and see his face blanch at the thought of what he had missed.)

They did not keep a 'nine-to-five' schedule; they worked as long as the group was alerted, the ground crews would return around nine or ten at night to gas up the ships and to check the engines, the electrical systems, the radios, the hydraulic systems, and to load up the bomb bay with whatever combination of incendiaries and high explosives was ordered by the squadron armament officer upon his receipt of the frag orders transmitted to our Headquarters.

Some of the indices coming from Headquarters were interrelated, of course. The tonnage of bombs dropped on targets was related most immediately to the number of planes the group could put up in response to orders. Essentially this depended on the damages sustained in previous raids. There were frequently some planes that would be totaled when brought back to base by their determined crews. Perhaps a wing spar had been cut by a flak shell and nevertheless, thanks to the aluminum skin, the wing had held, but that plane would never fly again. Instead, it would be 'cannibalized' before being sent to the scrap heap. So the replenishment of our stock of flyable airplanes would also depend upon the ability of our group operations officers to secure from Bassingbourn new wings, new engines, new propellers, new landing gear, new ailerons, new tail surfaces, and sometimes entire new planes.

Our airplanes, especially our engines, were constantly being used at the limit of their capacity. Practice missions were often scheduled for late morning or early afternoon, with bombardiers being taken to bomb a small rocky island in the Wash Estuary. For the pilots and copilots it would be the opportunity to fly formation. (The replacements who came after us had perhaps more occasion to fly these practice maneuvers; we flew raids so frequently that we had little time for practice missions. At least I never did.) When the planes came back, a pilot might note on his form, 'Engine #1 runs a bit rough.' To this a crew chief might reply, 'Changed all the plugs on #1 engine.' Plugs got changed rather frequently, and I sometimes felt that the remedy of 'new plugs' was equivalent to a doctor's 'Take two aspirins and call me in the morning.' But I was not about to say so too loudly.

When a new engine was put in, or after a major overhaul, either the pilot or copilot, or possibly another pilot or copilot more easily available to Operations at the moment, would be asked to take the plane up to test it. This was called 'slow timing the engine.' We would take along our engineer and our radio man, and we would do certain tests at various altitudes. Sometimes there were obdurate malfunctions. Back on the ground, these would be discussed with the engineering officer and the crew chief. These discussions with the ground specialists could prove very enlightening for the pilot, because they looked into the ambiguities of each malfunction and its possible causes. It provided for the pilot a chance to see how the mechanical wizards thought and get an insight into their world.

There was always some apparatus that needed verification, calibration, maintenance, junking, or repair. And, of course, there was not a lot of time to get it fixed. Once in a while, on take-off, a crew would not succeed in getting their plane off the ground. The pilots were not professional diag-nosticians, but they put a certain intensity behind their concerns, which the ground crew often heard as 'complaints'.

One of the problems that we had in communicating with the ground crews was that our mechanical knowledge was not very extensive. In the peacetime Air Corps, there had been sergeant pilots who were often ex-mechanics, and officer pilots received more training in the structure and functioning of their engines and superchargers,[1] but here on base, we were like patients trying to explain to the doctor the site and nature of the pain. We knew there was something wrong – 'There, you hear that?' – but aside from asking if a high cylinder-head temperature was an instrument failure or a reality, we could not go much beyond that.

Our own skill was elsewhere. It was in the intimate and instantaneous coordination of hands and feet responding to our eyes and to our inner feeling of position. It was in the immediate solution of a tridimensional problem of space, speed and time, and with this was also the feeling, never far from consciousness, that we were moving in a dangerous game. Like flying off the face of a cliff, it was exhilarating, but once in a while it took you by the throat, and that's when you had to show your mettle. You missed a collision by half a foot; through display of super-quick reaction time and shrewd crossing of the controls, you side-slipped out of the reach of a friend's wing.

Once in a while you would hear of a crew chief who had volunteered for air-crew duty and took gunnery training at the school the Eighth Air Force maintained at the Wash. When it happened, it reminded everyone of the distinction between the flyers and the 'paddlefeet' which made a crew chief willing to chance becoming a waist gunner on an air crew and to surrender in return, if not his rank of master sergeant, certainly his power, for the privilege of wearing the silver wings.

If asked why they did it, they would reply, however, that it was because the air crews were through their tours in four or five months, while the ground crews would have to stay at the base and eat brussels sprouts until the end of the war, which meant at least eighteen more months. It was out of the question for them to answer that 'the gunners were fighting a more exciting war' or that they wanted 'to contribute more directly to the defeat of Germany.' You had to volunteer while still avoid-ing the stigma of being thought an eager beaver. Nevertheless there was a constant trickle of ground crew members who wanted to take to the air. Some ground officers and also some enlisted men would sometimes arrange clandestinely, as it remained illegal, to become passengers on ships bound for a mission. They wanted to see 'what it was like.' I imagine that the number of these volunteers would be a good index of morale. And for the crew chosen by the paddlefeet for their initiation to combat, it would also be an indication of its reputation in the squadron. If you were a 'lucky crew' you would bring them back alive. The pilot who took it upon himself to accept them aboard was certified 'a good egg'; they owed him one.

This was one instance where the pilot's violation of discipline did not threaten military order. On the contrary, it proved to the ground crews that we cared more about their dignity than about our privileges and that we would go to the limit to help them reassure themselves as to their worth. Our violation of standing orders went to strengthen the ultimate commitment that was at the core of military discipline. When the paddlefoot came back from that 'illegal' mission, his commitment to duty was reinforced, and his respect for officers was increased.

The ground crews were 'true believers', and other enlisted men would not dare josh them about it, because they would get physical in no time and frequently with a good deal of weight to back it up. The devotion of the crew chiefs and their subordinates must have worked like a positive osmotic force upon the rest of the ground forces, opposing the similarly osmotic but negative forces of the goofing off and anti-authoritarian, 'f--k-the-officers' culture that existed on every American base.

How did you motivate the ground personnel to give maximum effort when you did not have much opportunity to supervise their work and when they were not rewarded, like the air crews were, by the prestige of their calling and public adulation?

Colonel Preston, in a one-page foreword to *Shades of Kimbolton*, gives credit to a spirit that prompted the men of the 379th to fight the war not for individual glory '... but simply for the satisfaction which comes from doing a worthy job.'

We were never lectured on 'how to get the best results from the ground crews'. We knew that our lives depended on them. Still, what could we do about it? We were not about to flatter them, that would be beneath our dignity. How did Colonel Preston treat us? Business, business. So we did the same, except that we were not as aloof as he was. We tried to corral the mechanics in as many photographic occasions as we could, in front of the ship with the ground crew and the air crew together.

The ground crew worked out of a large tent with a plywood floor and a seventy-five-watt electric bulb. A table, four chairs, two bunks, and a file cabinet completed the furniture. They would get some warmth from the homemade contraptions with which they fueled their stoves, through tubings of gasoline and oil, at the cost of the occasional explosions or fires. Otherwise, they worked in the cold, the mist, the drizzle; sometimes even snowflakes would fall on their noses while they were hunting for a burnt bearing with an inspection lamp, armed with their wrenches, hammers, and screwdrivers.

We were officers; they were enlisted men. We were free of the grime, the grease, and we were special because we were masters of the air, like eagles. But the ground crew loved their ship. In the air it was ours, but on the ground it was theirs. They knew its nooks and crannies. In many ways, they had rebuilt it with their own hands. I have seen crew chiefs and the members of their crew cry when their ship did not return from a mission and they were not crying for the crew – a little perhaps, but we came and went – but for their ship.

Our own ship had arrived from overseas on November 19, 1943. Just before our crew took charge, the crew chief gave Streit a penny, asking him to return it after each mission, a kind of lucky charm. Streit decided to call the plane *Penny Ante* after the game of poker. After every mission we flew, Streit returned the penny to the crew chief. And our *Penny Ante*, for us, was charmed, gaining her the reputation of being a lucky ship and us the reputation of being a lucky crew.

The ground crew's love for their ship meant that we could take for granted that they would take good care of her: that they would not forget an essential detail, that when a screw would not go in easily, they would not simply hammer it in only to have it vibrate out at 21,000 feet. I never heard them complain about the cold, the long hours, or having to redo a task for the third or fourth time. They were proud of their ship's prowess, of her victories for the country, victories that they chronicled by painting on the fuselage below the pilot's window a bomb for every mission accomplished or a swastika for every enemy fighter downed. Whatever work they did for the ship, whatever labors they performed, they were mostly the labors of love.

We, the air crew, should be worthy of her.

10

AFTER YOU, GASTON

PREPARATION FOR THE MISSION

The air crew utilized the tent of the ground crew to dress. The gunners would clean their guns, including the gun of the navigator, who always arrived late from his navigators' briefing. He would use the time instead to draw three miniature mission maps for the bombardier, the pilot, and the copilot. That would normally be his major contribution to the mission – we might have to use these maps, with their magnetic headings and distances, if we had to leave the shelter and guidance of the formation to try for home alone.

We left our valuables – our money, letters, pictures – with the supply people near the briefing room, but we changed clothes in the ground crew's tent. This was where we completed our psychological preparation for the mission. In deliberate, slow gestures we took off our clothes down to the long underwear we always wore on the base. Some of us put on sweaters on top of our underwear. Then we put on the blue electric suit whose connection and plug hung like a tail between our legs. The suit came with a pair of light slippers, connected to it by plugs.

We put back over it our GI pants and shirts and, over that, our tan flight overalls with all the pockets and zippers. And I would also wrap around my neck a white silk scarf. I would have distributed escape kits to each member of the crew, and my own I put in my knee pocket along with the navigator's map. Then I would put my candy bar in an inside pocket to keep it warm, otherwise it became hard like stone at high altitude, with cold that could reach minus seventy degrees Fahrenheit.

As long as the electric suit worked, we were sufficiently warm with our three layers of clothing. If the electric suit burned out, however, or if a piece of flak or a bullet cut our wire connection, then we would have to put on the mutton-lined jackets and perhaps even the fleece-lined trousers, something we hoped to avoid, as they were bulky and hampered quick movements. We also had fleece-lined boots that we put over our blue electric slippers. The trouble with the boots was, if you were shot down, they were not the best equipment for walking long distances. You might even lose them when your parachute jacked open, and they slipped off your feet. Most of us tied our regular GI shoes to our parachute harness, so we would be sure to have them once we had landed in enemy territory.

Once I had put on my fleece-lined boots, I was ready to pull up the main zipper of the flight suit. Remained then to put on the parachute harness and the yellow life jacket – the 'Mae West'. The parachute type most favored by the crews was the chest pack, which you did not wear but would hook to the harness when you were ready to jump. Meanwhile, you were not encumbered by the pack while you were doing your jobs in the ship. I preferred the back pack, though, because you could wear it without being uncomfortable. It was flat, the length of your back, and it was always there on your back in normal flight and in any emergency. I worried about explosions and finding my chest pack floating just beyond my reach. The very thought of it made me shiver. True, most explosions killed you or rendered you unconscious, but I did not want to be faced, in a bail-out situation, with the possibility of grabbing under my seat and finding nothing there – *Did I put it elsewhere, and if so, where?*

'Finicle, have you seen my chest pack? I thought I placed it under my seat. Did you move it, per chance?'

Meanwhile the altimeter would be rapidly unwinding, but it would not be the ground I was worried about, but the explosion of all that gasoline sloshing in the wings.

'Lieutenant, I found it!'

'Finicle, you have yours?'

'Yes, sir.'

'Are the others gone?'

'Yes, sir.'

'Well, let's go. We have ten seconds. After you, Gaston …'

These dialogues did take place, if not in our lucky *Penny Ante*, then certainly in other ships. And the lessons I drew from the raids reinforced my belief that the control of fear depended a lot on not being caught by surprise – the 'unexpected terror'. Controlling fear required a certain state of readiness, an awareness that whatever else we might be doing, a difficult duty was always present in the shadows of our psyches, so that we could mobilize ourselves to accomplish that duty at a moment's notice.

There are basically two ways to control fear. One is the repression of fear, excluding it from consciousness so that all that surfaces is perhaps a bit of tenseness, a sign that something is going on in the psyche that is not cost free. The 'naturally brave' were those whose fear rarely reached their consciousness. Blindness to peril and the illusion of immortality, which are often the prerogative of youth, would make some junior birdmen naturally brave – until they had been through a tough mission where they discovered that they too could die. The veterans did not like this courage of ignorance or blindness, which devalued their own. Their courage was based in reality and had been gained by the sweat of their brow (and an occasional tremor in their hands). For some, long sessions of poker, accompanied by alcohol, served as tranquilizers.

The second way is the suppression of fear. Suppression is when one has become aware of one's fear, and it takes a conscious act of will to contain it and still do one's duty. Suppression of fear is much harder, more exhausting than repression. Those, like me, who were not blessed with a calm temperament, could cope by constant rehearsal of what to do if a nasty situation developed. *What do I do if we are attacked head-on in a two-o'clock position? What do I do if we lose #4 engine?*

Successful control is based largely upon membership in communities, subjective and objective, and most chiefly in the subjective. These are the invisible communities with which we identify, such as our country, our social class, our religion. Those who are deeply committed to their country or their faith have entrusted their fate to groups that do not die and where a single member's death is of little consequence compared to the enduring survival of the subjective community.

For the committed, courage comes relatively easy. In the Japanese and German armed forces, I imagine this was a common form of courage, what we would call courage-exaltation. Against it, we had high fire power and discipline, a 'don't fire till you see the white of their eyes' inheritance.

Families have many features of the subjective communities, including prestige capital that is actually enhanced by the member's death. This is particularly true of the upper classes and, of course, the military families. Here, it is expected that you will 'return with your shield or on it' – *You will not run and throw away your shield, but you will let your friends use it as a stretcher to return your body for ceremonial burial. You will retreat from the enemy in orderly fashion and only under orders. You will not get rid of your shield in order to run faster and abdicate your responsibility for your squad, your platoon, or your company. You will choose death rather than run away from the battlefield.* This conditioning of the young adult begins in childhood, as our parents put iodine on our scraped knee and kiss away our tears, telling us, 'There's a brave boy. We don't cry, do we? Mommy and Daddy are so proud.'

And though most American families are not military families, they did share, as evidenced through the popularity of the cowboy and war movies, an admiration for the warlike virtues. In our backyards in 1927, when we played 'Statues': the most popular pose was that of the soldier charging the enemy or the flyer crashing to his death.

So the ability to repress or suppress fear is based on these meaningful memberships. However, in extreme situations such as war, surprise will often not permit the mind to mobilize its repressive capacity, and suppression will be the only mechanism available. In that moment, we are looking desperately for someone to tell us what the group wants from us. If someone starts to run to the rear, we might all begin to run, because running is an affirmation of membership. If it is possible to stop the running, by the action of officers and noncoms who have symbolized the group to its members, the rout might be stopped, and the men who were running to the rear will be running back to the front. The awareness of what the group wants, combined with guilt, will make determined soldiers out of a rabble united only in its panicked flight a few minutes before.

When do communities we know merge with the communities we feel? The military attempted to make the objective community more palpable to us through weekly award ceremonies, inspections by Colonel, daily Taps with that trumpet sound that went smack to our entrails, communications to our home newspapers of our assignments and our medals. But it was the band of brothers, and particularly our friends, our inner circle within that band, that was by far the most present and powerful of all the objective groups.

Chaplains tried to activate the religious communities, except that funerals were not done on the base; the dead were whisked away by the back door. I have often wondered about this policy. Did it leave us more vulnerable to ghosts? It was among our friends that we buried the dead in secret ceremonies not visible even to ourselves.

The family was also a powerful group, so powerful it could interfere with our dedication to the military group. It was more difficult to risk death when we remembered our mothers waiting for us, or our wives and children waiting for us to come back home to them. No doubt war is a young man's business, where ignoring our mothers and fathers was a necessary way to assert our autonomy as adults. If we died, we broke their hearts. But we brought them imperishable honor, from which they, our brothers and sisters, and our own children, would benefit. As they used to say, a father who died in the war is watching you from heaven. Also, now that unemployment had disappeared, American soldiers could more afford to repress the thoughts of their families, who were enjoying a higher standard of living and who were far away and safe from the battlefield. The Germans had a harder problem, especially when bombings became heavier and more frequent.

Both repression and suppression use up psychic energy, the latter much more than the former. The more you flew combat, the more it took out of you. German aces would accumulate forty, fifty, seventy, 100 victories, but eventually they made a mistake, like a great surgeon will sometimes make a mistake. Or they were simply overwhelmed by the numbers, and their luck ran out; or their desire to live ran out; or they became tired of the killing, which their own survival usually implied. The crucial factor in operational fatigue was not the hours flown – after all we did not fly much more than airline pilots in the States – but the control of fear. The psychological work required to control our fears drew on our psychic capital, a depletion that was largely invisible. As McCall said, a symptom of operational fatigue was the increasing indifference to your fate, rather than the incidence of conscious fear. Those who had good repressive mechanisms rarely became quivering wrecks, but one day, they just might let go.

Once you surrender in the spirit, the rest doesn't take long. One morning I had been on the verge of giving up, and it was Tex who saved me. We were to be low diamond, low squadron, low group, for the third time in a row. It was the most exposed position in the formation. Waiting in line with the other copilots to get my ten escape kits and ten candy bars, I spotted Tex.

'Tex,' I complained, 'we are low diamond again.'

'Rough.'

'God damn it! We are through; we won't get back. We don't stand a chance.'

Tex reprimanded me at once. 'Don't talk that way, Pitts. If you feel that way, you will get it. Snap out of it! Don't be a damned fool.'

'But, man, three times in a row!' I lamented. 'What have they got against us?'

'We had the same deal once, and we got through it. You'll do the same.' He gave me a long, steady look. 'But if you keep on moaning like a jerk, you're sure to get it.'

All I had wanted was some sympathy, I thought. I certainly did not want to get scragged. Better cut it out.

'I guess you're right,' I agreed. 'Somebody will abort, and we shall take his place. Hell, they can't shoot us down – we are too good a crew!'

'Now you're talking, Pitts. You'll be all right.'

Which I was, but if it had not been for Tex, I might have gone to the ground crew's tent having talked myself into complete demoralization, a disease that would spread only too quickly to the rest of the crew.

As it was, everything turned out okay.

One way to avoid being frozen by the fears that pursued me even in bed was to rehearse in my mind, *What should I do if …?* I had all sorts of mind games for various possible situations in which I might find myself. In this way I hoped I could avoid being caught by surprise, before I could mobilize my faculties and take action.

Until I switched from a chest-pack parachute to a backpack, I wondered what would happen if I could not find my chest pack under my seat, or if someone had misplaced or forgotten his. Could we use one chute for two people? I understood it could be done – we would bail out from the bomb bay, the crewman attached to my back and my neck by his arms and legs. If the initial jerk of the parachute's opening did not break his hold on me, we would make it to the ground together would have to be careful of the landing, because we would be falling faster than usual. If I wore a backpack, it was probably wiser that he not straddle my back. Better that he should straddle my chest like a child clutching his father.

I even had a mind game for the usually fatal loss of an engine on take-off. If I were in the left seat, which would happen if we were to fly the mission on someone's right wing, and it was too late to abort the take-off, I would lower the flaps a third of the way and salvo the bombs on the runway by pulling the handle on the left of the pilot's seat. On three engines with six-thousand pounds of bombs released – I could imagine them ricocheting on the runway like dogs running after their master – we should easily beat them and lift off before we ran into the target embankment, which blocked the end of the runway and where Schuenemann and Ratcliff had found their end.

The question was, *Would the bomb-bay doors being down and the one-third flaps cut our speed in such a way as to negate the reduction in weight?* When I shared my idea with Streit, he just listened and smiled.

Anyway I chose to believe these mind games of mine. I would rehearse them in the twilight while falling asleep in my bunk: *What if we were attacked from two-o'clock level, or from twelve-o'clock high? What if a propeller runs away? What if …?* – until I would slip into sleep, to be wakened in my single room by the gentle voice of our operations officer: 'Breakfast at three, briefing at four …'

11

ELEMENTS OF SURVIVAL

Combat fighting in heavy bombers was, of course, different from flying combat in fighters. The major difference was that the fighter pilot fought alone. The bomber pilot fought with a team of nine crewmen in his ship, each with his own specialty He shared his cockpit with a copilot who could substitute for him at any moment. His plane was usually in formation with the *squadron* made up of seven planes; with the *group*, which comprised eighteen to twenty-one planes; with the *wing*, which totaled fifty-four to sixty-two planes. With each ship carrying twelve guns, the formation was, for the pilot and his crew, the best insurance of both security and bombing effectiveness.

For the fighter pilot, solitude was the dominant experience. He would be assigned to a flight consisting of seven or eight pilots, half of whom would be flying on any given day, while the other half rested, and that flight of four would be integrated into a squadron of sixteen, and the squadron into a group of forty-eight to fifty planes.

Twenty-five percent of the fighter pilots accounted for seventy-five percent of the enemy planes shot down. Woe to the replacement pilot who came up against a German fighter whose rudder surface was covered with victory symbols But those became rarer and rarer as 1944 melted into 1945; American fighters were more and more apt to encounter a German novice, who had no more than 100 hours of flight training and perhaps less than twenty hours of time in his fighter. The American had 180 hours of training and probably eighty additional hours in his P-38, P-47, or P-51. The Germans never ran out of planes, which from 1944 onward were built in underground workshops or factories.

They ran out of gasoline, and above all, they ran out of trained young men.

Three American pilots who were comparative novices could dispose of a skillful German pilot they caught out alone, because they knew how to coordinate an attack. They had rehearsed the procedure over and over in practice flights. Situations like this developed more often, from March 1944 onward, and neutralized the German superiority in flying skills. That was the Germans' bad luck, and that was the story of the war. The Germans had better tanks, better light machine guns, better bazookas, better artillery, better infantry officers, but we had much more of everything, and superiority in quantity usually pays off better than superiority in quality. In the air, the German jets were at least two years ahead of us in jet design, but they were a year behind us in their ability to get those jets to the front in quantities that could make a difference. The P-51 was a somewhat better plane than the Me-109 or the Focke-Wulf 190, and from February 1944 onward, we had masses of them. We also had the trained pilots to fly them. That is what decided the air war in 1944 through 1945.

The fighter pilot was the modern incarnation of the knight of old. The British flyers of the Battle of Britain lifted the reputation of the whole order to its highest peak. Whatever orders Hitler gave in his many fits of anger, the German Air Force tried to maintain the traditions of chivalrous warfare. There was a fraternity of airmen that transcended national hatreds. Even so, there were times that German fighters shot down enemy parachutes or attempted to spill the air out of them so they would 'torch' to the ground. Even Americans did it if they caught a German flyer at it. They would pounce on him, blow him out of the air, and if he had been able to bail out, give him a full taste of his own medicine. But I don't think an American flyer would boast of doing it without provocation. (If a German pilot had given you great fear and barely missed sending you to the carpet, it was possible that your fear could turn to rage, and then you would not be a gentleman to that pilot who had given you the runs. And if you were a German and had lost your family to daylight bombing, I can understand, although not forgive, shooting an American in his parachute.)

Fighters were our 'little friends'. Their pilots considered themselves the ramrods and the B-17 formations the 'cattle', except that they always gave us credit for our fortitude. (Remember, it comes from Flying Fortress.) We loved our little friends, but we beefed (indeed!) when they were not there at the rendezvous point, or when they would zigzag 3,000 feet above us while the German flyers would come from below, spraying our formation and split 'S'-ing (reversing their direction and diving) before the fighters could come down to stop them. And until June of 1944, the American fighters in hot pursuit were forbidden to go down below 18,000 feet.

Top: 2. Cadet training: Ryan PT-19.

Left: 3. Cadet training: Ryan PT-19.

Above: 4. Cadet: before graduation.

5. Thirty-seven 379th Flying Fortresses returning to Kimbolton, March 12, 1945, Mission #300. This is the largest number of 379th BG Aircraft in one photo. (Courtesy of 379th Association and Turner Publishing Co.)

6. Aerial view of USAAF Station 117, 379th Bomb Group (H) Airbase, at Kimbolton, England, 1943–45. Main gate is off upper right side of photograph. (Courtesy of 379th Association and Turner Publishing Co.)

7. *Penny Ante*'s crew. Sitting, left to right: Streit, Pitts, Kundin, Marcott. Standing: Snell, Owens, Boyovitch, Chruby, Williams, Finicle.

8. *Penny Ante*'s ground crew, November 18, 1943.

9. Lopez painting bombs on *Penny Ante*, March 5, 1944.

Top: 10. Our crew and *Penny Ante* (January or February 1944). Standing, left to right: Finicle, Boyovitch, Chruby, Snell, Owens. First row: Streit, Pitts, Kundin, Marcott (missing: Williams).

Above: 11. Cockpit of a B-17.
Right: 12. Catwalk of a B-17.

Above left: 13. Col. Maurice A. Preston, 1st Commander of the 379th BG. (Courtesy of 379th Association and Turner Publishing Co.)

Above right: 14. Lieutenent Colonel Rohr (facing left) and Colonel Preston (right), March 3, 1944.

15. Thanksgiving Dinner, November 25, 1943. Jesse Pitts sitting far left; Colonel Preston far right.

16. General Travis.

17. James E. Williams, Left Waist Gunner, December 20, 1943.

18. Colonel Preston and staff watch the return to base of B-17s to Kimbolton after a combat mission. (Courtesy of 379th Association and Turner Publishing Co.)

19. Operations Board in Operations Room of 379th Bomb Group. Under the clock are crew details of current mission #61 to Frankfurt on January 29, 1944. Details of previous mission #60 on January 21, 1944, are in column on right. (Courtesy of 379th Association and Turner Publishing Co.)

We would cheer at briefing when we were told that Polish Spitfires would meet us over Belgium and take us home. The Polish had the reputation of being lions in the air and would ignore their fuel gauges when they were in a fight, bailing out or ditching when they ran out of gas, rather than giving up the chase. When this happened, we would try to get them an Air-Sea Rescue plane or boat before we left them, if we had the gas to circle. If our navigator was on the ball, he would have the radio wire to Air-Sea Rescue with good map coordinates.

When an American fighter squadron tangled with a German squadron, the actual fighting would *theoretically* take place between the flight leaders, and those leaders would be assisted by their wing men, who protected their rear and doubled their fire power in front, each fighter having about twenty-three seconds of fire power. A good wing man would duplicate the moves of his flight leader regardless of the speed and violence of those maneuvers. If he could do that, time and again, he could also keep on the tail of an enemy fighter trying to shake him off. He was ready to become an element leader himself, if he had that extra aggressiveness that makes a good fighter pilot.

Theoretically is the right word, because the closure rate of the two formations, in a frontal encounter, was 700 miles an hour: about 340 yards per second. In twenty seconds, a speck in the sky would loom large against the windshield, and pilots could even see the eyeballs of their opponent for a brief fraction of that time. The major danger, for the first few seconds of the encounter, was collision, usually fatal to both pilots.

So, the two hostile formations would try to approach each other from the rear, at a height of 2,000 feet above the opponent. But the advantage of height was hard for the Americans to achieve, because the Germans profited from controllers with good radar, and they knew the position of the Americans at all times: their number, their altitude, and their location close to the bomber stream.

Fighter groups tried to coordinate their planes as much as possible through orders given on the radio, but usually a clash between an American group and a German group, or even sometimes between two squadrons, would become a mêlée. A good wing man, despite whatever scraps the wing leader might toss to him as reward for being in on a kill, itched for the chance to be his own boss, and that wish could not be denied for long. Given the independent spirit of many fighter pilots, he would soon be doing what he wanted to do – shooting down as many enemy fighters as possible under the safest conditions compatible with hot pursuit. During these free-for-alls, the best fighters on either side would pick their victims, who would usually make a run for the deck before being shot down. If the victors came back for more, one might see some terrific dogfights between veterans. But I have a feeling that they preferred, when possible, to fight the greenhorn who was not flying a very tight formation. Among fighters, it was often the novice who would stay and fight when the odds were definitely against him. He could not bear the thought of running away. The veteran did not have to prove himself on that score. Fighters would not hesitate to run away from a fight where they did not have the advantage, once the formations had broken down into individual dogfights. All a pilot in a P-47 needed to do was put the nose down, and it could outrun any German fighter except the jet.

Fighter pilots did not experience flak as bomber crews did. They went through it at about twice our speed, which reduced their exposure. Flak was fate, and the ace was as vulnerable as the novice on his first mission. Each relied on the wisdom of his group leader to keep him out of it. German fighters were sometimes killed by their own flak when they attacked us on the bomb run or over the target. But this was an activity I don't remember having seen very often; all experienced fighter pilots, on both sides, knew better than to make a second pass on a ground target they had awakened by their first pass, unless they had specific orders to do so.

Bomber formations had no autonomy, of course, in the altitude at which we flew, or in the choice of target, although the wing leader or the division leader had a choice of an alternate target if, as happened frequently, the initial target was covered by clouds. If the wing or division navigator took us unnecessarily through the Ruhr, that was our tough luck. There was always more safety in sticking to a formation led by a navigator suffering from lack of oxygen than in striking out on our own. If a leader, like Travis or LeMay, of a bomber formation decided to go around the target for a second pass rather than drop his bombs on the first one, all the bombers would be forced to do the same. It was said that B-17 formations never turned back from a target – a noble and true image. Again, it was safer to stay in formation than to try to run away alone. Bomber crews were used to this 'bureaucratic heroism'. After all, the lives of eight crewmen were constantly in the hands of the pilot-copilot team.

In fighters, the individual skill of the pilot was not diluted by the weight of the group as it was in bombers. In bombers I might be a first-rate flyer, but if my tail gunner could not shoot straight or warn me in time of a German attack and tell me, at the right moment, to 'jump it' I would get a swat of 20mm cannon shells, which the armor plate in the back of my seat could not handle. (In the latter stages of the war, a single 30mm shell from a jet could put an end to my career.) My navigator could get me lost. My formation leader could whip me all over the sky by making too sharp a turn or could make me use twice as much gas as the mission was programmed for by changing airspeed too often.

Flying tight formation was a crucial skill that involved not straining our engines and our propeller governors. The more we did it, the better we were at it. That is why we kept flying, as often as weather and combat missions allowed, many practice missions. When enemy fighters had a choice of targets they avoided the groups that flew in tight formations. It said something about the quality of the training the bomber crews had undergone, from pilots to gunners. Any enemy fighter who wanted to get at the leader from the rear had to fly through several layers of fire. Head-on attacks avoided this problem, but the speed of closure did not give much time for adjusting one's aim, and when the German fighter flipped on his back to begin the inverted loop that would put him in position for another go, he became vulnerable to the ball turret's fire, which might or might not bounce off the armor plate on his belly.

In a formation there were good spots and spots where we were more likely to meet fighter fire. The closer we were to the group leader, the better off we were. A low-diamond, low-squadron, low-group position, often called 'Coffin's Corner' or 'Tail-end Charlie', would be assigned to our crew by the operations officer, supervised by the squadron commander. In a way, it was a compliment, for they preferred having in this position a crew they knew was unlikely to abort. Nevertheless, regardless of how good we were, our chances of coming back were somewhat reduced, though not to the extent of the position's reputation. If the ship ahead of us aborted or was shot down, and we were the closest to the empty slot, we were entitled to take his place. Nobody ever asked the question, but it was understood.

In my opinion (and these are numbers that I draw out of thin air), a bomber pilot depended, for survival, fifteen percent on his flying skill, twenty percent on the skill and discipline of his crew, fifteen percent on the skill of the group and wing leaders, and forty percent on luck. Translated into operational terms, these numbers mean just this: you could be a hot bomber pilot, but if a German fighter with fortitude made a pass at you, breaking away only at 150 yards, your chances of survival would be small. And why did he attack you rather than your neighbor? Because you were at the tail end of the formation. And why were you at the tail end of the formation? Because you did not have the seniority of the element leader or the squadron leader. That would be the intelligent explanation of why you were low diamond that day. But it could be because you were at the end of the list that the typist had received. Or maybe it was because you were reliable, and the operations officer knew that you were less likely to abort than some of your colleagues.

'In those summer months of 1943, abortions were a serious problem,' Colonel Mo (Preston) admits.[1] Formations would reach the battle area already depleted by some ten to twenty percent of their original number. (I remember especially the third Schweinfurt where aborts ran a steady flow from such an infamous target.) To cope with this problem, our Colonel inaugurated the 'spares system' sending along on a mission, rather like alternates on a jury, three or four B-17s as extra planes for his group. The spares were supposed to accompany the formation to the enemy coast and then either return to base or replace those who aborted. (I don't believe the spares were allowed to decline the honor, even if the only spot left to them was Tail-end Charlie.) The result was that the 379th had the lowest official rate of aborts of the whole Air Force. Eventually other group commanders caught on to the statistical trick until General Doolittle put an end to it in April 1944.

(The infantry had a similar problem. When the lieutenant would blow his whistle and yell, 'Charge,' a certain percentage of the troops would remain in the fox holes. During the First World War, when nationalism was more powerful, the medals fewer, and the standards of bravery higher, some soldiers would play dead on the battlefield. At Verdun, one of the greatest slaughterhouses of all times, perhaps worse than the Russian Front in the Second World War, a French sergeant taking his platoon over the top is reputed to have cried out, '*Debout les morts!*' – 'Rise up, the dead!' This became a public relations triumph because the civilians understood it as being a passionate appeal to all the dead of France to rise up in the defense of the motherland, a magnificent example of the type of rhetoric that galvanizes the French. Returning veterans, however, clued in their civilian relatives as to the true meaning of the sergeant's cry, which was, 'Get up, you phony dead!' This gave, of course, a sarcastic twist to what is still, to this day, a part of French folklore. In the French schools, I received the laundered version.)

If I had to ride as an observer in a plane, I would prefer a lucky crew to a masterful one. Better be in a plane flown by an average pilot that endured two or three fighter attacks in a raid, than in a plane that might have a top-notch pilot but endured ten attacks. There was a limit to what skill could do against firepower.

Where skill made a difference was when we had lost two engines to flak or fighters, and we had to return to England on our own. Then it took good flying, good crew coordination, determination, and good luck to make it, especially on the crash landing in the beet fields. In bombers, the pilot-copilot team with experience was more likely to come out alive from a raid than a novice crew. Emergencies were now more familiar, as well as the techniques to cope with them. We read our instruments with more skepticism. Pilot and copilot communicated better; the copilot did automatically what had to be done even if the pilot forgot to order it.

And no doubt a team that was not panicked by the structural damage that a B-17 can endure would not bail out the crew prematurely. I have seen some B-17s blown out of the sky by a direct flak hit, although the more frequent disaster was to have a wing or the tail blown off by flak. Probably fifteen to twenty percent of the B-17s shot down were direct victims of flak, but the most common fate was to have an engine or two knocked out by shell fragments.

Then the crucial skill for a bomber team was the capacity to bring a B-17 on three or two engines with, it was to be hoped, the dead propellers feathered. It might require at times that pilot and copilot handle the controls simultaneously, with their combined strength, especially if the two engines that were knocked out were on the same side of the plane. Unless there was a cloud bank to hide in, it was better to fly over Germany very low so as not to allow their radar stations to get a fix on us. The navigator was very strategic in guiding us over Germany at tree-top level, avoiding airdromes, cities, factories, harbors, and other areas of high flak concentration. To help confuse the German radar, the course had to change fairly often; this and the low altitude added to their problems in attempting to vector a fighter to our tail. If they sent only one, we were lucky. Two, and our dangers were doubled. Three, and our goose was cooked. This was the time we needed a cool navigator who could give us headings home regardless of how many times we changed course. And if we did make it to England, our crash landing in the beet fields should not end in a gas explosion. What could we do to increase the odds in our favor? Cut the main switch at the last moment and hope that the ship would not make too many sparks as its belly scraped the ground. This was also a time we prayed for the thick English mud.

During all this, the copilot had to maintain the morale of the crew through appropriate comments. Over the intercom, he would urge, 'Gunners, only short bursts,' because there was a tendency for the gunners to use their machine guns as if they were hoses, fingers locked on the triggers. Good crew morale would be indicated in the accuracy of the gunners' fire and in their ability to conserve ammunition, especially if much of it had been jettisoned in order to make the ship lighter.

Gunners had had training in the States, just like our ground crew had. We did not intrude into their specialty nor would they intrude in ours. We took each other's skills for granted, which was the wisest attitude given our mutual dependency on one another. After all, when a German fighter attacked us from the rear, there was a maximum of eight guns from our own ship bearing on him, and if our gunners were not such good shots, it could be compensated for by the eight guns from each other ship in our element – a total of thirty-two machine guns if we still had our Tail-end Charlie with us.

(Even so, gunners' claims of German fighters they had shot down should have been scaled down to about ten to twenty percent of the asserted totals, something few of our 'paddlefeet' intelligence officers had the audacity to do. Headquarters was always surprised to see so many German fighters take off the morning after a raid where gunners had claimed shooting down one to two hundred of them.)

Some crew members might decide on their own that it was better to bail out rather than risk getting killed by the fire of German fighters; bureaucratic heroism had its limits. (Of course, if we were hedge-hopping, bailing out was not an option anyway.) So good crew morale was also evidenced by no one bailing out unless he heard the bail-out signal, and usually a good crew required a direct verbal order from the pilot or copilot, especially if there were wounded on board. There were crews where the gunners preferred to die together rather than survive alone. Faced with a refusal to bail out, there was nothing for the pilot to do but ride the ship down, to get back to England on two engines, or try ditching or crash-landing. It was a great honor to have served with such men.

One can argue whether the raids undertaken in 1943 were worthwhile in terms of damage to German factories versus the loss of squadrons, but the by-products of these raids were many. First they trained the generals and colonels of the Eighth Air Force in the difficult art of leading wing formation and division formation, and there was no other way to train but by doing. There was no link trainer equivalent for flying wing formation.

Second, they established standards for the Army as well as for the Air Corps. At the moment of attack, we went through the enemy fire and trusted our luck. There was no other way. It forced the Germans to divert the equivalent of fifteen artillery divisions to the defense of their fatherland. In the first ten weeks of 1944, with a leadership in training, we broke the back of the Luftwaffe and ensured the success of the D-Day landings.

12

THE PITFALLS OF ASSEMBLY

In 1936, I was crossing the Atlantic for my first visit to America in nine years. I was traveling alone to see my father and spend summer vacation with him. We had not seen each other since my mother and I left for France in December 1927. I was fifteen, already a passionate fan of aviation, and on board the ship at my assigned dinner table, I met a man named Burt Acosta. He turned out to be a French pilot who had flown in the First World War and who had been on long-distance raids during the 1920s. He had also survived a crash on take-off in an attempt, with René Fonck, Admiral Byrd, and a navigator, to cross the Atlantic before Lindbergh. Between my adoring questions and his eager answers, I don't think we allowed our table companions much opportunity to speak.

Acosta related how René Fonck, who was the top French ace of the war, had won all his seventy-five confirmed victories because he was a remarkable shot with his machine gun, sometimes disabling an enemy plane or killing its pilot with only two or three bullets. However, Acosta told me, Fonck was just an average pilot. In the attempt to cross the Atlantic, it would have been better for the four of them to have let Acosta take the controls during take-off, but Admiral Byrd, who was the airplane commander, wanted to have Fonck do it, because in 1927 Fonck was the best-known figure in the crew, and for that reason the newspapers would give them bigger play. The result of that decision had been that the over-loaded multi-engine plane had crashed on take-off, killing the navigator and sending Burt Acosta to the hospital.

He answered my many questions about what flying had been like in the First World War. When I asked especially about formation flying, he

explained that toward the end of the war the French Air Force had experi-
mented with large formations of fighters and bombers, but that it took
close to two hours to assemble them. In World War I, planes would have
run through most of their fuel by the time the formation had finally
come together.

When I was flying combat, years later, the rendezvous and assembly
– into squadron formation, then into group formation, and finally, shortly
before departing the British coast, into wing formation – still took about
the same two hours. But then the big difference was that our bombers
would still have about eight hours of gas left.

But we still had the identical risks of collision and of getting lost. These
two phases of a mission, rendezvous and assembly, were very delicate and
often as dangerous as meeting with enemy flak and fighters. As eager as I
was to do landings and take-offs, I remained only moderately interested in
flying the rendezvous and assembly. I did not learn much about it anyway,
as Streit, the first pilot, kept the controls during all of these procedures and,
on more than one occasion, saved our asses from disaster.

To assist the first pilots in assembly, we had large code letters painted
on our vertical stabilizers; multi-colored flares shot by the copilots of the
lead ships; radio beacons, called splashers; and radio compasses with needles
that would home into the splashers. Normally, after take-off, the group
leader would climb to the assigned altitude for the first splasher and circle
it for about an hour while the lead squadron formed behind him, first the
deputy lead on his left and then his other wing man on his right. The first
element of three being complete, the second element would form behind.
When the lead squadron was then assembled, it was the turn of the low
squadron, which formed about 200 to 250 feet below the group leader, to
his left and somewhat to his rear. And after that, the high squadron would
form, 200 to 250 feet higher than the group leader and to his right.

After the group was formed, it would depart at a specific time for the
second splasher and climb to the altitude assigned to that group. If a group
leader also was to be wing leader, he would arrive at the second splasher
with his group and assume the right altitude; the other two groups would
then take their positions, one above and the other below him, keeping a
separation of about 250 feet above the high squadron of the lead group,
or 250 feet below the low squadron of the lead group, respectively. At that
moment the 41st Combat Wing would have formed. At the appointed time
the wing would stop circling the splasher and head on toward the British
coast before crossing into occupied Europe.

If all was well with the 41st Combat Wing, and it was scheduled to lead
the First Division into Germany, other wings would fall in behind it at
intervals of about two minutes. The trouble was that events rarely followed

smoothly the scenario given to the leaders. Clouds and contrails would often reduce visibility; ships would not be able to find their squadron leader, who took off two-and-a-half minutes ahead of them; squadrons would not find their group leader; group leaders would not find their wing leader. Wing leaders left with only two groups assembled for their command were forbidden to proceed into Germany with this reduced formation. Meanwhile, formation leaders were supposed to be flying 'precision.' If the orders said 150 miles per hour, it was not 149 or 151, but 150!

(Wing leaders varied in their aggressiveness. General Travis did not hesitate to go on with only two groups, regardless of what general orders said. Sometimes the third group would catch up with him over the Channel, sometimes not.)

The progress of a group formation into wing formation, and from then on into the division procession of wings, was settled by Eighth Air Force Headquarters and came to us in the form of 'frag orders' (so called because they were fragments of the long official order, which could run twenty pages and which included radio channels; code names, like Fatgal White, Cowboy Blue; main targets and possible alternatives; specific orders for the different wings and their component groups; and so forth).

Our itinerary had to be timed minute by minute so as to ensure smooth integration of the various wings and ensure also a reliable rendezvous with our fighter formations, which left their bases later than we left ours but cruised a hundred miles an hour faster. If we missed rendezvous with them, there would be hell to pay, and the payment would be exacted by the enemy fighters. Sometimes the friendly fighters would wait for the bomber wings, but for how long? The bomber wings could not wait for the fighter groups, so the greatest care had to be taken to meet the schedule set by the frag orders. If the wing was early, it would try to kill some time by reducing its airspeed by one or two miles per hour or by making a broad 'S' or two in the sky and hope that this would not disrupt the procession.

Slowing down by two miles per hour by the formation leader meant that ships further behind would see their own speed vary, for short times, from ten to twenty miles per hour. A decrease of twenty miles per hour could bring a heavily loaded bomber to the edge of a stall, and it would be at the mercy of the turbulence caused by the airflow from the propellers of the ship in front. A formation leader who created too much work to his followers was apt to lose some of them to aborts or to 'getting lost' or because they decided to latch onto a formation that seemed better led.

A major problem for our leaders was that, although they may have been outstanding pilots in a solo B-17 or in a flight of three or even in a squadron of six or seven, they were being asked to show mastery in leading a group of twenty or twenty-two planes or, even more challenging, an entire wing of fifty-four. A wing extended some 1,500 feet above them and some 1,500 feet below; it also extended 1,500 feet to the right and 1,500 feet to the left. This was the area of command over which each lead pilot had to spread his imaginary Icarus wings.

Sometimes a wing leader would forget he was combing the sky with such an enormous and deadly rake. Twice I saw such formations rake two, four, and even six ships into flaming collisions – the price of a change of direction that had not taken into account the reach of the wing and the proximity of another wing.

Bad weather created problems for a lone ship and even more for an element leader or a squadron leader who was trying to follow his radio-compass so as to circle the invisible splasher. Suddenly the simplicity of a solid overcast transformed into a world of peaks and valleys. The peaks were made of boiling clouds aiming for the sky above and looming like anvils, and the valleys were the space below, with clouds like a huge carpet of bubbles sticking somehow to the floor beneath.

The crew in that ship, looking for its appointed formation (or failing to find that, for any formation it could latch onto), might have a hard time orienting itself. The sheer majesty of the cloud formation was in itself a distracting, if not an intimidating element. Here, we would be intruding into a world that was definitely not our own. We would try to stay in the valleys and away from the boiling white columns. How reliable were the readings of the radio-compass, with the needle oscillating between two columns of clouds trying to choose between them? In which of the columns would the turbulence be bearable?

There were no clues except the horizon line and the chance of discerning the outline of our leader's plane through the fog. For a while we would fly blind, surrounded by other ships also flying blind, each of us carrying for the other the possibility of deadly collision. The wisest course was to catch the profile of our leader or to see his flares and follow our heading for five or ten seconds, hoping to recover the visual cues. Failing this, the best policy was to get out of the assembly by climbing 2,000 or even 3,000 feet – anything to get some perspective on the formation in order to rejoin it or to abort the mission and return to base to try again the next day.

Getting lost while chasing one's formation was no crime if it did not become a habit. Bad weather permitted a crippled ship to hide from the Luftwaffe; it also provided excuses and escapes for those who did not feel very eager that day. Let's face it, a bomber pilot did pretty much what he wanted to do once he was in the air. He was a free agent, and his consent to the formation and to the silent direction from the formation leader was that of a man who could not be forced if his will ceased to agree with what he was asked to do. As a pilot he was partly very skilled craftsman and partly a professional; every situation he faced had a high component of the unpredictable in it. As with a doctor, we had to trust his skill and his commitment to duty, which included his willingness to put his life on the line as a matter of course. In fact, the latter component was never mentioned by his immediate superiors. Our generals were the only ones who ever spoke to us of 'sacrifice' and 'death' and the necessity of facing both as they led us in hazardous missions like Schweinfurt or Berlin, and it never helped our morale. The exhortations broke the implicit contract that we had with the group leaders: *You lead, and we follow to the limit of our lives and of our ship's capacity; we don't ask any questions, even if they burn our lips.* This was part of the day's work, and what the foreman said went. It was up to him to keep the formation clear of enemy flak concentrations and to ensure our fighter support. In return, we had the formidable support of the band of brothers. With it, we would brave any walls of flak, any group of German fighters.

When the generals made speeches they immediately went beyond that consensus. Most of us would still follow, but it was an individual decision. Those who took off for Sweden or Switzerland, those 'who could not find the formation' or whose engines 'vibrated' or 'heated up', those whose oxygen supply had 'leaked too badly to permit completing the mission', would not be judged too harshly by us. Half the time their problems were real, half the time perhaps not very real, at least to the engineering officer, who often would fudge the issue to protect the first pilot, or to the group leader who would look the other way if it were the first time or if the pilot had had a bad string of tough missions where it had been touch and go whether he would make it back to the base.

Furthermore, there was the fact that the first pilot was responsible for the lives of nine other individuals, and that always weighed in favor of aborting the mission if he was in doubt. He would bear the guilt and the sanctions if the Colonel decided that the pilot's actions 'showed poor determination to complete the mission.' But if he did not abort and, over Schweinfurt or Anklam or Haberstadt, the engine he had suspected quit on them, and he could not stay with the formation – if the enemy fighters crowded in on him and the tail gunner ceased to answer the copilot's call for oxygen check, then what? When he received the sledgehammer blows of 20mm shells in his back through his armor plate, and consciousness began to fade into black, was his last thought to ask the crew for forgiveness? Was that less painful than to ask the Colonel for *his* forgiveness because you aborted the mission without sufficient justification?

Among the first pilots themselves were differences in priority. About ten to twenty percent were eager and determined to complete the mission; about the same percentage were 'less than eager' and ready to abort on any pretext. The majority of missions were flown by pilots who were not especially eager, but who were not about to just quit either. They were people who would not put down their brethren for the choices they made and who would always give them the benefit of the doubt. Their own courage did not need to be bolstered by the contempt for or rejection of others. I deeply admired them, but, although I mellowed toward the end of my tour, I could not then join them in their forgiveness of human frailty. At that time, I needed to kill the coward in me by killing it also in those around me.

13

COPING WITH FAILURES

Controlling one's fear was not too hard, so far, yet there were some who could not do it, the cost of self-control being so great that they were not able to function as aircraft commanders or fly a mission effectively.

In the original cadre that came over from Wendover with Colonel Preston, there was a group operations officer I will call 'Major X'. He went on two missions with the Colonel, who noticed that his major had a bad habit of covering his eyes when enemy fighters came his way. The Colonel took him off flying duty and made him head of the Officers' Club, known as 'Duffy's Tavern'.

Major 'Duffy', as he came to be known, did an excellent job of running the club and in stocking the bar with liquor; apparently, the 379th had the best choice of brands in the whole Eighth Air Force, with the exception, perhaps, of Wycombe Abbey. Major Duffy had found his niche; those who knew about his *de facto* demotion became fewer with time. He was a man without complexes, not eaten up by shame or remorse, happy to serve where the Colonel had placed him. The Colonel, in being able to recuperate combat failures and make them useful, was smart – and/or lucky.

There were two scandals in our squadron, we discovered. The first was the fact that our squadron CO was a coward and refused to make himself available for any mission except milk runs to the French coast. A good and handsome flyer, Major Culpepper[1] had been unable to schedule himself to lead the squadron; we could not say he was suffering from battle fatigue, since in seven months he only succeeded in going on ten, mostly easy, missions. He had little prestige with the veterans, and the replacement crews soon caught on to him. In fact, the whole group had caught on to him, and we took for granted that the Colonel was only waiting for a chance to get rid of him.

In the fall of 1943, after the Air Corps discovered that in ninety days of summer it had been able to fly only thirty-eight days of visual missions, a pathfinder group was created to train bombardiers and navigators to recognize their targets through clouds and bomb effectively through use of the radar screen.[2] In December, our Colonel let it be known that Major Culpepper would be sent down to join them.

It gave the Major a graceful exit. Except that he never left. January, February, March passed, and our *François* Major (the nickname given to all those squadron commanders who seemed to be fixated on French targets only) was still in Kimbolton, with his elegant moustache, his well-tailored uniforms, and his cordial demeanor. The day after my twenty-fifth mission, he was still there, and I took him in poker for $250. (How could anybody stay mad at a man like that! He was a hedonist for himself and for all of us.)

Eventually Colonel Preston was able to fob him off on one of his friends who commanded a bomber group. I guess the Major was not able to schedule himself for missions there anymore frequently than at Kimbolton, otherwise he would have completed his quota and been back in the States well before November 1944. But in November 1944, Culpepper was still a major and a squadron commander. In the memoirs of Colonel Preston's friend, the only mention of him is that he fried eggs on a stove with great competence.

Most of us had no inkling of the Culpepper scandal, which was not so glaring after all. The gossip vine was broken by those in the know being shot down or being rotated out after having finished their tours. Elmer Bendiner, a navigator who had been through two missions to Schweinfurt and one ditching in the Channel, left for the States the very week we arrived as fresh replacements. It was not until years later, reading his book, that I learned of Major Culpepper's cowardice. Titled *The Fall of Fortresses*, it was not published until 1980, after the death of Colonel Preston, by then a four-star general. Centered around the Second Schweinfurt raid, it is one of the better books about our group.

The second scandal in our squadron involved a pilot named Gray, who had come to Kimbolton practically with the original crews. Gray was constantly accusing our CO of systematically giving him the low-diamond position in the squadron's order of battle and threatened to go to his native Sweden at the first occasion that presented itself. Gray did not keep his beefs for his original buddies either; he shared them with the junior birdmen as well.

There was no excuse for our squadron leadership not to have been on Gray's case. Granted that his complaints about his assignments in the order of battle were largely trumped up, there could still have been some discussion as to whether it was true that the low-diamond position was more dangerous than others. (In fact, against frontal attacks it was probably one of the safest.) If confronted about his threats to go to Sweden, he would have had to claim that they were not meant seriously, and perhaps he would have been led to believe it himself. A good talk with the flight surgeon and the squadron commander might have worked.

But our squadron commander was hardly in a good position to counsel reason or to buck up Gray's spine, since he shared his reluctance for combat. Major Culpepper, if anything, was probably a covert supporter of Gray's mission-avoidance techniques – colds, toothaches, sick calls, bureaucratic snafus requiring visits to wing headquarters or even to Pinetree – since they reduced the guilt of his own methods, which were more subtle than those available to Gray.

The enlisted men suffered acutely from situations like this. They did not like aborts (although they might not mind too much if the target was Schweinfurt or Berlin); they did not like going through the wrenching of 'the night before' and the briefing for nothing. After that, the mission was half over. But they didn't get half credit for the night before and the briefing. For the enlisted crew, their war aim was to do their jobs and get back home as soon as possible. A pilot who aborted often made that goal more elusive. Although they would not share his punishment if the Colonel got wise to his behavior, they would have to do many of their missions as spares on other crews where they knew comparatively little of their companions. They would not have the support of their own crew, their own first circle in the band of brothers.

Normally a pilot would have had about 180 hours more of flying B-17s than the copilot had. He would have been trained for emergencies. The copilot could catch up with him, and there was an unknown percentage of copilots who were better flyers than their first pilots. It was basically the requirements of Headquarters for 100 copilots that made the determination. A certain number of the young graduates would go to B-17 school, and the rest would go directly to a staging area, where the only training they would get would be the training that their first pilots would give them (and, of course, ground school, but the ground school program was very haphazard). But it was rare that a pilot or copilot was found deficient in basic flying skills. At that level, what made the difference was how he behaved under fire.

An ambitious copilot, eager to take over the aircraft commander's seat, had to be careful. He could not go and squeal on his first pilot to the squadron commander. What would usually happen when a first pilot was 'suffering from battle fatigue', as we would say, is that the bombardier and/or the navigator would talk to the enlisted crew and make a delegation to Brownlow, our operations officer. A real aristocrat, whose grandfather had been governor of Tennessee, William Brownlow III had rather taken over the *de facto* direction of the squadron. With the help of good sergeant McCormick, he made up the order of battle, sent crews to 'flak home;' scheduled our forty-eight-hour passes, and supervised our training. Instead of delegating the job of waking us on the mornings of missions to some clerk in his office, or even to his assistant operations officer, Brownlow would most often do it himself, rousing us with the familiar, 'Breakfast at three, briefing at four.'

I would always be awake before he tapped on my door, because the entrance to our barracks had a squeaking door in the best tradition of *The Inner Sanctum*. I often wondered if he was ever greeted by an officer pleading, 'Not this time, please, not this time. I have no stomach for it.' If it did happen, Brownlow never said a word, even when the principals were long gone – shot down or finished with their tour of missions or removed from their crews to be made PX officers. You could talk to Brownlow. He would not squeal on you.

Often flying as a last-minute replacement for the officer to whom he had granted a reprieve, Brownlow was rumored to have flown something like thirty missions. From the copilot seat he took movies of the formation, of the crew, of the enemy fighters. The crews that he would fly with would be so astonished by this, by his cool, his white moustache, and his elegance that they would put on a show for him. Of course, without seeming to, he was checking on their performance. He chose the crews he flew with very well; when seventy to eighty percent of the crews that were flying in July 1943 had been shot down by the end of the year, he managed to make it back with his camera every time. He had the quiet courage that spread like a positive osmotic force throughout the squadron. We all fed on it at one time or another, and it made up for the leadership vacuum left by the 'overlooked' failure of Major Culpepper.

So, to discuss the problems of a first pilot, a delegation would go and see Brownlow. After having talked with the delegation, Brownlow would then call in the copilot and try to get the true picture from him. To overcome the taboo against 'squealing,' he might pull out the American flag: 'It is your duty to tell us the facts as you see them.' If the copilot remained silent, or noncommittal, his silence spoke for him. ('I don't know … I never noticed anything amiss. If the first pilot decided to abort, I suppose he must have had a good reason.') There was no stigma in defending the first pilot, hence if the copilot said nothing, he said plenty. He was driving in the knife without showing that he held the handle. And he became the first pilot. Who said that the path of honor was obvious and easy?

Within a week the old first pilot would be gone, often made into copilot, usually in another squadron. For many it was sufficient to have been relieved of the responsibility of command to become operational again. For others, the psychic wounds were too deep and compounded by the public humiliation. If they could not take it anymore, they would be grounded. Major Duffy was certainly a greater asset to the group as a splendid head of the Officers' Club than as a mediocre first pilot, and he did not put in danger the lives of others.

Frey was the first obvious failure of our group. He would fall asleep at the controls as the formation would approach the French coast. His copilot did not have as yet the know-how and the self-confidence necessary to take over the leadership of the mission, and there would be nothing left to do but abort. It was not fatigue but fear. Curiously enough, Frey used to complain that his radio man had no nerve for combat, while all the time it was he whose courage had run out. The responsibilities of commanding a crew in combat were beyond him. He had already too much on his hands taking care of himself. For that matter he could not even take care of himself.

Falling asleep at the controls could be deadly when you are flying tight formation. It had fallen to Brownlow, after consulting with the Colonel, to call in Frey after his second abort and say, 'We have a good job for you, where you will be most useful. How would you like to be the tail gunner on the squadron lead crew and be observer for the Colonel?' Frey's crew was broken up, and he was made tail gunner-observer on the lead ship, where his job was to keep the group or the wing commander informed as to fighter attacks from the rear: who had aborted, who was shot down, and how the formation looked. From all accounts he did a very good job of it, and he kept his commission. True enough, the job of tail gunner in the lead ship was reputed to be the safest in the formation, but to be relieved of responsibility, to not have to bear the loneliness of command, was all that Frey needed, and as tail gunner he was a success. I think Frey regarded the job as a deserved advancement. No wonder he was surprised not to be promoted with the rest of the first pilots.

How could we feel toward him? Some, like Fowler, did not hide their contempt. On the day we went to Oschersleben, Duvall's radio gunner, the one Frey had complained about, had his arm crippled for life when a 20mm shell went through it before lodging itself in the radio. Fowler had been riding with Duvall as well and kept the disarmed shell as a souvenir. He would pull it out when we were in the dayroom, making various comments on life in general and Frey's lack of guts in particular. Fowler had guts, but he also had a foul mouth and an ugly disposition, and it was a bit embarrassing. The rest of us did sympathize with Frey up to a certain point; we knew too well ourselves the fragility of a man's courage. Who were we to throw the first stone? But sometimes we hated him for his soft job, and we vented our jealous fury by laughing with each other at how surprised he had been on not being promoted with the rest of the first pilots: 'Ha, ha, can you imagine? Rather takes the cake doesn't it?' But Frey kept on living unashamed having made peace with himself, apparently immune to our judgment.

I saw Frey once more, back in the States, when I was in the Transport Command, flying the Brass and civilian dignitaries out of Washington, DC. I was in a chow line and who is coming toward me but Frey, ready to shake hands. I looked not at him, but through him. Frey did not insist and turned away.

McCall, Gurney, O'Neil, Tex, and Barrett would probably have disapproved of what I did to Frey, and later, I would realize that a certain component in my attitude was that I was trying to kill the Frey I had in me. Add to this the jealousy of a copilot toward a pilot who could not live up to the expectations of his status.

But for a while I congratulated myself on showing my icy contempt toward a man who did not have what it takes and who seemed to have no compunction about it. How, I thought, could you maintain high standards if those who did not meet them suffered no guilt and had little or no shame?

14

FIFTH MISSION

The first time we took off for Kiel, on January 4, we were supposed to assemble in squadron formation before dawn. However, this night take-off and assembly was not coming off any too well. Maresh's ship took off in front of us, shot a red flare, and vanished. We got ready to move on but were ordered to wait. When we finally roared over the end of the runway, we could see small flames outlining the shadow of a mangled ship. They must have lost an engine, I thought. On take-off that was deadly. I guess they held us up to see whether or not it would explode. After five minutes, they decided they were willing to take a chance, and we were given the green light. They could not delay the assembly any longer.

In the air, it was a nightmare, dodging planes, trying to find the leader and fall in with him. A passing red light would zoom in out of nowhere, and we'd flash our landing lights and haul back on the stick just in time to see a shadow ship pass gracefully and precariously beneath us.

Our throats dry and hands a bit shaky, our eyes straining for the lights that might mean an impending collision, we decided to climb to 10,000 feet and wait for daylight. There was no use milling around here, risking death for nothing and scaring the crew. 'Orders is orders' but the first order was to use one's head.

At 10,000 feet we found comparative peace. The tremor in our hands subsided, and we found time to grin and complain. *Snafu!* We were all right.

Waiting for dawn, we watched the crash at the end of the runway still burning, rather gently as fires go, a red glow on the ground.

… And I am remembering the same glow that evening on the lake, canoeing with Ann, both of us using the same paddle, our bodies close, her blond hair against my cheek, tingling it like a baby's fingertips. And bound for shore, the charm soon to be broken, I watched what I at first thought was a fire on some distant house. It grew larger, too big to be a fire; it was the moon coming up, and I felt rather silly …

So this time I decided I would not be fooled; what I was seeing was the sun coming up. But the red glow suddenly sprang into an enormous mushroom of fire and smoke, and I knew I had been tricked once more. It was another B-17 exploding.

And it was beautiful, terribly. For a moment you forgot all about the war, watching that so murderous mushroom, born, growing, and dying, all in a few seconds.

And the moonrise on Lake Michigan and the warmth of Ann's body were so near that I ached with longing.

Boyovitch had reported another plane afire on the ground near the one that had exploded; it must have been a collision. We wouldn't know who had died until our return. Radio silence was strictly enforced during missions – for 'security reasons'. Although I thought the real reason was probably to tell us: *Don't bother the others with your problems; solve them on your own. Die, if need be, without disturbing the others with your screams.*

Finally, with daylight, formations came together; but as we left the British coast, three planes lay burning on the ground, killed by the quiet cool darkness, blind having stumbled upon blind. Blind having rammed the ground while trying desperately to rise above it.

This first raid to Kiel is my first encounter with real fear.

We are carrying a bomb bay tank. Two hours or so into the mission. I want to transfer gas from it to our engines' reservoirs. But Streit says he prefers to go over the target with the bomb bay tank full, because when a tank is empty but still full of fumes, it becomes a bomb. It makes a lot of sense, and our tank remains full.

Over the target Marcott goofs. Instead of toggling our six 500 pounders, he salvoes. Having also forgotten that we still have our bomb bay tank, everything goes out at once, all of the bombs and the full bomb bay tank. This little mishap is followed by our discovery that our squadron leader does not realize that, since we, being low diamond (what else!) are echeloned downward, we can be in the cloud bank while he, 150 feet higher, is in the clear. Eventually Streit, who is flying the plane, calls, 'Fat Gal White Leader from Enamel K for King. I'm in the soup. I don't want a collision. I'm leaving formation. See you at home. Over and out.'

And he puts the nose down. I reduce the RPM to 1,800, and he reduces the manifold pressure to eighteen; might as well begin to save gas for the long trip home. I also turn on the carburetor's heat to keep it from icing.

We do not know how thick the cloud bank is. From 21,000 feet we down to 10,000, and we are still in it.

I call up the navigator: 'Copilot to Navigator, over.'

There is no answer.

'Copilot to Bombardier, over?'

Voice of Marcott, returning, 'Go ahead, Copilot.'

'I'm not getting any reply from the Navigator. What's he doing?'

'He appears to be asleep on his table.'

'Does he have his earphones on?'

'Yes he has them on. Do you want me to wake him up?'

'Never mind, he gave us a miniature map of the mission – should we make do with that.'

To Streit I say, 'Copilot to Pilot; 320 magnetic should take us further away from the German coast and enemy fighters. On the other hand, it will lengthen our road back – 290 should do it, at least for a while.' Streit nods and turns to 290. On the intercom he adds, 'And the others will not be on that route.'

He flies by the artificial horizon, keeping the plane below the horizon bar. 'Copilot to crew,' I call. 'We are at 10,000 feet and going down. You can remove your oxygen masks.'

At 2,000 feet, the cloud bank begins to thin, but the windshield and side windows are iced up. I turn on the defrost control, but it does not seem to work.

At 1,200 feet, we break out of the cloud bank, and Streit and I both open our cockpit windows so that we can see outside. I set the RPM at 2,300, Streit pushes the throttles to forty-four inches of manifold pressure and the airspeed goes up to 240 miles per hour. We are over a little island covered with green meadows, and we can see a small village, its houses clustered around a white church.

Suddenly, Marcott is shouting, 'We've got machine guns shooting at us!'

Tracer bullets pass in front of and below the ship. From the open cockpit window I can see the blinking lights of machine guns as they fire at us. And then, WHAM! – an 88 shell bursts! I see on my side the red flash of the explosion and black smoke uncoiling fifty yards ahead of the ship on my side. Five seconds later, another shell bursts, closer, its fragments peppering the bomb bay. I duck my head below the cockpit window. Streit is corkscrewing the plane while diving for the deck and the ocean side of the island. WHAM! Another 88 shell, but on Streit's side. This time, I do not duck, and neither does he.

WHAM! Another shell on my side.

And I duck.

My guts are twisted and my knees and feet are jittering up and down. Several machine-gun bullets go through the cockpit. They make a delicate noise and leave holes through which daylight appears. In the midst of my fear, the noise reminds me of glass Christmas ornaments falling on the floor. Then I am yelling, 'Shoot these sons of bitches. Tail Gun, shoot; all turrets – shoot!'

The staccato of machine-gun fire is my answer. Another shell on my side – WHAM – but too high. As I duck again, I notice my window has defrosted. I close it; Streit closes his. And the windshield is clear, thank God, now that we are hedge-hopping below tree-top level.

My knees stop shivering. We are over the beach and over the water, ten feet above it.

Streit says to me, 'Take it.' And I take the controls.

Kundin gives us a bearing, an ETA. We land at Oulton, refuel, and are home – only one hour behind the group formation.

The next day we went back to Kiel, but this time we assembled in daylight. It was the second time in two days – the Germans were ready for us. A twin-engine fighter tried to drag a cable bomb through our formation but lost his nerve and let go of the bomb way out of range. When it blew, its explosion was ten times that of an 88 shell. Germans were experimenting with ways to get at our formations without exposing their flyers, just like we were trying to find a way to bomb their cities by dropping flying bombs from an area well out of reach of their flak guns.

Many seemed to dread flak more than fighters on the theory that you could do something about the fighters but little about flak. Actually, when one thought about it, flak rarely killed us; it just crippled us and left us easier prey for the fighters. And a fighter was a man out to kill us. All the PR communiqués to the contrary, an isolated bomber did not stand too good a chance against a determined fighter attack. The high number of planes claimed shot down by our gunners was just that: claims. 'Intelligence' usually scaled the numbers down by a quarter or a third, and they were still too high. There could easily have been eight gunners all claiming the same enemy fighter.

So flak was part of fate, part of the general picture of things, like the sky, the water, the plane. It started as a black seahorse uncoiling, at first small and then becoming frozen and white. We could spot the target from way back by the concentration of little white and black puffs like a rash in a corner of the sky.

Sometimes it seemed that a flak battery was zeroing on a particular plane. We would watch the first bursts of four shells explode being too high and above us, the second too low and behind, the third right on the nose but to the side. Then we would wait eight or nine seconds for the fourth salvo, which we are sure will burst smack inside the cockpit. But the fourth salvo doesn't come, perhaps because it was again too high and too far forward, or perhaps because we were out of range already. Or perhaps because it was a random barrage. Much flak, especially on the bomb run, came from box barrages, where the gunners or their radar aiming devices were filling a geometric box in the sky rather than aiming at a specific plane or squadron.

This time, on our second raid to Kiel, the fourth salvo, still a bit low, caught our right wing. The #4 engine threw oil, and fire started coming out of the cowl flaps. We feathered the engine before the oil pressure gave out completely. To stay in formation, we needed to gain more power. We released our bombs immediately. I felt rather sorry to waste the mission but the remainder of our group released its bombs on a turn anyway, succeeding, as a result, in missing not only our target, the submarine pens, but the whole town of Kiel.

The Supercharger on #3 gave out completely, and we had to leave the formation. I don't remember any fighter escort that day; in any case we didn't see any. Our trip home would have to be made alone. We let down to a lower altitude in order to get some power out of #3; a slow descent brought us down to 2,500 feet.

Owens, from the ball turret, told us we were losing gas. Apparently the flak had ripped some pretty good chunks out of the self-sealing gas tanks. It became obvious the return home would be touch and go. Our gas consumption was increased by the loss of an engine, our inability to transfer gas from the dead engine, and the leaks sprung by the flak holes while Finicle was trying to transfer gas from the #4 engine to #2. I warned the crew we might have to ditch.

Ditching in the North Sea in full winter was no cinch. Wet, you could die of exposure in just a few minutes. Dry and warmly clothed, you might last a couple of hours. An Air-Sea Rescue man had once told me of a B-17 ditching. They had all the information as to location and so forth and were able to lose no time in their search, but it was winter, and the dinghies had not inflated. A fighter pilot following the bomber reported that all he could see after the plane hit the water was a gunner astride on the tail of the wreck, embracing the tall vertical stabilizer as if it were an indifferent mother. Ninety minutes later, when they got to him, he was dead – of fear, shock, exposure, what have you. We would have to really want to live to survive a winter ditching. Furthermore, we had to be careful to not ditch too close to shore; too close and we might blow ourselves up on the sea coast mines of the British. We did not know it then, but on the average, a ditching resulted in only thirty to fifty percent of the crew being picked up alive.

Over the intercom I called, 'Copilot to crew, jettison all unnecessary equipment – machine guns, ammunition, anything that you can carry to an open window.'

'Right Waist to Copilot. Excuse me, what does 'jettison' mean?'

'Excuse me. I meant throw out anything that is not bolted down the ship.'

And soon the #3 engine quit cold. Out of gas? We checked carefully before feathering: switches all right; oil temperature falling, of course fuel pressure fluctuating around five pounds instead of the normal twelve – we feathered. How long before the two remaining engines, now giving their maximum power, would run out of gas? We had the lights lit up on the fuel gauges, though these gauges were chronically inaccurate. There was nothing to do but give the order to prep ditching. The crew needed to be ready in case one more engine quit, we had to hit the water – an altitude of 2,000 feet would allow us but a small margin of warning. They had already been jettisoning flak suits, guns, and ammunition trying to make the airplane as light as possible and save some gas. They were too busy to be very afraid. As soon as everything that could be jettisoned was out of the plane, I turned on the emergency IFF: 'Identification, Friend or Foe,' the automatic radio signal that would identify us to Allied gunners as friendly. I called out, 'Copilot to crew, Copilot to crew: prepare to ditch, prepare to ditch.' I had to snicker at the theatrical ring of my order. Life imitating melodrama.

Often on our raids, an hour and a half would elapse between take-off and our entering the enemy zone. So when the Dutch coast came in sight, I would say, 'Copilot to crew, copilot to crew: battle stations, battle stations.' It didn't mean anything more than, 'Get on the ball; from now on, it could get rough anytime.' But I would say it very much like the skipper in the movies; I really gave it that old earnestness of a Cecil B. De Mille melodrama, and the crew would answer in a short, rapid fire: 'Tail Gun ready. Right Waist ready,' and so on.

In the same vein, I would call out, 'Copilot to crew, Copilot to crew: standby for take-off, standby for take-off.' Totally unnecessary. The gunners knew damn well we were taking off. Still, it sounded kind of urgent; old glory. 'You may fire when ready Digby.' And the crew responded instinctively to it, taking up the movie attitudes, getting up the movie courage, secure in the movie happy ending.

A fighter pilot would call out for all posterity to hear, 'So long, fellows. I'm going to see what the Krauts are having for dinner tonight.' Where the flesh might not be willing to take us, the Pixies would; if we couldn't be brave in silence, we could always be Errol Flynn in *Dawn Patrol*. And as I called out now, 'Prepare for ditching, prepare for ditching,' I wondered what the hell is this, the war or a radio show? Even the networks couldn't do better, and I would not have been very surprised if Boyovitch had answered, 'Sir, I am sorry I have but one life to give to my country!' or if Chruby had declaimed, 'Tell them back home we died fighting!' or if Williams had shouted, 'Don't give up the ship … yet.'

The movie voice was tolerable, because in its excess of zeal, it was a parody. It was not the 'eager beavering' that would put you on the side of the Brass and alienate you from your band of brothers. It was half serious and half joke. The joke was the meaning that you were obeying but under enough protest to retain your individuality – you weren't being taken in.

Now, everyone except the radio man took his position for ditching. When I asked navigation to give our exact position to the radio, Kundin was ready. We were forty-five minutes to the coast, probably too far for us to make it. Everyone in the crew was huddled in the radio room, his head protected with seat cushions.

We had no more contact with the crew except through the radio man. Everything was okay back there; all we could do now was sweat out the gas.

I am remembering the mission to Beauvoir. We had had little flak and no fighters. Hearing Boyovitch calling out, 'Fighter escort coming up from six o'clock low,' I hadn't been able to resist joshing him about the raid to Emden.

'Sergeant Boyovitch,' I had called to him.

'Go ahead, Copilot?'

'Sergeant Boyovitch, I wish to congratulate you upon your voice finding again its normal tonality.'

'Thank you, sir.'

And today, returning from Kiel, the bass has not wavered when Boyovitch answered, 'Tail Gun ditching.' Perhaps I had been right to tease him, although I had regretted it then two seconds after having spoken. Survival in a ditching would depend a lot on firm resolve. If fear was under control the cold and the fatigue would not overwhelm you so easily.

Forty minutes to go before the coast, waiting for an engine to miss for the lurch that would indicate the beginning of the glide into the water. Chruby is sending continuous signals from which our position can be plotted. On the ground, they are drawing our course on maps alerting the coastal patrol boats.

It is not too hard to wait. All you have to do is to freeze your imagination. There is still no fighter escort, which could circle above us to guide the Air-Sea Rescue boats to our dinghies if we have to ditch. We have things to do, watching the cylinder-head temperature on our two good engines, keeping the bad wing up, staying on course, maintaining every foot of altitude. It is harder for the crew now that they are in ditching position – all they can do is sit and wait. We might have delayed the order to prepare for ditching and thus have lessened strain. But, on the other hand, we might have been caught by surprise and the carefully rehearsed drill could have suffered from too much haste.

We are ready. We have a head wind. If we have to ditch, it is preferable to turn in such a way as will land us in the trough of a wave. Landing at sea – water, air, fire, ground – the elements of life and war and the incongruities of man's grammar trying to tie himself to them.

We have thirty minutes to go. If one of our remaining engines quits, we could stretch our glide a bit; we might glide for sixty seconds at 115 miles per hour. Perhaps. Neither Streit nor I have ever tried it before. They say it might be a good idea to land crosswind, but here the wind is easily around twenty miles an hour, and if we hit at eighty-five or ninety miles per hour, that would give us sixty-five to seventy miles per hour ground speed – or in this case, sea speed – but we should avoid ramming a wave. We should land in a trough even if it means facing a crosswind.

Flaps. We could use half flaps and put the rest full down when ready to hit, trying to hit flat so as not to break the tail off if possible. As soon as we start to glide, we will have to unfeather the dead engines if we can. I've heard that windmilling props absorb shock more easily than feathered ones. *Will #4 unfeather? Or have we lost all our oil? Or perhaps the oil in the prop dome is frozen?* It is minus twelve degrees centigrade; they will probably not unfeather. The right wing, already weakened by flak, might tear off. If we have thirty seconds before the ship sinks, we will be okay.

Twenty minutes to go. About forty-two miles away from the coast. The gauges on #2's gas tank indicate twenty gallons, enough for about ten minutes at our present consumption. All we can do is hope that the gauge, almost always inaccurate, is wrong this time as well. I keep shooting red flares at regular intervals, hoping to stir up a fighter out of nowhere. The cockpit smells of powder.

Fifteen minutes. The radio is giving us a course to steer for if we can make it. Applebridge, sounds like *Alice in Wonderland*. Sounds too good to be true.

Chruby comes back, 'It's not Applebridge, but Attlebridge. 'T' as in 'tare.' 'Okay.'

Marcott is crawling into the cockpit. What in hell is he doing here instead of remaining at his ditching position? He wants to know 'What's going on?'

'Damn it! The same thing – sweating out the gas!'

'Are we going to make it?' he wants to know.

'I don't know. You know as well as I do. Get back to your post and stay there.'

He wants the flare pistol; it's part of his ditching duties. What's he trying to do, show off? We already know he can take it. Somehow or other I resent his presence in the intimate chamber of the cockpit. This is our battle, our problem, not his.

'Hell, we need it right now,' I reply, and he goes back laughing.

Right now, we must make up our minds whether to ditch this minute of our own free will or risk being forced to ditch later, perhaps on the mine fields. In the back of my mind, I have been always sure we will make it to the coast, but I have also learned not to mistake a subjective invulnerability for the wishes of fate. As I anticipate landing at Attlebridge, the #1 engine may quit and force us into the water. Our drill is well prepared, but the ship may break in two; the dinghies might not pop out of their hatches; or our cockpit windows may wedge shut, trapping pilot and copilot. I will not dare look our danger in the face and scoff. What confidence I have I will keep to myself.

Still … we have ten minutes to go, and now just eight. The #1 gas gauge indicates zero. Our minds are made up: we shall try for Attlebridge.

Five minutes. We can see the coast through the haze. *O, now let us not fail!* We must not fail, for now it is the coast, and it is also the beach works, the mines. Closer and closer. Everything in us is pushing the plane forward. All my heart pours love on these engines that are taking us home. I check every instrument. I handle the stick as if it were the raw nerves of this wounded ship. Streit is letting me take the ship home, a proof of confidence that helps to contain my fear.

Over the beach, over the cliffs. Here is Attlebridge, right into the wind – an enormous runway, right into the wind, about five miles with a tower operator who sounds like an Oxford graduate. I love Oxford. I love everybody. I undo some of the trim; decrease the power; and start letting down, straining on the rudder pedals. Wheels down. The wheels come down okay. What about the right tire? Is it ok? Half flaps, full flaps. The engines conk out as the *Penny Ante* hits the ground but the tires hold.

Halfway down the runway, I swing out and park, and Streit and I shake hands and smile tired smiles. Everybody piles out, yelling and embracing each other. I hug Boyovitch, Marcott, and Kundin. A British truck driven by a cute WAAF (more screams and more yells) comes to get us. A tug starts pulling the ship out of the way.

'Hi, Pitts. That was a damn nice landing!'

'Thanks, Marcott. I bet you our bombs were the only ones to hit the town.'

'Right. Frank sure screwed up the detail on that one.'

'Pretty soon you'll have your chance.'

'Well it won't be hard to do better.'

Another ship comes in bearing the 'Triangle K' of our base. As he lands, one of his props flies off. It's Duvall. Jennkovitz is with him, still in one piece and still owes me five pounds. We never cared too much for each other, but now we fall into each other's arms.

We had seen Eaton let a fighter come within 400 yards of his tail shooting rockets. One of them had taken his left wing right off, and he had gone down in a crazy spin. Back at the base, we learn that Maresh and Chamberlain had crashed on take-off. All were killed but two. The ship's bombs blew up at noon. Killion, we learned, had collided with a bomber from Molesworth whose traffic pattern overlapped with ours. That mushroom of fire had killed nineteen men.

I had known Killion pretty well from back in Texas. There had been a waitress in Amarillo I had been giving the eye, but Killion was dashing and had beaten me to her. So we had dinner together, the girl waiting on us, very sweet, very demure; Killion thought she was nice. And we had become good friends, meaning that we had talked a total of perhaps one hour since then (he belonged to the next squadron). I had never asked about the waitress and he had never mentioned her. Had she become a part of his sacred, or had she just been a good lay and that the was end of it. Now Killion was dead, with nothing left but a hole in ground you could put a four-story building into.

They gave us our first forty-eight-hour pass that night. I grabbed a bag and my money – did not even bother to shave or shine – within hours after being over Kiel, I was in London with a room at St James Court.

15

PASS TO LONDON

BRÛLER LES ETAPES

The pass we were given on our return from Kiel was the first I had received since I had arrived in England ten weeks before. We had had the pleasant surprise of finding Brownlow waiting for us at our dispersal area to announce the news. The officers he just told, but to each of our six enlisted men, he handed out regular passes, signed, dated, and stamped, which would satisfy the MPs that they were not AWOL. The officers were never stopped by MPs unless it was an emergency and everyone was being recalled to the base.

We retrieved our B-4 bags from the ground crew's tent and hopped on a truck that took us to the interrogation room, where the whole crew was debriefed by an intelligence officer about the mission. *How was the flak? How many attacks by enemy fighters?* Our interrogator seemed interested in the bomb that a German fighter tried to drop on the formation ahead of us. With an explosion easily equivalent to eight or ten flak bursts, it must have been a substantial bomb.

After interrogation, we went into the room where we changed back into our regular clothes: regular pants, regular shirt, tie, leather jacket, and rubber overshoes. Journalists were there trying to get a story out of us. I was interviewed by one while I was trying to get my flying suit off and my pants on – one leg in and the other still out. I told him, 'It wasn't too bad, we only lost one ship to enemy action.' I did not tell him about the snafu of the night take-off and assembly and the twenty-seven airmen killed.

I noticed from the corner of my eye one man from our squadron who had a big brown spot on the back of his long johns – no need to ask what that meant. But there was a loud-voiced, horse-faced woman journalist circulating among us, smelling our sweat, sneaking glances at our crotches, who went up to the guy and said, 'Well, lieutenant, did you have a bad time up there?'

The man did not answer. He ducked into the men's room, and she gave up the chase at the door. She turned to face several airmen glaring at her and muttering curses under their breath. She finally left; our group was not going to give her the time of day.

I found out later that 'they' had let her in because she bulldozed our senior intelligence officer and pleaded unfairness. Not being allowed in our dressing room with the male journalists gave them an edge in getting stories from us, while half our brains were still back in Germany with the flak, the fighter attacks, and the planes of our squadron going down with few chutes coming out. This failed, however, to warm my feelings about her.

So, this time, no complaints, no stories, nothing juicy enough to make the AP wires. If the censor had not screened the copy, the public might have heard about the crash on the runway, the mid-air collision. We were warned about keeping our mouths shut when talking to the press – 'You don't want to frighten your mothers, do you?' And it was true; we did not want to frighten our mothers. Death had to remain evanescent, fleshless – no screams or even shitting in your pants when 20mm cannon fire came right through your cockpit. And I think that was the best policy. But how long could the nightmares be repressed? I sometimes woke in the middle of the night, drenched with sweat but unable to remember what I had been dreaming. Perhaps it is all coming out now while I write this and think of the twenty-two and twenty-three-year-old I was then, without, I hope, too much self-pity.

Once dressed I lugged my B-4 bag to the squadron barracks, far down the road. Luckily, the B-4 bag contained only flight clothes and equipment: boots, heavy muttoned-lined trousers, jacket, gloves, parachute, oxygen mask, and leather helmet. When we went on a mission we left our B-4s, full of regular clothing, personal papers, pictures, and billfolds, in the custody of our ground crew. (Would those who were shot down and returned to England by the French underground railway find their billfolds and their money?) When we came back, we took our bags to our respective rooms after going through interrogation and change of clothes. It would have been simpler if we had all had our own lockers in the dressing room. *Could not be done,* 'they' said.

We were rarely finished before five o'clock, unless the mission had been a short one. Then it would take only five or six hours instead of the eight to ten we were getting accustomed to. Coming out of the dressing room with our B-4 bags, we would pass the Red Cross mobile, where two young women would offer coffee and donuts. A percentage of airmen did not care much for coffee, so they could have hot chocolate. Nobody would cast aspersions on their dislike for coffee, because, after all, an airman's virility was taken for granted. The Red Cross girls were often pretty, but they gravitated in their dating to the Headquarters' staff. All things of value gravitated toward the Headquarters' staff. That's life.

Back in the squadron dayroom (our salon), we would check to see whether we had any mail or packages and then walk to our officers' mess, which was nothing but a huge cafeteria (and resembled not at all the British mess with its rituals). Then back to the dayroom to play poker or gin rummy or, more often, to write letters and kibitz with some of the others. Then, after an hour or so, to bed, especially if we were stood up, on alert for the following morning.

But on this evening, after checking the mail (I had none), I went to my room, picked up my kit bag (what the French call a musette bag), and stuck into it my toothbrush, a clean shirt, two changes of underwear, two pairs of khaki socks, and two cartons of cigarettes. I did not smoke, but I knew from hearsay the discomforts created by deprivation and I thought that these two cartons would make some smokers happy. I also wrapped in a towel a bottle of Sauterne that I had been lugging all the way from the States. You never knew when that would prove handy. I grabbed my heavy, long, British-style coat that I had bought in Bedford to keep out the damp cold that prevailed in the English winter. I had in addition a white silk scarf, given to me by the German wife of one of my favorite professors. She used to invite some of us to tea at her house, and after graduation I had kept in touch, going back to see the professional couple once prior to joining the Army Air Corps. Before going overseas, she made me a present of the scarf, saying she hoped it would keep me safe and warm. (While I now pounded her motherland to bits.) I was moved that she would do this, and I wrote to her that I would never part from the scarf, which became my good-luck charm. After fifty-nine years, I still have it.

I was finally ready to run for the truck that was taking off for the Bedford railroad station. I threw in it my kit bag, and the guys already in the truck hoisted me aboard while others yelled and banged on the driver's cab to make him stop. But he didn't stop; he was also in a hurry. Anyway, we made the next train to London.

Once on the train, in my near-empty compartment, I bundled in my greatcoat and started to think out the strategy of my leave. I could expect a pass every three weeks, during which I would have four goals: first, to take a real bath; second, to get laid; third, I wanted to meet whatever friends from school might be in London; and fourth, I wanted to speak French with whatever members of the Free French Forces I could meet in their hangouts, such as the Petit Club Français, the French headquarters' mess at St James Court, or the Air Force mess at Kensington Park. In those days, I was definitely more French than American, and I suffered from a certain *mal du pays*, cultural sickness in my case rather than home sickness.

To get a bath and a room, I went to the Hotel St James, recommended to me by Brownlow, a hotel as classy as an English dowager: rooms with tall ceilings, large lobby full of antique furniture, and halls adjoining the reception room. The bedrooms were always well heated and had plenty of hot water, and I would always come back to this hotel sure of my welcome, regardless of whether I had a reservation or not.

To get laid, I had a wide choice. I could turn to one of the thousands of prostitutes who hung around Piccadilly Circus and Hyde Park or to the better trade who could be found in the lounges of the better hotels, Claridge's or the Ritz being the top! (But here they could not look too tarty or they would get bounced, even if their tips to the staff were lavish.)

I might even meet a good-looking woman, well dressed and wearing little makeup, presenting herself as a 'sister' – a nurse from a local hospital. After an hour of drinks, dancing, and courting, it would turn out that she was hustling, without benefit of a pimp. Five pounds would be her fee for the whole night, bed and breakfast included. Anyway, that was how O'Neil had described it. In those days, five pounds was a substantial amount of money; one tenth of my monthly pay and probably the equivalent of a month's pay for the 'nurse'. O'Neil also said she was worth it.

If I wanted to combine sex and French-speaking 'culture', I might try to find one of the French professionals who made up about twenty percent of the available pool. They had been smuggled into England in fishing boats by their pimps – in 1940, 1941, 1942, and even 1943 – by bribing guards and harbor police, probably on both sides of the Channel, some of the girls paying the police inspectors, whether German or French, *en nature* – a quick 'in kind'. As far as the French policemen went anyway, I am nearly sure; for the British Constabulary, I am not so certain. In those days, the British police were still the elite of the British working class, with a great deal of pride and self-respect in their profession, and everyone treated them with consideration. In the French police, it was not uncommon to find some of the inspectors of the sex brigade, *La Brigade des Mœurs*, or even plain policemen, moonlighting as pimps.

Furthermore, the French and the Italian males had a greater culturally legitimate – though not necessarily legally legitimate – demand for sex. They were less likely to turn down a free feminine offer. The British demand for sex was definitely lower. (Since the Second World War, and especially since the 1960s the cultural acceptance of sexual demand has risen for both the British and the Americans – still without catching up to that of the French and Italians.)

The toleration of the 'white slave' trade on the British side of the Channel was not a result of local corruption but a matter of policy. The French pimps were not about to spoil their racket by allowing the Germans to use the trade as ways to smuggle agents into England. They had to guarantee their product was as free of German allegiance as of disease. Their ways of determining this were nearly as good as those of the 'Patriotic School' closed building where all foreigners coming into England had to pass through a demanding schedule of interviews, often lasting several days, to check out their good faith. (Some left the Patriotic School 'feet first', hanged after the Brits became convinced they were German agents.)

The Brits welcomed the French prostitutes as a way to preserve their own women from unwanted advances and sinful suggestions about better-paying jobs, especially in view of the growing American demand: 'Overdressed, oversexed, overpaid and over here.'

I suspect that the better looking and the smarter of the French imports found their way into the Free French Women's Volunteers (AFAT) where one did not have to work so hard as on the streets, especially if one could wiggle one's way into a white-collar assignment. And the Free French had ways to rid them of their pimps. Then it was up to them. A girl might marry a sergeant on his way to a battle-field commission, who might discover with delight (and perhaps a fleeting wonderment) the uncommon erotic skills of his loved one. I know of at least one of these cases – an AFAT who began her career quite differently and married a sergeant. He survived the war as a well-decorated general, and they had four successful children.

Anyway, I was repelled by commercial sex, and I never used it know-ingly in my life. In college when I had been hard up (so to speak), I relied upon *la veuve main gauche*, the 'widow left hand', and the occasional date with one of the nymphomaniacs that every campus harbored, whether at the Oberlin of 1860 or 1940. (I knew one who suffered from halitosis, but when I was sufficiently desperate, I would invite her to my room and feed her some strong minted chocolates.)

Another outlet was necking and petting with a girl 'who can't say no'. Probably five to ten percent of girls are that way, whether they live on an American campus or in Saudi Arabia. The difference is that in Saudi Arabia these girls can be chaperoned more effectively and married off early enough for their lack of will power not to create any trouble for the family. In many cases in America, they will be saved by their escorts' sense of honor or fears of impregnating them. If you got a girl pregnant, you were expected to make it right by marrying her (unless her family arranged for an abortion). Often enough, if the pregnancy had not been faked – what the French call *le coup du canapé*, the 'sofa trick' – it did not work out so badly in the end.

In the United States, college dorms were under parietal rule. You had to sign the girl in, you had to keep both sets of feet on the floor at all times, and your door had to be kept ajar at least the width of a book – some daredevils took this to mean a matchbook. Americans, of course, had cars, and many colleges did not allow you to have a car until you were a junior. I did not have a car, but I had something better: a room of my own in the basement of a law-student cooperative where I earned my rent by stoking the antique coal furnace. It was a large room without 'parietal rules', which I had decorated in the Bohemian style.

Of course, a room of your own was convenient, but it had much less prestige than sharing a room in one of the 'Houses': Adams, Eliot, Lowell, Kirkland, Leverett, and the rest. Commuters and 'people who lived outside the Houses', like myself, were not 'true' Harvard men, but at that time I was thinking of my sexual opportunities more than my lost social opportunities. I was not a club man. I did not live in a Harvard House. I was a 'greaseball.' However, I did not feel put down, because I marginalized myself further by being a Trotskyist, the leader of the Harvard Socialist League Fourth International. I transformed a social disability into an imagined ethical and political superiority.

Harvard was tolerant of radicals (in a way, no College today is tolerant of conservatives); in those days it was a magnificent institution. It was run by Boston Wasps who believed completely in their right to rule the people in the name of their Puritan values, but they knew how to listen, which is at least half, and perhaps the real essence of democracy. The great force of democracy is that the separation of powers, and their modulated conflict, forces them to listen to one another. Not by preaching, but by osmosis, Harvard gave us – the greaseballs, the House members, and the club men – much of the moral equipment that sustained us (and especially me, who had had little family life) in war and in peace.

The rules of the American game of 'dating and rating,' which began in high school, were not known to the Europeans. Except in Scandinavia, marriageable girls above working-class status, their fans and dance books in hand, were chaperoned, either directly or by the 'mother's bench' at formal dances. If a girl violated the European code by allowing herself to be kissed passionately, or by petting, out of sight of family and friends, she was considered fair game. She had committed herself to go the whole way.

Many European men, wild-eyed with excitement when an American girl while dancing would lean her forehead against the cheek of her escort, discovered, when they undertook *de brûler les étapes* – 'skip the intermediary steps' – a firm resistance against further explorations in the darker recesses of the park. (There were many exceptions and violations of these rules, especially in wartime; nevertheless they held for most.) In New York, at a 1941 cocktail party for the officers of the submarine *Surcouf* the prize ship of the Free French Navy, I had heard a dashing *lieutenant de vaisseau* (lieutenant junior grade) complain bitterly that 'with American girls it is always *'la main dans la chose ou le chose dans la main mais jamais le chose dans la chose'* – 'the hand in the thing, or the thing in the hand, but never the thing in the thing.' He told me of an ancestor, who wintered in 1781 at Newport with the French fleet, who already had complained of the same problem in his letters to a cousin. I thought such wit deserved better luck. (Alas, the *Surcouf* went down with all hands a couple of months afterwards in the Panama Canal Zone, under the depth charges of an eager American destroyer who had not received the proper signal of recognition.)

I was thinking all these burning thoughts while idling in my fifteen-inch bath, triple what we were allowed for hot water. Then I thought I'd better phone Margaret, a secretary at the American Embassy in London. Of course, the embassy was closed now, so I tried the phone at the apartment she shared with two other girls in London.

She picked up, and I greeted her. 'Hello, Margaret. It's Dick, Dick Pitts. I got your phone number from your mother.'

'Oh, my God!' she exclaimed. 'Where have you been? I've been worried about you. Mother told me you were a B-17 pilot.'

'Yes, that's true. At noon today I was over a German harbor named Kiel at 21,000 feet. And now I'm here.'

'That's wonderful. When will I see you?'

'Are you free tonight?' I hoped.

'Yes, but don't you want to get some sleep and all that?'

'I just took a long bath, and I'm going to take a quick nap. I haven't eaten since four o'clock this morning, and as I unwind I get more hungry, but it will wait until you get here.'

'Well, you are in luck. The embassy just had a party, and we brought all sorts of leftovers back to the apartment – sandwiches with *foie gras* and caviar and little pastries. You know, *petits fours*, as you taught me to say. I'll bring them with me.'

'That's perfect. If we're still hungry after that, we'll go to a restaurant in Soho.'

'Oh, yes, and I know a few; I've even been to a black-market restaurant where you can order real steaks.'

'Terrific! Be here at nine o'clock, and we will have a great time.'

'Sounds wonderful. I'm sure you have great stories to tell. Things have been kind of dull here, but now that you have arrived, life will be more exciting.'

We hung up, and I called the porter and asked him to make a fire in my hearth and shine my shoes. Then I slept for an hour. I dressed in my Class A uniform. I wanted to do honor to Margaret and not arouse her apprehension by opening the door in a state of negligent dress.

Margaret and I had met when I was at Harvard. A Radcliffe girl, nevertheless showed little interest in intellectual things. She was pretty, probably a nine on the ten-point scale of beauty, with a black ribbon over her old-gold hair. She also had a body and a pair of legs that were beautiful without being provocative. Her grades had not been very good, until the year when she surrounded herself with a crew of escorts who tutored her in various subjects and rewrote her papers for her. An Indian Sikh, an American boy from Boston, and I tutored her in French and sociology. We offered to tutor her for free, but we were not as disinterested as we made out. For me, making out in my own room with a pretty Radcliffe girl was reward enough.

Commencement and the invasion of Soviet Russia by the Germans came at about the same time; I departed for New York and my job at R.H. Macy & Co. Margaret's family and I exchanged Christmas cards, and I came back up to witness the graduation of the class of 1942, having a few friends graduating that year and a couple of weddings to attend as well. I saw Margaret in cap and gown and made an appearance at her graduation party where I recognized the Sikh and the handsome American who gave me a pregnant wink. Margaret gave me a peck on the cheek and a long squeeze on my hand that was a summation; after that, silence. When I came up to Cambridge in June 1943 with my Wings and the bar of a second lieutenant, I saw her mother, who gave me Margaret's address and phone numbers in London. One and a half years after her graduation Margaret was due at my door.

The bell rang. I opened the door to Margaret, who was dressed in civilian clothing. I gave her a mock salute. We kissed on the lips; her mouth had an adorable melting feel. She had a bag of goodies left from the embassy par and we sat on the carpet in front of the fire. I brought out the bottle of Sauterne, nice and cool, and two glasses. We both ate and drank while she gave me news of her family. Her job at the embassy was not very interesting per se, but she and the two other Wellesley graduates who were her roommates had positions on the staff that were commensurate with their social status and so were able to meet all sorts of interesting people, including the heads of our Air Force – who, of course, tried to put the make on them. They were also privy to much juicy gossip, but I did not ask her, 'For example?' even though it was on the tip of my tongue. Margaret was not catty; I never heard her speak ill of anyone.

She wanted to know all about me. I told her some anecdotes about our crew, and I decided to tell her about this morning's crash and collision, relating it with a mixture of horror and detachment. Margaret had a kind heart, and she was moved. I saw tears in her eyes. Would this morning's gore and the Sauterne open the way to the 'Holy of Holies'? Could we pick up where we left off two and a half years before?

We kissed. I caressed her. And at that point fatigue overwhelmed me – I had been up for twenty-two hours. My last chance was to offer her my room for the night, counting on an invitation to sleep on the couch or, even, to share the wide bed. She accepted the offer of the room; she did not, however, say 'I'll let you share the bed with me if you promise to behave.' I would have promised anything, without much commitment to living up to the promise. I was a combat man; she was not a coed anymore. In fact, she was a year older than I. I thought, *Enough of this American love making! Take off your clothes!*

So I went downstairs with my kit bag and told the desk clerk to give me another room, that I had given mine to a lady friend. No problem. And I went to bed, a tired but pissed-off young man.

In the morning we met in the lobby. We had a copious English breakfast of powdered eggs and bacon (we ignored the kippers), and in a conference room next to the lobby, I kissed her melting lips goodbye. I clasped her ever more closely, and it took a little while to disengage ourselves.

She said, 'Let's sit down a minute. I must tell you something. I have a fellow who has been taking me out for the last three months and who will be popping the question fairly soon. He's a career man in the State Department, and I don't want to do anything to jeopardize this. After all, I am not getting any younger; most of my girlfriends are engaged or married already. I know you are disappointed, and I'm sorry, believe me. Here you are, flying and risking your life, and I'm thinking of my own problems, which are nothing compared to yours. You didn't deserve this.'

At this she began to cry, real tears, real sobs and I felt terrible. 'As you know,' she wept, 'it's difficult for me to resist you. A part of me wants you very badly. If I had let you stay last night, we were bound to go the whole way. And I couldn't face him if I had done that. Believe me I cried in my bed after you left. I hoped you would come back, and if you had, I would have fallen into your arms. You know I shall always be fond of you. Don't leave me now.'

I gave her a clean handkerchief, and she wiped her eyes and blew her nose.

The thought of Margaret in her nightgown, falling in my arms, was overwhelming. But I did not love her, and I could not love her. I would have exploited her, which would have been nearly as bad as running away under fire. My American friends would understand me. My French friends would think I was nuts to have forsaken such an occasion. Even now it was not too late, if I took her upstairs. But I had cooled off somewhat. I tried to console her. 'Listen to me,' I told her. 'I understand fully well what you did, and I think it took as much guts as flying a mission. Especially for you, who has the temperament of a volcano.'

'What do you mean by temperament?' she sniffed. 'Please don't make fun of me.'

'It means your amorous disposition, your sexual capacity. I think your husband will be enchanted to discover it. You have more temperament than ninety-five percent of New England girls.'

She started to smile. 'How do you know?'

'I've done a survey over the years.'

'I can believe that!'

'It certainly took a lot of will power to kick me out of the room when the temptation was so strong. But your sense of duty was more powerful, and I admire that, even more than your temperament. Your boyfriend should marry you. He's a fool if he doesn't.'

'I think so too.'

'You will be a great wife and a great mother. People will drive fifty miles to come to your teas. I will always think of you with tenderness and pride.'

'Pride?'

'I let you go, and I will probably regret it the rest of my life.'

At that, she cried again and took my hand and kissed it.

I spotted a hotel groom, and I asked him to get a cab, then I inquired of Margaret, 'You are covered as to where you spent the night?'

She nodded.

'Okay,' I said. 'Well, it's time to go. And good luck to you! Goodbye, Margaret.'

She hesitated and made as if to fall into my arms again.

'No, no,' I said. 'I have a cab for you. I'll see you later.'

'Oh, do that,' she urged. 'Do that, please.'

She was finally gone and I never saw her again. Some time later, my invitation to her London wedding arrived at base; it caught up with me in Atlantic City where returnees were being assessed for reassignment.

16

MISSION ABORTED

DUTY AND DEFECTION

Usually aborts were caused by some mechanical failure that reduced drastically the chances of a crew to carry out its mission successfully and get back home. However, it was not always so easy to decide whether the failure was crucial enough to warrant turning back, for in aviation the human and the mechanical are closely intertwined; careful handling of the engines will go far towards preventing its breakdown, and a determined crew will often overcome damage that would discourage another crew.

It also depended on the whole situation. In the old days, when we had no fighter escort, the failure of the turrets to function properly might be legitimate cause for aborting, because the guns of the formation were the only ones we had at our disposal. Being low diamond with the top turret and ball turret out, one was a dead duck. But now, when fighter cover was taken for granted, the malfunction of twelve machine guns would not be sufficient grounds, though the gunners would find it rather sour. I did not think that anyone would let the loss of one engine prevent him from going on a milk run to the French coast, where the risks were quite low, the exposure to enemy fire quite short, and there was little fighter opposition to fear. On the other hand, just the probability of engine failure – indicated by the oil pressure falling and the cylinder-head temperature rising – not even the actual failure itself, might be sufficient reason to turn around if the target was Berlin or Stuttgart.

Engine failure was like a disease. We lost one, and soon we lost two. It could be caused by some systematic oversight of the ground crew in its maintenance, or it could be because we had overworked the remaining three engines by the excessive use of power needed to keep in formation. A feathered engine acted like a beacon light upon enemy fighters, and if a crew had lost the protection of the group, this would single them out for special treatment. If it was a long run, three hours over enemy territory, they were in for a pretty bad time.

A bomber pilot in the air was his own boss. He could really do what he wanted to do, leave the formation, or stay with it, or 'lose' the formation. If he decided to go to Sweden, it was because something in the constellation of factors told him that that was the best answer to his problem. And he would deny the legitimacy of anyone's challenges to the correctness of his decision.

There is no doubt that it was also a way to cover up cowardice or, as Colonel Preston would have said, 'poor determination to complete the mission.' But the first presumption of our group and wing leadership was that the pilot had but cogent reasons for going to a neutral territory.

In January of 1944, on our first mission to Kiel, Gray aborted. On the second raid the day after, just as we turned for the bomb run, and before we had encountered any enemy action, he left for Sweden.

The then veterans closed ranks around his defection and accredited the story that his plane had caught a piece of rocket shortly before we turned into the bomb run. Since he flew very close to us, our gunners had seen Gray leave the formation. They had not, however, reported any rocket exploding nearby. Given the fact that a rocket made an explosion several times larger than a flak shell, it seemed unlikely it would have been something they would have missed. This meant desertion in the face of the enemy, a capital offense in any army.

It is unlikely that Gray polled his crew before deciding to go to Sweden. At the time he left formation, when pieces of the rocket were supposed to have hit him, he had 230 miles to fly to get the tip of Sweden at Slättorp. To fly back to the British coast would have required only another seventy miles with sufficient time to alert the Air-Sea Rescue people if he had to ditch before reaching Great Yarmouth. When Gray made the choice to go to Sweden, many of the veterans refused to judge him too harshly, provoking, of course, many conversations and debates amongst us.

'One never knows; you might have to go to Sweden one day yourself rather than ditch in the North Sea and get scragged.'

'Yes, but Gray protected our tail, and he left us in the lurch. If you were element leader and I left the diamond position, you wouldn't be so happy. That desertion in front of the enemy. We were only ten in our group going over the target instead of eighteen; when he left we became a group of nine. It was sheer luck that the German fighters didn't single us out for destruction.'

'Well, I won't condemn him until I know all the facts; you never know what may have happened to that plane of his.'

'Of course. But I still have my own ideas as to the reasons for his going to Sweden.'

'He sure was a fool to land, though, because they have the plane, and they can see whether it was sufficiently damaged to justifying his landing in Sweden.'

'The best deal is still to act a bit flak-happy. They'll send you back home as battle fatigued.'

'It depends on the flight surgeon. You try and pull that stunt on Powell and see how far you get.'

'The real flak-happy character doesn't know it and tries hard to stay on operational status. It's hard indeed to judge a man. Courage, fright. One never knows when he himself will crack up.'

Brownlow had asked me once to fly copilot for a pilot named Holt so that we could fly a colonel to another field. I had flown with Holt once in the States, and he was a pretty good formation flyer, although he had cracked up on take-off one night. Nobody had been hurt, although the ship was totalled. On this mission, we also had his engineer and radio man, just back from a little jaunt of AWOL. Holt had had quite a lot of trouble with his crew about AWOL but they seemed sincerely repentant, and it was overlooked.

We landed at Polebrook around five o'clock. We went out to eat, leaving the engineer and radio man to guard the ship. On the way back, I hunted up and down to get some sandwiches for them. (Thinking back, I realized it was not my business to do so – they were his crew, and they were his responsibility. I was surprised he did not think of it himself.) As a result, I came back a bit late. Holt was waiting impatiently, the engines turning.

'I went out and got some sandwiches for the crew.'

'To hell with that – let's go. It's getting dark, and there are no lights on this runway.'

We took off. He got the ship off the ground but flew right back onto it. Luckily the wheels were down, and we just bounced right up again. If I had pulled the wheels right up, we would have been in for the same accident he had had in the States.

It got pretty dark, and we were having a bit of trouble finding the field. Finally, after he had fiddled around with the radio, I asked his radio man for a heading and took it. After all, radio men know all the codes and how to get directions from ground stations, and this guy was all right. But Holt wouldn't trust him. What kind of a crew was this? The ceiling was around

1,200 feet, and here we were flying at 1,400 asking for flares. But how in the hell can you see flares if you are right in the soup?

He gave me the controls, and I started a shallow dive to get out of it. Suddenly, he yanked back the controls and headed straight back for the clouds again. Did he think I was going to dive for the ground? Finally, he quieted down and got out of the clouds, blurting all kinds of apologies and excuses. When I got out of that ship, I knew Holt wouldn't last long.

That morning, he was supposed to fly on McCall's right wing. He got lost in the overcast. On another mission where our crew was stood down, Holt was given our ship to fly. They had oxygen trouble; someone in their crew opened up the emergency valve and let it drain out.

They tried sending up the crew without Holt, and the ball turret gunner started to bawl and refused to fly combat anymore. It was a mess. Holt's crew was broken up and Holt made a permanent copilot, a move that the other copilots resented as an insult to their position, which, of course, it was.

As I reflect back some fifty years after the events, I have come to admire how my colleagues went to war without demanding that their more pusil-lanimous fellow officers should be punished for their lack of combat ardor. If a flying officer in the Air Force could not hack it, he would be let out on the diagnosis of 'battle fatigue' and given ground duty. Enlisted men were sent to the kitchen. The one advantage for the Air Force that I see in this mansuetude is that it maintained the belief that everything one did was voluntary. It was an expression of yourself, starting with your solo flight and ending with you pushing the throttles forward for a mission to Bremen, to Stuttgart, to Anklam, to Schweinfurt, Munster, or Oschersleben. You did it because you wanted to, and your crew did it because you were 'the best pilot in the group,' and because they knew that their pilot and copilot would bring them back alive if it were at all possible, that they certainly would bail out last because they cared, and the crew cared in return.

The reality was more complex, and less decorative. For instance, con-cerning the crews who had flown to Sweden, American Consulate Officer William W. Corcoran in Göteborg had interviewed a small (and probably not random) sample of pilots and crews. Among other things, Corcoran wrote that interned American flyers expressed opposition to further flying, seemed cynical or apathetic in outlook, and distrusted and expressed hatred for General Doolittle, who was seen as being unsympathetic and sending them to certain doom. More damning still was Corcoran's allegation that flying to Switzerland or Sweden as a means of getting out of the war with impunity was 'openly discussed among bomber crews in Great Britain.'[1]

It is obvious that Mark K. Wells cannot believe the last statement, yet the fact of the matter is that I participated in bull sessions where going to Sweden or Switzerland was openly discussed, with advice given by veterans: 'Burn up one or two engines before you land.' 'Let out all the oxygen from the system.'

I was a willing participant in these bull sessions even though I was one of the ten to twenty percent who were eager beavers, and this in a group that contributed only two crews to neutral countries during the course of its combat duty in the European Theater of Operations, while the average group contributed about ten, and with much less exposure to tough raids. But I also listened to a discussion between a bombardier and a copilot who decided they would kill their first pilot if he tried to take them to a neutral country without full justification. They were reacting to certain patterns of speech on his part that could be interpreted as trying to prepare the crew for a trip to Sweden. They never had to carry out their threat.

Bull sessions were situations when all sorts of fantasies were freely expressed. There was no division of the participants into pro-internment or anti-internment partisans; ideas and suggestions came from everyone. We were genuinely interested in finding out what worked and what did not work. We were not interested in winning an argument. I think it was the minority of cases when the bull sessions reinforced a delinquent motivation. Usually it merely ventilated them, and thereby weakened them, and there was sufficient basic trust between everyone that no one worried about tattletales to the Brass.

The generals at Wycombe Abbey did not have the same level of identification with the pilots as did the group and even the wing leaders. The latter, who led our battle formations and were usually 'super eager beavers,' still identified with our first pilots. Any implication that many of the crews interned had not been forced to leave their formation by overwhelming damage to plane and/or crew was resented by the band of brothers and by group and wing leaders as a slur on their airmanship or on their leadership. Coming to the defense of these internees would prove to everyone in the groups that they would go to bat for their people, thereby, it was hoped, improving morale.

This also meant that defectors did not have to worry about their return, home. In the case of Gray, a deal with the Germans at the highest level must have allowed the Swedes to release him. He was returned three months after his internment, along with the rest of his crew, and they were offered the opportunity to finish their tour. All but the pilot and his copilot accepted the opportunity and finished their twenty-five missions. I think Gray lost his Wings and was given a permanent desk job. He should have been court-martialed.

On March 16, 1944, four heavy bombers landed in Switzerland, and three more crashed-landed there – a bad omen for the leadership if they could read the signs.

Two days later, on March 18, *Stars and Stripes* (the newspaper of our European Theater of Operations) reported, sarcastically perhaps, thirty US bombers down in Switzerland; *The Mighty Eighth War Diary* reports that four B-17s and twelve B-24s landed in Switzerland that day. These desertions – nobody used these words, but I will, and I believe it to be valid for at least three-quarters of the pilots and copilots; how else explain the fact that the 379th had five times fewer internees than the other groups? – must have been the result of a feeling that General Doolittle was breaking an agreement when he increased the quota for a tour of duty, from twenty-five missions, first to thirty and then to thirty-five missions.

There was actually no such agreement since Wycombe Abbey decided unilaterally, ever since the creation of the Eighth Air Force, what the quota of missions an air crew had to do was. But in the minds of the air crews, twenty-five missions had become a right, not a convention. Even though those who flew thirty missions in the summer and fall of 1944 were definitely less exposed to death than those who flew twenty-five in 1943 through the winter of 1944, I could still sympathize with their feelings. I cannot understand how General Doolittle put through these changes in mission quotas without asking the group leaders to discuss them first with their flying officers, to present the statistics that would justify the changes.

The loss of contact between the top leadership and the flying troops came to a crisis point in early 1944, when division headquarters and Wycombe Abbey asked certain fighter pilots on an individual basis to check out any bomber they saw leaving the formation because of structural damages.[2] It was an order that could not be made public, and it was unenforceable What fighter pilot would rat on a bomber pilot and behave like a stool pigeon? At any rate, the crisis disappeared as losses diminished, solving the problem for Doolittle and for the groups.

Meanwhile, the cover-up, in the sense of not facing the fact that the bulk of internees were deserters, has continued to this very day. Col. Mark Wells, although too young to see combat during World War II, has done an excellent research in the Air Force archives and in the books and letters written by survivors, and his authoritative book, *Courage and Air Warfare*, demonstrates Air Force solidarity in defending its good name. You can't go wrong by praising the courage of the air crews. 'Everybody is a hero' is the covert hypothesis, and anybody who goes against that good opinion is wide open to the hostility of the band of 'elderly' brothers.

17

REMINISCENCE

THE THOUGHTS THAT GO THROUGH ONE'S HEAD

I had my granddaughter on my lap, her long blonde hair flowing down her back, and I was reading to her from *Snow White and the Seven Dwarfs*, the American version of the *Snow White* tale.

Instead of focusing on Snow White's rivalry with the bad queen and waiting for the young prince, the American version is focused on group relations. And as I was reading to her, my mind started meandering, prompted by the dwarf called 'Dopey'.

Dopey – every small group has a dopey, the one who goofs up all the time. And when something goes wrong, immediately Dopey becomes the scapegoat: *He did it wrong; he is late; he forgot*. The others of us remain faultless because he assumes the burden of our mistakes and of our guilt. Sometimes there is a price to pay for the mistake, and so we all hustle to cope. We cooperate on the fly, without instructions, and we come through brilliantly, to our pride, I must say.

Dopey sets the bottom level of performance, and since we are all better than that, we bask in the security of our competence.

Why not get rid of Dopey and raise our level of performance even higher? The fact is, if we get rid of Dopey, someone else has to be 'it'. Who is second in line to occupy the damnable spot? Better not ask the question. Dopey finally does more good than harm. He is a negative focus of solidarity; he gives us security in our personal rating. He shows how far we will go in extending our protection to group members that are not up to par. And let's face it, there are times when we are all below par, thank God not all at the same time.

When we first started flying combat, we had our Dopey. He was the one afflicted with the fear that none of us could afford to assume. When fear was afloat in the plane, it would come and stick to him, bypassing nervous guys like me. I had the steadiest hands of any, no sweat in my palms, no tremor of my fingers. Just my stomach would get into painful knots, invisible to others, and my knees would quiver, also not too obvious. When he started jumping up and down, I would have taken on all the German 'yellow noses' of Northern France and not sweated a bit.

'Grandpa, Grandpa!' I heard. 'Why don't you keep on reading to me?'

I had fallen asleep, until Lea brought me back to my duties by her protest. But I did not resume my reading.

I asked her, 'Who is the leader of the dwarfs?' She replied, 'Doc.'

'You are right, but what about Grumpy?'

'He always sees the bad things. Doc's not like that.'

'What about Happy?' I asked.

'He always sees the good in things, like Uncle Christopher.'

'That's pretty smart, perhaps too smart for an eight-year-old like you. But what about Snow White?'

Lea squinted up at me. 'She is the mother, and you know how mothers are. They always want things right – wash your hands, wait till everybody is seated, don't grab the food, watch your manners.'

'But she is also the one,' I smiled, 'who provides the goodies. She is the one who cooks these fabulous desserts, which I am not allowed to eat anymore. She will sneak upstairs with a piece of cake after you've been sent to your room without dessert.'

'How do you know that? You're not supposed to know!'

'Because all mothers do that, because they can't stand your suffering alone upstairs without your dessert.' (In America, perhaps the threat of no dessert is no big deal; in France it is a very big deal.)

'And she tucks you in bed,' I continued.

'And, Grandpa, Snow White kisses the boys' heads and makes everything right.'

'That's right, she calms Grumpy; she can even make him smile.'

And on this I slid back into sleep and went back to my ghosts. This time Lea gave up on me and went to see if Grandma would read to her. Grandpa was fun, but too unreliable.

Every human organization had its 'father' and its 'mother'. The 379th had 'Mo' Preston as its father, rather aloof as fathers go; the mother, or Virgin Mary in this case, was Lieutenant Colonel Rohr (Lieutenant Colonel Kittle was another mother). Of course, the organization will be stronger if father and mother get along. I am not sure that Colonel Preston very much liked Colonel Rohr, but each did his work very well, and it would not come into anyone's mind to try and play one against the other. What went on between these two was not affection but duty. When duty is hard, what you exchange is as good as affection. In a family in the hills or in the prairie, it made the difference between having enough to eat and having to swallow oatmeal fourteen times a week. In his native Kentucky Williams would tell us, the church's supper or someone's wedding would often have to provide the proteins for the week.

Half the Southerners never ate so well as they did in the Army, especially the Army Air Corps, with chicken three times a week, meat twice a day, white bread, ice cream and unlimited coffee. But they would not confess it to anyone outside the crew; they did not want to look poor.

Just as I was grateful to the Air Corps for giving me a chance to fly, I thought they would be grateful to the Army for giving them a taste of the good life, but they complained all the time about the food. Of my own initiative, I ate once a month with them in their mess, and I found it definitely superior to what I had got in the French boarding schools, tasty in fact, especially the chicken and pie *à la mode*.

And suddenly it struck me. What they were complaining about was not the food per se, but the fact that they were far away from home, and it was not their mothers' food. Nothing could taste as good as Mother's hominy grits and apple pie. It was all to their credit! Ice cream, chicken, and real coffee could not make them forget their mothers' food.

I kept on listening to their complaints and never clued them in on to my explanation of the reason for these complaints. I had learned that speech was given to man so that he may hide his thoughts, first from himself.

I had also learned that you can't do anything about most complaints, except listen.

Every crew has its leader, the first pilot, who made the major decisions, essentially. *Do we abort the take-off or try to make it into the air?* He had less than a second to make up his mind. *How tight a formation do we fly? Do we abort the mission, or do we go on? Do we bail out or stick to the ship and try to make it home? Do we land at the first British base on the coast, or do we try to make it back to our own base?*

If we were a family, we were a family short of food and living in insecure territory, and these were, one way or the other, life or death decisions. Aborts were deliberated between pilot and copilot – at least it was between Streit and me the only time we aborted. Whether to land at a British base or try for home was deliberated in the 'front office' usually with the engineer as a consultant, and we would also involve the navigator. (*Distance? Winds? Alternate fields?*) I don't remember any two-to-one decisions. It was like a good marriage; you rarely had to say, 'We'll do it this way because I say so.'

The first pilot related the crew to the outside world, including the world of the enemy. He related the crew to the world of colonels and generals, of orders coming in at night over the teletype. Usually he represented the crew at critique.

We were there to execute the orders, orders that created fears and tensions, rivalries also, when some would get complimented and others would get chewed out. The important thing was to preserve the cohesion of the group, to ventilate the anxieties, to make the punished accept their punishment.

All of this was the job of the copilot. He dealt with the personnel problems and developed a fine ear for the feelings, spoken or unspoken, of the crew. He was closer to them. In some crews the enlisted men called their copilot by his first name. I never went for that, but when the crew had a beef, a request, they would approach me first. The only time a crew would not approach the copilot first was when they wanted the removal of the first pilot.

What happened when the pilot was killed or replaced, and the copilot moved over into the left seat? Not infrequently you would get copious complaints from the enlisted men that the former copilot had become less friendly, that 'power had gone to his head.' They forgot that in his new position the ex-copilot could not afford to be as friendly as he used to be when he did not have first responsibility for the mission. He looked outward now rather than inward, and he developed some insensitivity to the crew's moods.

On a mission when the boys wanted to turn back, you could not afford to hear them, even with your 'third ear.' You could not afford to be too close to those you might have to punish, or to those you might lead to their deaths. Your new copilot would have to learn his duties on the job, and there were few guidelines. The image of the copilot in the Eighth Air Force was a happy-go-lucky fellow, somebody who would get to the piano and lead everyone in songs about drink and women, and who was always good for a five-pound loan to someone short.

It was a profound stereotype, for it underlined the copilot's contribution to the strength and cohesion of the group, his willingness to help out his crewmates. No, he could not be a mother. We were in a tough business. Over the interphone you would not hear any therapeutic lingo, rather injunctions such as 'Be sharp,' or 'Stay on the ball.' Or 'Get your head out of your ass!'

There was a story in the Air Force concerning a famous college athlete. He became a pilot and, of course, was a public relations hit. But during a mission he bailed out and all his crew were found dead in the crashed plane. He was moved to another theater, where something similar happened again. After that, no one would fly with him.

I do not know how true the story was. There were all kinds of tales running around their Corps in the early 1940s stories about injection carburetors that 'some people' had not wanted us to use, and tires that would never wear out and were not being manufactured because of pressures by industrialists. There was a story about Carmen Miranda dancing with no panties. And there were photos of her, skirt flying, lending proof that some rumors were true.

I don't know about the story of the athlete. It could very possibly have been mere slander. There was a lot of secret jealousy felt toward such famous figures, and we resisted very little the opportunity of tearing them down. (Jimmy Stewart was an exception, because everybody who had met him said he was for real.)

The story about the college athlete also had a populist function (besides demonstrating that 'these college boys were no good'). It reminded us of our duties toward the crew, that pilots bail out last, a silent injunction so powerful that we never spoke of it. Nor did we argue, *What about the co-pilot? Must he wait his turn? Can he use his knowledge of the situation to gain a precious few seconds?* After all, the pilot can usually do the last flying himself or use the automatic pilot to keep the nose up and the wings level.

What really did happen in these circumstances? Nobody knows. We do know that in the 379th, out of 150 planes shot down, only 450 crewmen did not make it to the prison camp. Thirty percent, which means that seventy percent lived. I would never have thought it was that much, after all the horror stories we heard about crewmen bailing out and being killed by the tail section or the big stabilizer, or worse, by the propellers of the ship behind them. The average number of survivors for the whole bomber force was much lower, closer to fifty percent.

Why was the 379th so lucky? Was it because we had turned in our forty-fives and did not even think of fighting with the German farmers or their wives, coming at you with their pitchforks and shotguns? I would think that the average crew tended to stick to the ship out of solidarity; as well as the fear of bailing out. If the 379th crews bailed out earlier, is it because the copilots kept more in touch with the crew in combat and were able to order them to bail out, thus backing up or substituting for the bail-out signal?

I wonder how often the pilot, in his desperate attempt to keep the plane flying or get it out of a spin, would forget the toggle switch on his panel that signaled bailing out? And pushing the toggle switch down meant also that he knew he was defeated. And I guess that most copilots fought the plane alongside their first pilots, synchronizing their movements so as to bring more strength to the controls, giving up the opportunity to bail out. You don't deliberate these things; you do them or you don't do them. If we were fighting against our plane – against our controls, against our engines, against our wings – from which the aluminum skin was peeling, or, worse, against a gasoline fire devouring the trailing edge of our wings, we might not think about the possibility that we were beaten and that the best thing left to do was to get the crew out before they were pinned to the plane by centrifugal force or killed by the gasoline explosion. After all, it was for them that the first pilot fought to the last the plane's desire to fall into its final spin.

There comes a moment when someone has to say, 'Let's bail out the crew!'

And our crew knew that if things were bad, and we were still alive, Streit and I would keep the plane steady as long as possible so that they could bail out, even if it meant that Streit and I would be riveted to our seats by the final spin.

18

SEVENTH MISSION

OSCHERSLEBEN: GRADUATION

The veterans in the squadron apparently needed their moments with the band of brothers more than we, the new replacements and junior birdmen, still sure of the immortality of youth and sheltered by our lack of experience. They would play cards sometimes all night, bringing a bottle to the Officers' Club and sharing it with their poker partners, even when the alert was on, until the cutting edge of anxiety was sufficiently dulled for them to go to briefing or to sleep. The card game was good conduit for talk, because half the mind was on the cards and the money, and the emotions raised by both would compete with fear of the mission to come.

The veteran flyers had seen more danger than we had. We had been on six to eight missions in the last month, they had been on twenty or more over the last six, at a time when B-17s would be sent on 'deep penetrations' with little or no fighter escort. They had been to Schweinfurt twice, to Kassel, to Munster, to Anklam Less than twenty-five percent were still in their squadron the other seventy-five percent had been shot down. They had been in combat since the middle of 1943. The rate of combat missions was lower then, when the groups had fewer planes to substitute for the ones that came back from raids full of holes from flak and fighters, and for those who did not make it back to the base. There were fewer new engines to replace those that had been brutalized by running at full power for a couple of hours to keep a ship flying that had lost one or two engines to enemy fire. The ground crews would have to cannibalize the 'hangar queens' (those ships with chronic problems that eventually wound up permanently grounded and used for spare parts) in order to keep the planes assigned to crews in flying condition. On average, a crew would be sent out on a mission once a week, which I thought was harder on the nerves than the twice or three times a week we were sent out, because we got into a system of emotional mobilization and demobilization, which made an alert something of a routine.

At the rate we were going, our twenty-five missions would be over, one way or the other, in little more than three months. And after that, what? To tell the truth we didn't think much beyond the thirty-day leave that would be coming to us when we finished our tour, and no one dared to think about that seriously till we were on our last five missions. We took it for granted that we would not become available for combat again until many months had lapsed after our leave. The British combat crewmen were less fortunate than we were; within six months they would be flying their second tour. From what we knew of German fighters, there were no real tours for them. With the exception of some leave time here and there, they would fly until they dropped, were shot down or killed in some stupid formation or landing accident, when the odds were quietly waiting for them to pass by.

And then, on January 11, came the raid on Oschersleben, where the three groups of our wing lost nearly as many crews as at Schweinfurt. After that the veterans, their prestige already besmirched by the desertion of Gray, could no longer maintain the legitimacy of their self-imposed separation from the junior birdmen, and the epithet vanished from the language.

Oschersleben was the only time I felt any real panic. It was my seventh mission. It did not turn out well. Our fighter escort had not been able to take off as scheduled; weather had gotten bad in England, and they recalled whatever fighters had taken off already, before the fog overtook the airfields. By that time, however, we were already deep into Germany. The Germans thought we were bound for Berlin and threw us every aircraft they could get a hold of, from their latest models to old aircraft. Me-109s went right through our formations in vertical slow rolls, spraying lead like a revolving garden hose.

Within two minutes, four B-17s exploded. I felt my eyes burning and checked the harness of my chute. My insides were melting; now I knew what blind fear was. Yet its very paroxysm seemed to kill it as soon as it was born. I went back to my work, keeping us in tight formation, and refused to think of anything else. Our tail gunner's window was frosted; he couldn't see too well attacks from the rear, so we stuck close to our element leader and 'jumped' with him. Under our wing we saw row after row of 20mm shells burst where we had been half a second before.

The whole group at times will jump as one, just like a covey of ducks surprised by a hunter on the surface of the lake. Jumping is even better when you are faced by a head-on attack, because the speed is so great that once the target has moved, it is already too late for the fighter to correct his aim; all he can do is roll on his back, split 'S' (like finishing a loop), and start over again.

For two hours we were under continuous attacks, but what was most painful were not the actual attacks but the short lulls in between while the fighter turned around to get into a new position. With each lull, fatigue became heavier. The rattle of our guns, the smell of powder, the shivering jump that was exhilarating. It was like a game. We were the animal hunted, and we were smarter, more skillful. A fighter trailing smoke spun through our formation and we cheered.

The 303rd beneath us was being cut to pieces, the German fighter planes going through their formation as if they were a circus act. They were good – often after one had gone through, we could see a fort hesitate, stumble, just like a person, raise a wing, oscillate once, and then fall out in a slow majestic spin. One or two chutes would come out, and suddenly there would be nothing but black smoke and a little debris; the fort had exploded. And the German fighters kept coming in.

We were the low diamond in the low squadron, but we were in the high group that day, which is overall a good position. Furthermore the group leader, Major Sipes, kept us a little higher than normal. This deprived the lead and low group, Molesworth, of the protection of our guns, but decreased somewhat the chances of our catching their disease. It wasn't perhaps altogether good military behavior, especially when Sipes kept sliding in order to put the low group between us and the sun, which added to the low group's misery, of course. No, Major Sipes was defending our interest, but this had nothing to do with the heroic manner; this was not conforming to the war-like virtues.

But what did I do myself? The plane in front of us belonged to another squadron and had received a chunk of flak in its rudder. It made maneuvering more difficult and he started to lag. Following him, we found ourselves out of the group formation. So we just cut him out and took his position, relegating him to the position where we had been – low diamond, low squadron, but in the high group. He kept on lagging until he was well behind the formation. The German fighters soon concentrated on him.

The attacks made upon our group were not pressed with the determination evidenced below. They would start shooting at 7,000 yards and break away at 200. They had to run the gauntlet, as they dove underneath us, of the lead and low group stacked below.

At the target, we saw four P-51s; what they were doing there, only God knows. Super eager beavers, they were the only friendly fighters we were to see during the whole mission. I saw the leader start after a Jerry. You could see, way out, two vapor trails, one chasing the other at very high speed, until suddenly the one ahead exploded in a huge white puff, and what looked like a battery came sailing by our wing. That puff hung there in the sky. We passed right under it.

(I found out later that they had been led by Major Howard, a real flyer who had refused the order to return to base. He got the Medal of Honor for his performance on that day.)

We landed at a B-24 base. Watson, famous for buzzing the World Series on his way to Scotland, came in with a fire in his wing. On the way back, all his crew had bailed out. When his turn came, he felt rather dubious whether he was still over land or over the North Sea. Rather than jump in the water and die, he preferred to chance the possibility of the plane exploding. But the fire in the wing did not touch off the awaited explosion, and he was able to land with us. Now he was anxiously checking with the navigators to find out the chances of his crew having parachuted to the earth of Holland or into the North Sea.

Our group had lost two ships, which was nothing compared with our neighbor, the 303rd, who lost half of the lead group they had put up, flying with General Travis. Another ship came limping in, the one whose position we had taken. The left stabilizer had been sliced off, the tail gunner was dead, and blood kept oozing out on the ground, like a trace, as the plane taxied off the runway. The ball turret gunner also was dead. They had already taken him to the radio room. A puddle of blood remained in the bottom of the ball turret. The radio man's head been removed by a 20mm shell, his brains were all over the cabin. One of the waist gunners, when he saw the headless body still clutching his guns, had bailed out in sheer panic. The copilot was half-mad and threatened to kill us for having taken their position. The others tried to restrain him and justify our action.

I felt sorry, and guilty, though we had been right. We couldn't lag because of him. Their pilot agreed we had been right. The copilot was taken away in an ambulance. The waist gunner, alone in that ship with two corpses, had done his job well. He said nothing, just stood there tall and white, with blood and specks of gray matter all over his flight suit, so tired.

After supper, a truck convoy came to take us back to our base. The convoy got lost, what with the blackout, the false signs put up by the British to foil the German invasion, and general snafu. We finally arrived at the base at dawn. The enlisted men still had to clean their guns. We went with them because we couldn't sleep while they worked. Then we had breakfast in the enlisted mess, sharing between the ten of us the tin ware Boyovitch and Williams always kept with them, always ready to eat at a moment's notice. This time, we had 'had it'. Only the new crews had been out on this mission. We were alive, we had fought well, and luck had been with us. The ground officers had cooked up an award ceremony; we had air medals coming for our first five aids. But today we were above that. Our modesty was never so well meant. No one showed up; we slept.

We too had become veterans. We knew we were not immortal anymore. The older crews acknowledged us as members of their fraternity. No more would we wonder why they couldn't sleep on the eve of a mission; no more would we ask them for advice or 'how it was'. We knew. We had graduated. We had returned from a slaughter we had experienced real fear. We had discovered our fragility.

19

GOOD LUCK, GOOD SHOOTING AND GOOD BOMBING

We learned from Major Culpepper, our squadron CO, that General Travis, who had been leading our wing on the mission to Oschersleben, had received the order to return to base twenty minutes before we reached our target. The General decided to bomb the target regardless of the order, since we had lost already a good number of ships, including his two wing men, who had been shot down, and it would have been stupid to waste the mission. (It was obvious that Major Culpepper did not approve of this decision, which seemed to me rather like a rabbit passing judgment on a lion.)

However, the bombing had not been extraordinary. One group had missed by three miles, and we had been a bit too far to the right. We had lost sixty planes out of approximately 220. The same losses as at Schweinfurt and for more dubious results.

Back in the States, before coming to England, General Travis used to insist on a lot of brass and polish, saluting and so forth. In combat, he behaved like a real soldier, a true believer in the virtues of the warrior. He believed in hitting targets and not turning back, in duty rigidly accomplished. And he knew when to disobey. The boys didn't like him at all, just as most of his troops did not like Patton, because the qualities that made him a good general made him also a demanding 'iron ass'.

General Travis was a real eager beaver who was not afraid of taking chances, but we expected that from his behavior at the briefing for the aborted mission to Berlin. He would have gone over Berlin on three engines.

The great majority didn't care where the bombs fell, as long as they were credited with a mission. They were fighting to get their quota of twenty-five and then go home. Few ever bothered to look up the target photos. After all the hoopla about the famous Norden bombsight and 'precision bombing' they, of course, were often disappointing. Schweinfurt had already conclusively proven that deep penetrations without fighter escort were too costly for the results obtained, and now Oschersleben, where we had expected that fighter coverage all the way to our target and back, had turned out to be a repeat of Schweinfurt.

It was from the veterans that we learned of the first missions of the group. At Saint-Nazaire, instead of the submarine pens, we had plastered the town. One of our pilots had been able to bail out of his disabled ship through the cockpit window but had a hard time connecting with the French escape network – it had been the group's first mission, and the country was still under the shock of the 379th bombings. Eventually, when French tempers had cooled, he was passed on to the escape network. Within a month or so he was back in England, only to be sent immediately back to the States, because the policy was not to use in combat flying personnel who had been in touch with the French (or Dutch or Belgian) underground, to spare them the possibility of blackmail or torture or reprisals against the native population. We were, in fact, asking the occupied people to put in jeopardy their own lives to send back home those who would not be fighting anymore, at least not in the European theater.

Unable to bomb the Munster Marshalling Yards, the group had been sent on a mission to bomb instead the airfield at Enschede, Holland. We missed the airfield but hit the town, killing 155 Dutch civilians. Some of the crewmen thought they had converted that town to Nazism. Actually the Dutch understood that it was part of the misfortunes of war. Nevertheless, some guilt pervaded the band of brothers.

When we, the replacement crews arrived at the base, the whole Eighth Air Force was recuperating from a series of raids to Frankfurt, to Bremen, to Anklam, to Munster, to Stuttgart, and especially from two raids to Schweinfurt (the first one combined with a raid to Regensburg), which between them had seen the loss of sixteen percent of the attacking forces. At the second Schweinfurt alone, out of 292 planes dispatched, the force lost twenty percent. At Anklam, of an attacking force of 115 planes, sixteen percent also were lost – at Munster, twenty-two percent of the Third Division, with the 100th Group alone losing twelve of the fourteen ships dispatched.

A major factor affecting morale was the fact that precision bombing had been vastly oversold to the crews. It was done in good faith by the top Brass of the Air Force, who thought that precision bombing could win the war without killing many civilians and requiring mass armies of infantrymen. The war waged by the Air Force was to be swift and relatively painless.

There was ideology behind this belief, the ideology of Gen. Billy Mitchell, the martyr of the Air Corps' cause, and also of bureaucratic self-interest since the Air Force would have to grow at the expense of the Army and Navy. To a democracy that had joined the war with more resignation than enthusiasm, this offered a way of winning without much expenditure of blood. It also offered for the 3,000 to 4,000 ground personnel at the air bases a way to bask in the glory of the 500 airmen whose ships they serviced while stationed at one of the safest postings of the war. (We must remember that the movie that best depicted the average American experience of World War II was *Mr Roberts*, certainly not *The Sands of Iwo Jima*.)

Lieutenant Colonel Rohr went so far as to say, when he participated in the briefing for the first Schweinfurt which Colonel Preston led, that it was up to us to end the bloody war that Tuesday morning of August 17, 1943, by the destruction of the Germans' ball bearing supply.[1]

We did not know then that fourteen percent of our bombs were duds. (Was it because the bombardiers forgot to take out the safety wires, preventing the fuses from arming themselves on the way down to the target? Was it malfunction due to bad workmanship at the factory?) On the second Schweinfurt '... of the 1,222 high explosive bombs we let fly, eighty-eight scored direct hits on the factory buildings designated as prime targets and fifty-five other bombs landed within the factory area ...'[2] Which means that less than twelve percent of our bombs were effective. This was a very good day.

Even though we did not know the full scope of the PR deception mounted around the Norden bombsight, we suspected it. Precision bombing was largely a hoax. Did we care? We did not want to know. At critique I don't ever remember a discussion of target photos (though I presume the photo of the Regensburg strike must have been used extensively by PR to show us and the American public what could be done). I read in 1944, in *Impact*, an in-house Eighth Air Force magazine read by half a dozen airmen curious about the big picture, that 'Eighty percent of the drops were made with a factor of gross error': gyros left caged, trails improperly set, errors of sometimes 2,000 feet in the determination of our true altitude. Did we have reconnaissance planes buzzing the target in order to transmit to our oncoming formations the barometric pressure on the ground to give us greater approximation to true altitude? Our bombardiers toggled or salvoed their bombs as soon as the lead plane, which had a bombsight, let go of its bombs.

When we asked the tail gunner, 'How did the bombing look?' he usually answered that we had 'plastered it'. It was like gunners' claims of fighter kills – the wish was often father to the thought, or sight.

The Eighth Air Force would certainly not end the 'bloody war' on August 17, nor on any other day. Our most strategic contribution would be to have given our side control of the air for the D-Day landings, when the Germans had only two fighters and four bombers available with which to confront our armada, the result of our bleeding the German fighters white and also of monumental staff errors and oversights on the other side. (They should have mobilized all their fighters and bombers in Western Europe, but the commanders of their various fleets, in Italy, in Southern France, in Eastern Germany, in Norway, must have resisted the mobilization with all the strength of bureaucratic inertia.)

At briefing for the second Schweinfurt, the air crews were read a telegram from Gen. Fred L. Anderson of the Eighth Bomber Command, who led the First Division at that time:

SECRET.

TO ALL LEADERS AND COMBAT CREWS, TO BE READ AT BRIEFING.

THIS AIR OPERATION TODAY IS THE MOST IMPORTANT AIR OPERATION YET CONDUCTED IN THIS WAR. THE TARGET MUST BE DESTROYED, IT IS OF VITAL IMPORTANCE TO THE ENEMY. YOUR FRIENDS AND COMRADES THAT HAVE BEEN LOST AND WILL BE LOST TODAY ARE DEPENDING ON YOU. THEIR SACRIFICE MUST NOT BE IN VAIN. GOOD LUCK, GOOD SHOOTING, AND GOOD BOMBING.

ANDERSON

I doubt if this call for the crews to live up to the dead's sacrifice (instead of dead they were called 'lost') which would include, of course, those among themselves who might be killed that October 14, was very effective in raising the determination of the troops. In the Air Force, the professional officers lived in a world where the speech to the troops, often drawn from the Napoleonic tradition of the continent, was much appreciated by the, speakers. But for the troops, this was bullshit, and the troops did not like to be suckered.[3]

What was more effective in lifting morale was the bundle of compliments that Eighth Air Force Headquarters sent to each group's staff, which they forwarded to all their crews with an additional endorsement from their own group commanders. That was the first time the troops got a thank you note from such leaders as Winston Churchill or General Marshall, who spoke of 'brilliant, punishing blows.' To Gen. Hap Arnold it was clear that we were moving toward supremacy in the air. Our Own General Eaker, commanding general of the Eighth Air Force, expressed his 'unbounded admiration' for what his crews had done. Colonel Preston had all these compliments mimeographed, stapled, and distributed with his own expressions of pride.[4] According to my friend Barrett, this had a very powerful impact upon morale. I was ready to give Colonel Preston credit for the initiative, when the reading of Bendiner's book made me realize this initiative was the result of Wycombe Abbey's planning.

It is a brilliant commander who knows when and how much to congratulate his troops. He knows easily when to chew them out. (Goering was a master at that.) It takes talent to know when to compliment them. A commander is always asking for more. If he compliments his troops, is he jeopardizing his right to ask for that 'more'?

Any one of our superiors who faced us with the facts was likely to make a much more positive impression and to keep our trust. What if the facts were, 'Today we expect to lose a quarter of our crews'?

Morale was not such as to permit the group to lose fifteen to twenty-five percent of its flying personnel on each raid. Even if the original plans for training had been to provide the replacements for such losses – and they had not – it would have been difficult to get the crews to carry out the missions in an effective way. The sick-call list would have lengthened, and so would the number of abortions, or simply the desertions to Switzerland and Sweden.

It was rather easy for us to desert. There is Sweden, where Gray went on the second raid to Kiel. As we turned right towards Kiel to start a four-minute bomb run, he just turned left. This was desertion characterized, and yet he probably would get away with it. In a fashion, he did. This fight was a luxury for us; you couldn't shoot a man for refusing to indulge in a luxury.

'Why are we here?' I would ask McCall. And McCall, who had won the DSO, would answer, 'Sometimes I wonder.' And from Gurney, 'Damned if I know!' I guess we all wondered, particularly when the going had been rough, when our lives seemed more precarious, when we started feeling for a way out of it.

Our heads were supposedly given to us to clarify situations, to simplify our task. But it didn't work that way; the more we thought, the more confused we got, the more aware of the deceptions and stupidity of our side. Instead of drawing from our thinking any reasons for more fortitude, we found ourselves less sure of our duty, more doubtful, more cynical. And the more education we had been exposed to, the more confused we were apt to be, because we could find more rationalizations for refusing to do our share. The best thing was not to think at all.

When the chronic dampness and the cold became too overwhelming, when all became an accomplice to desertion, I thought of my lover's body, curled up in the precarious privacy of some park, a body quivering in the complicated assemblage of cells and blood, bone and muscle, pleasure and pain, and I longed to be the prisoner of her body and of her loving me. Here is where I searched for strength.

There was an evening, as we were shooting the breeze in McCall and Gurney's room, we got into a discussion about Frey. Soon I was lost in my own thoughts. I was jolted back out of them by Tex saying, 'Hey, Pitts, where are you? You've left us!'

'Sorry, I was thinking of something.'

Tex was continuing with his story. 'You didn't know Remy, Killion's bombardier. He knew he was going to get it. He told me several times, 'Tex, I know I won't live through it, I know it in my bones.' But he kept on, never had himself grounded and he finally got it. He was a brave man, a real brave man. I don't know if I could do that. Even when it looks terribly bad, you still believe you'll get out of it. Lots of people praying for you back home. I pray myself. But when you get back, you can be sure there was somebody saying some good prayers for you back home.'

Tonight, why should I argue? Why should I tell him I never pray? I don't even believe in God, although I consider Christianity to be the greatest of the world religions. Tex, my good friend Tex, who comes and wakes me at two o'clock in the morning to celebrate his coming back from the hospital, or his coming back from a tough mission, or his promotion to first lieutenant, or his birthday, or his Texan's right to 'get stinkin''. In fact, Tex's life seems to be full of occasions to celebrate and to pull down my covers at odd hours of the night, which gets me mad and just makes him laugh all the more. Tex, so enormous and yet so gentle in the confidence of his strength.

Tonight we shall agree: it sure takes lots of praying to get us back.

20

THE FLAK OVER THE RUHR

On a raid to Brunswick, McCall and Gurney lost two engines, shot down three German fighters, and barely made it home. There was a lot of PR hoopla in the States and in *Stars and Stripes* about their performance, and the rumor was they were up for a big medal.

They had totaled their ship and were given a B-17 F in replacement, which they liked because it was identical to the one they had lost, and also because it was more maneuverable and a bit faster than the B-17 G. On the other hand, it did not have the thick glass of the B-17 G. Gurney, like me, was always careful to put all the chances on his side, and right now he was trying to get some bullet-proof glass, like the kind we had in the *Penny Ante*, for his cockpit.

'Gurney, old hero, did you ever find that bullet-proof glass you've been hunting for?' I asked one night when we were all hanging out in his room.

'Rough, old boy, rough.'

'You bet your life it's rough,' Gurney complained. 'I like that old thick glass in front of me like *Penny Ante* has.'

Ralston piped up. 'You make me laugh with your armor plate. Very rarely does it do any good. What's going to get you will get you!'

'Well, I believe,' I argued back, 'in taking as few chances as possible.'

Gurney added, ' after Brunswick, I am becoming more careful than ever.'

'If you can't find the bullet-proof glass here,' O'Neil suggested, 'Why don't you try the material depot at Burtenwood? Just take a couple bottles of whiskey along. I'm sure Brownley will let you take your new plane there for a couple of days.

'O'Neil is right,' I agreed. 'I doubt whether they will let you fly operational before the next awards ceremony, of which you and McCall will be the stars.'

'Do I detect a note of envy in your voice?' asked O'Neil sarcastically.

'Yes, I guess so. By the way, do you know what medal they will get?'

'I think the Distinguished Service Order, which is right after the Congressional Medal of Honor.'

'Terrific!'

McCall asked, 'Do you know how a teetotaler like me can get a couple bottles of whiskey?'

O'Neil shook his head. 'I might get you some help in Burtenwood, but I can't help with the whiskey. Why don't you ask Pitts here, he's got a conduit.'

'I don't drink whiskey either. Wine is my drink. But my tail gunner has a conduit. I'll put you in touch with him.'

'We appreciate that, old buddy. Where is your tail gunner likely to be this evening?'

'At the enlisted men's club' I replied. 'But we are alerted for tomorrow, remember?'

'Well, then, I'll see him at interrogation after you guys return from tomorrow's mission' Gurney said. 'But what about you, Pitts? No armor plate on your seat? Don't you feel rather naked?'

I had had the ground crew cut me a piece of armor plate the size of my seat and had been using it on every mission. 'You bet I feel naked,' I growled. 'Some bastard, probably from Holt's crew, if not Holt himself, swiped it. So now I'm using a piece of flak suit to protect the family jewels, but it is not as convenient as the armor plate. Over enemy territory I wear my flak suit and my helmet all the time.'

'What about Streit?' asked McCall.

'Streit,' I replied, 'flies in his flight suit and bareheaded. That's his business. I guess he is naturally brave. There are guys like that, probably five to ten percent of the male population. About another eighty percent will follow their leaders, or even more so, their buddies, out of the foxholes and charge. With Streit on my left, I don't have the right to be openly scared, though it has happened to me.'

'Streit is lucky; I'm not naturally brave.' said McCall.

Gurney added, 'Nor am I.

'Nor am I,' announced O'Neil.

I said, 'I'm not either.'

'Streit has never been put through the ringer like McCall and Gurney,' Ralston pointed out. 'So we really don't know, do we?'

'I am satisfied to be a member of the armor-plated chicken brigade,' O'Neil proclaimed. 'But, Pitts, ten percent plus eighty percent makes ninety. What about the other ten percent?'

'That,' said McCall 'is the real chicken brigade. The naturally cowardly, right, Pitts?'

'Right,' I answered. 'We have them on the base, although they tend to drift toward desk jobs in our Headquarters. Few are flying personnel, because the dangers of flying tend to discourage them from the start.'

O'Neil objected to this. 'But there are also guys who begin well and just wear out rapidly. We all have our breaking points, you know. For some the threshold of panic just happens to be much lower than for others. But with the wear and tear of combat, everyone's threshold tends to get lower and lower.'

'For some, it's panic,' McCall said thoughtfully. 'For others, it's the feeling of "I don't give a damn anymore." They let themselves be killed.'

'And the rest of the crew with them!' rejoined Ralston emphatically. 'But on the other hand, look at women, normally emotional and not very brave. But to defend their children, they can be tigresses. And pioneer women were brave, braver than city women.'

'That's true,' O'Neil added. 'And if you remember, you don't want to go falling into the hands of a bunch of German women. Unless you crave death by pitchfork.'

There then ensued a ten-second spell of heavy silence.

I finally broke into the quiet: 'Tell us, McCall, the story of your return from Brunswick.'

McCall settled into his chair and began. 'You remember the first pass of the German fighters?' he asked. We nodded as he continued. 'Well, they knocked out our #2 engine. You guys were going too fast for us, and we couldn't keep up. So we dove for a cloud bank, but we were immediately pounced on by three Me-109s, who knocked out our #1 engine. A lone P-51 appeared and chased the three Me-109s shooting one down. But the two remaining Germans then shot down the P-51. Meanwhile, we were able to reach the cloud bank and try for home, two engines dead on one side with the props windmilling because we couldn't feather them. We came down to 1,500 feet and passed the Ruhr, where the flak put holes under the #2 engine and broke the navigator's leg. It was like hail on a tin roof. We kept dodging in and out of the clouds and again were met by German fighters.'

'Were you ever attacked by several German fighters at once?' I asked.

'Once we had two after us, but they made the mistake of attacking us separately. We shot both of them down.'

'I guess they thought you were easy meat and didn't want to share a victory.'

'We were a bit tougher than they expected,' Gurney put in. 'One Me-109 met us down below the clouds, looked us over. We didn't shoot and neither did he. If he wasn't going to bother us, we weren't going to either. So –'

'So he might have been out of ammunition and simply called mission control with your coordinates,' interrupted Ralston.

'You may be right,' McCall admitted. 'But the fact is we had thrown overboard most of our ammunition and didn't have much left to spare. A while later, a little guy in a Focke Wulfe came up on us, and the tail gunner killed him. He went by and took five feet of our left wing with him. I saw him in the cockpit slumped; looked like a kid.'

McCall rubbed his face. 'I'll tell you one thing, when they start that invasion, it's going to be no picnic. The coast is full of concrete bunkers. I tried to find a corner where habitations were scarce. Finally I went near a casino over a beach. Boy! They opened up on us from every window. You could see them shooting at us with submachine guns, carbines, pistols. We passed over little concrete emplacements buried in the sand, probably machine guns or bazooka installations. Our altitude about was 200 feet. Finally we met some Spitfires. We must have been going the wrong way, for they started flying in front of us, turning to the left. We got rid of our machine guns, every piece of dead weight. We climbed to a thousand feet so that we could clear the cliffs. The good engines had been giving all they had for a long time. I guess they were exhausted and the maneuvering we had to do decreased our lift. It became harder to keep the left wing up. When we arrived in England the plane was really sluggish; we jumped a couple of high-tension wires and set her down in a beet field.'

'Did you ever think of putting your wheels down and surrendering?' I asked.

'No, it didn't come to my mind.'

'But if you had met seven fighters at once?'

'We should have had to give up then,' said Gurney. 'You don't stand a chance against seven. Two you might take care of, but seven? This is a war, not a movie. That P-51 sure saved our necks. He won't get any medals, though he certainly deserves half of ours. Well, from now on we want easy raids. France here I come!'

'You don't want to be a hero anymore, do you, Gurney?' Ralston inquired.

'Hell no! You do that once. Next time they get you. This hero stuff is dangerous.'

'It's a nice thing,' McCall added, 'to have behind you.'

'Your parents will be proud of you,' commented Ralston.

'My mother,' retorted McCall, 'would rather I fly low and slow.'

O'Neil announced, 'By the way, Pitts, you're low diamond tomorrow.'

'No kidding! Again?' It was not something I wanted to hear. 'Yep. Low diamond, low squadron, low group.'

'God! How do you know?' I demanded.

'My little finger.'

'You and your finger!'

'All right, don't believe me.'

'No kidding?' I asked mournfully.

'No kidding.'

'Now, why did you tell him that?' Ralston wanted to know. 'He won't find sleep so easy now, and he needs his sleep. We all do.'

'Oh, that's all right,' I said. 'I have more time to recover from the bad news. I remember one time I got that news, and Tex had to pull me out of a bad funk just after briefing. He sure is a swell guy.'

'That's true,' Ralston agreed.

'After all,' McCall pointed out, 'when you are low diamond, you don't have to worry about wing men when you take evasive action. It's a flexible position.'

'So flexible,' I rejoined, 'that your tail parts company with your wings.'

'You can move around a lot,' said O'Neil.

'So can your engines. I guess when one falls from its mount, it's just being extra flexible' I jested. 'But you sure have a very good tail gunner. If you guys are ever stood down, we'd like him as a replacement.'

'I am sure Brownlow will try to accommodate you' laughed Gurney. 'Especially since you have the reputation of being a lucky crew.'

'That's true, and we have to come back tomorrow. Otherwise Gurney might not get his bullet-proof glass.' I rose to leave for my bed. 'Goodnight, you guys!'

'Goodnight and sleep well, old buddy!'

As far as I was concerned, control of fear had gone through several stages. At the beginning of my tour of missions, the fear was checked by my belief in my immortality. As a young man, as my mother's son, I could not be scheduled to die. Hence I wouldn't. It was a security blanket, and I held on it with my thumb in my mouth.

After my fifth mission, I knew better. I had seen fellow young men go down with their ships. I let go of the blanket. I took my thumb out of my mouth. I knew that if I learned my trade and was careful, I would live. I would still play games with Gurney when we flew formation and our positions placed us in the line of sight with one another, Gurney in the right seat of his ship and I in the left seat of mine (because Streit wanted to have a better view of the formation's right side). Before we hit the enemy coast was a good time for horseplay; we would thumb our noses at each other and fly a very close formation, just to show off, just to prove that we possessed the skills most needed in a copilot. Streit would often catch a nap during these ten or twenty minutes. Sometimes a snooze would extend to an hour, or even more, giving me the chance to act as aircraft commander. I knew that the slightest change in our course or speed would wake him, like a mother wakes at the first whimper of her child in the next room.

Around my tenth or twelfth mission, the dullness of habit set in. As the French say, 'On s'habitue à tout' – 'You can get used to anything.' The Alert, the Briefing, the Take-off of our overloaded ship, the Target, the Enemy Fighters – all were experienced as a heavy rock to be carried carefully, each step foretelling the next step, each mission adding to the total that would soon amount to twenty-five, at which time I could let go of the rock. I would have 'been through it.' I would know how to handle routinely the incidents that were on the menu of the average mission: the overheating of one of the engines; the failure of a super-charger; a runaway propeller; somebody's propwash, which might flip our wings from ten to sixty degrees one way or the other; a ship on a collision course with us; a crewman not answering the oxygen check; a turret that failed its gunner; sometimes even a live bomb hanging from the bomb bay. By the time we had been to Halberstadt, to Schweinfurt, my fear of the missions had been routinized. And at that point, fear might be too strong a word; apprehension is perhaps a better description of what I felt.

On our twelfth mission, February 4, returning from a raid to Frankfurt, the wing leader had taken us through 'Happy Valley,' the Ruhr. Of course, Happy Valley was full of flak; on the briefing maps it was covered with a big red spot indicating huge concentrations of flak guns. There would be no relief until we had left the whole region.

If our leader chose to fly the length of Happy Valley rather than slice through it, he probably had a legitimate reason. Possibly it was to get a better photographic plot of the German anti-aircraft batteries; that way, at a later date, our fighters could give these batteries some individual attention. Or perhaps the leader was trying out a new electronic device, designed to confuse the enemy's radar that aimed the guns regardless of cloud cover.

Or perhaps, we wondered, our lead navigator had made this egregious mistake of guiding us through the Ruhr because his mask was not giving him enough oxygen.

I was imagining the 88mm guns located on the roofs of German high schools, guided by radar, but loaded and fired by students, who probably considered it a welcome diversion from class. Perhaps they jumped up and down when they scored a hit and saw a B-17 fall out of the sky in flaming pieces. I hoped they wore steel helmets so they wouldn't get killed by shell fragments falling from 21,000 feet in a deadly hail. It was difficult to think of these kids as the enemy.

At that moment, we began to see some of these 88mm shells bursting anywhere between one hundred to twenty feet in front of our cockpit.

If we were able to see them, however, we would be largely immune to their cores of splinters, discharging upwards like bouquets of flowers. If we were going to be done in, it would be by the bursts directly below us, the bursts we could not see. Although all sounds were muffled at this high altitude, we could still hear something like a woof, a sign that they were too close for safety. We flew through the smoke of the exploding shells, which hung ominous and intimate, familiar dark seahorses riding the sky. Some of the fragments smacked into our windows, and the windows would crack, just like they did in the gangster movies, under the impact of the bad guys' sub-machine-gun bullets. But here the glass was thicker, one inch, and it held for us, the good guys.

Though our pilot Streit flew usually without helmet, flak suit, and parachute, while I flew with all these accoutrements, including a backpack parachute that stayed on me from beginning to end of a mission, I was taking this more calmly than our first pilot. Normally a naturally brave flyer, he kept pointing at the cracks with surprise. But I was impassive; German fighters didn't dare attack us through such an impressive barrage, so it was a moment of comparative quiet, marred only by the occasional woof of a close burst.

We could do nothing to avoid this flak. It was not aimed at a particular plane but at the whole wing, in a scientifically apportioned box barrage. If it was going to get us, it would get us. I personally always feared the fighters more than the artillery. The fighters represented a human will out to get you. Flak was part of fate, and fate, so far, had been good to me.

For others, however, the woofs of close flak resonated all through their beings; each shell seemed closer to them. They suffered terribly during the bomb runs where, like in the interminable Ruhr, no evasive action was possible.

By now our wing was reduced to some forty-five planes. With my own eyes I saw two B-17s destroyed by flak, and then a third, most of his right wing shot off, rolling to his death. Was duty to follow blindly, or was duty to break radio silence? 'Cowboy Blue, this is Enamel K for King. Is this trip through the Ruhr really necessary? Shouldn't we be heading 280 degrees instead of 350 degrees? Can't the wing leader change course, or why don't we first take our group out of this mess?'

But I didn't call. Streit might decide to accept my seditious suggestions, which could turn out to be disastrous if German fighters waiting outside and picked us off as an isolated group. And besides, to tell the truth, I didn't even seriously think of calling up our fearless leader, Cowboy Blue; I had forgotten that today Cowboy Blue was Lieutenant Colonel Kittel. And we were the lead group of the wing, and through that, of the whole First Division. There was no escape, and I was not about to break the silence of the cathedral, where death was glorious, not stupid.

Out of nowhere came the scent of – *vanilla? My God, where was that smell coming from?*

And irresistibly, it took me back to college days, sitting on the ground with my back against a tree in the yard with Jill's head on my lap. A mild courtship on a pre-war campus, where Jill was one of the goddesses, and I was not one of the gods – just paying homage and helping her with her schoolwork. From her body came the scent of vanilla. Today, now that I belonged to the aristocracy of the sky, I wondered, would she give me a date? Would I ask her for one?

The smell of vanilla vanished when the first pilot shook the wheel to let me know it was time for me to take over. Two or three more cracks on the window, four more woofs, and we were out of the Ruhr. Streit called out to the crew, 'Watch out for fighters now, especially out of the sun!' I squeezed my oxygen mask to make sure I was getting a proper supply; lack of oxygen could play bad tricks on us because it hit the brain first, and we were rarely aware of it.

21

LOVE AND WAR,
AND ALL THAT'S FAIR

Tex had said once, 'You know, I feel sorry when I see a plane go down, even if it is a German fighter.'

'Well I can't, after all these bastards have done,' I had retorted.

'Then look at yourself, boy. We've been to Frankfurt, and what did we bomb? The heart of the walled city. And the word to us was to claim, in case we were shot down, that we were after the railroad station. We are terror flyers, Pitts, make no mistake about that.'

'That's what their interrogation officers use,' I argued, 'to scare us with, to try to make us talk.'

'Speaking of interrogation officers, were you there when that intelligence officer from Headquarters came to brief us on their methods for worming out information?'

'No, I was on pass.'

'Well, he told us they had got hold of a German flyer who had been captured with a bunch of letters on him, letters written to him by a French gal, and those letters were hot. At the first interrogation they told him, 'We are going to send home all your personal belongings. You can have your knife, your fountain pen, but your money and the letters we're going to send to your family through the Red Cross.' The guy got all red and said he didn't want those letters sent to his home. They replied they had to do it, "Rules, you know." The German begged them not to do it.' Tex paused to shoot me a look.

'Then this intelligence officer,' he continued, 'rubbed his hands and told us, "You know we made him pay for all the letters with information. One piece of information, one letter. If he told us something particularly valuable, we let him have two letters. Once they are broken, you get all you want from them." Then he went on telling us about how all you have to do to them is threaten to pass the word to the Germans that they've turned informer, and they get scared for their families and start to talk plenty.'

Hearing that, I felt sick. To fight, to kill, in a fair and open fight is one thing. But to blackmail, to break a man's soul? That disgusted me. That's when I felt sorry for the German pilot. I raised my voice and protested, 'To kill is bad enough, but to transform a man into a desperate and crawling dog — that's a business that repels me thoroughly.'

'Pitts, don't talk like a damn college boy with a French accent.' Tex's reply was, as usual, succinct.

'Touché.'

O'Neil, a copilot, interrupted: 'Listen, you guys are getting me down. Let's talk about something else. Let's talk about women.'

'You talk of women, you're the big lover here. What's new in your harem?'

'Or, more to the point, who's new?'

O'Neil sprang immediately to the change of subject. 'Well, I was at a party on a fighter base quartered in, get this, a Brit castle, nothing less. And when they organized a party they did not bring in the bags of Bedford. *These* were genteel WRENs[1] and they had class. And I latched on to one.'

O'Neil began warming to his story. 'She was young, around eighteen, and I come up and sit beside her in the dayroom. In a bit I put my arm around her waist, but she's rather stiff. Kind of scared, you know. So I ask, "Do you want a drink?" "No." So I go and get her a coke, and some ice, pour it for her. After a while I say, "Let's get out of here, it's too noisy." So we go upstairs to my room. She's kind of reticent, but I guess she's glad to get out of the room downstairs; probably scared somebody's going to get screwed right in there.'

He was grinning, remembering. 'Her fears were grounded. Those WRENs were losing their manners with the booze. They just don't have the training that our "good girls" get. So anyway, I'm sitting on the bed, with her on my knees, still timid and stiff, but I warm her up a wee bit and finally get her on the bed. After a while, I knock the light switch with my shoe. Well, right away she sits up and demands some light. I turn on a desk lamp, but manage to cram it down so it's only got an inch or so clearance with the table, and I started working on her slow.

At last, I get one knee between her legs, and I start on her skirt. You know how tight those Wrens' skirts are? I finally get her zipper loosened enough to raise her up and get the skirt off. Well, her slip is rather easy, and she's wearing these thin pants. Unusual for a British girl.'

We knew about the panties that the WREN's usually came furnished with, formidable objects with strong and wide latex bands around the waist and thighs, impossible to remove without the full cooperation of the 'victim'. It was certainly easier (and may still be) to complete a seduction if the girl did not have to give conscious and elaborate cooperation to her seducer; that's where liquor and flimsy underwear came in. *By not putting on her navy-issue 'chastity underwear'*, I thought, *the little lamb had already surrendered in spirit to the big bad wolf.* But I did not tell O'Neil that.

He continued, 'There was some mild sobbing, you know that stuff. When it's all finished, she says to me, "Do you know why I did that?" Well, I'm rather embarrassed, I can't say, "Yes, I know," but I can't look dumb and say, "No, I don't." So I just hang in there, waiting for her to go on. She isn't looking at me, and then she says, "Well, I kept on looking at those flyers' boots." She looks at me and says, "Well, they're British."

'And I say, "Yeah, they're better than ours – what does that have to do with it?"

'And she tells me,' O'Neil shook his head, 'she tells me, "I had a brother in the RAF." Or something of the sort. She's kind of watering in the eyes, so I don't want to ask her if he's alive or not. But I'm telling myself, "Well, from now on I am going to hang those boots on the ceiling so that they're in full view!"

'A few days later, I borrowed the Colonel's car and went down to the Wrennery. She got in the car; she's cold as ice. But back at the base she warmed up all right.'

I was sorry that O'Neil should have talked that way. And yet I felt an awkward dryness in my mouth, and I thought of Jackie.

One activity in which our dapper Major was effective was organizing dances. He would arrange for the transport of young women from Bedford or from some British women's auxiliary battalion, pick the best looking one for himself, and let us apportion the remainder amongst ourselves. An order from Colonel Preston set the limits to our pleasure: 'All ladies attending Saturday-night dances at the Officers' Club MUST be off the base by 0800 Monday morning.' I never went to the dances, though; most of the women were not very attractive, and it really looked like a meat market. I waited for the forty-eight-hour passes that came every three weeks and went to London.

I picked up French girls, some 'easy' such as a saucy AFAT (the French equivalent of the Women's Army Corps, or WAC) I had met at the Free French Air Force Headquarters in Kensington; some more 'difficult' to whom I would introduce myself at Le Petit Club Français, where my American uniform and wings had their fans.

But the first night of my pass, I would meet Jackie. She was stationed in London, a member of the WAC. On my first forty-eight-hour pass I had made a date with her and acted quite flak happy in order to exploit her pity and get her into bed (something that still bites into my conscience today).

I had chased Jackie for a long time back in the States. When I first met her in 1940, I was head of the Harvard Trotskyists, with my hair a trifle too long, and my twisted tie hanging loosely around my shirt with the top button undone. Jackie was putting in time with the Free French and with various committees that were promoting American intervention. She had been living in New York like a Bohemian and knew all of their haunts, but she remained a straight arrow, as morally naïve as they come. She always had money to give to a bum who asked for a dime to 'get a cup of coffee'.

We began as friends. I could talk to her more freely than to any other girl because we were both disinterested in one another. We were not involved in the secret but incessant bargaining between attachment and sex, which dominated the relations between boy and girl from the age of thirteen or fourteen to marriage. I confided to her my various adventures and misadventures with girls, and she 'moralized' me, complaining of my promiscuity. She acted as if she were my older sister, even though I was her senior by one year and was academically ahead of her by two years. For me, an only child, she was indeed my *sorellina*, my confidant.

Jackie was in love with Ivan, an airline pilot who was not terribly interested in her. He took her out when he had nothing better to do. This meant that any time he called to say he was in town, announcing, 'I'll be in New York at seven, and I'll pick you up at eight,' any other plans Jackie might have with me or another were off. She had little bargaining power left in relation to him. It bothered me, though I never brought it up.

In 1938, my last year in France and a year before the war between the Germans and the French resumed in September 1939, a series called *Les Thibault* by Roger Martin du Gard, had put out its last major publication called *The Summer of 1914*. In the story, a young girl, Jenny, falls in love with her brother's best friend, Jacques, when she is finally conquered by his rebellion and his courage, and also because she discovered him, when they were timid teenagers kissing her shadow on a wall. It had seemed very romantic to me, and as I grew to know Jackie, the story kept coming to mind. I knew I could have loved her, but also knowing that I did not have a chance, I kept my passions under lock and key.

During that time, my Trotskyism was receiving some hard blows from my favorite sociology professors Talcott Parsons, Robert K. Merton, N.S. Timasheff and L.J. Henderson, the latter a character with a beard and a stentorian voice right out of a Henry James novel.

The fall of Paris, which according to Trotskyist dogma was a minor event in the struggle between two imperialist powers, brought me back to reality.

But it was like falling out of love, and it took me several months before I could tell myself I wasn't a Trotskyist anymore. Trotskyism had defended my identity as a French revolutionary by denying the moral superiority of America, a land of robber barons, a land where strikers were shot down by the National Guard, a land where there were still ten million unemployed after ten years of depression.

After the Marxist-Bolshevik blinders had fallen from my eyes, I could look at America with new eyes. Now I was ready to fall in love with America, ready to fight for my country. This would not be a star-eyed love, rather it was more like the love a man has for his wife of many years, a love that would endure until I died.

I decided to get into the war by joining the British-American ambulance Corps along with my friend Mike, a move applauded by Jackie, and I became first alternate for the Corps' departure. But nobody fell ill or defected. Mike went, and I was left on the beach.

In June of 1941, I graduated from Harvard and went to see my father before taking a job on the R.H. Macy's Executive Training Squad. My preference would have been to take a job as errand-and-copy boy at *Time Life* but they only paid fifteen dollars a week, while Macy's paid thirty dollars and gave me a real snow job to entice me. I was a fool to choose them, and they were fools to hire me. Even though my mother was a buyer for her family's store, I had no predisposition for retail merchandising. It took Macy's about eight months to find out, and I was encouraged to resign. I packed my things and returned to Ohio to see my father prior to joining the Air Corps.

I had decided I would become a combat pilot. In my consciousness, my decision had nothing to do with Ivan's being an airline pilot. I had always been a big aviation fan. Nevertheless I wonder now. Before I left, I took Jackie out on a couple of dates. We spoke about love, and a certain amount of game-playing went on at the time. She did not speak very much about Ivan, because I kept telling her she was barking up the wrong tree and that her feelings were wasted.

Once I was in the Air Corps, I started writing to Jackie, as well as to other girls in order to get them to write to me. She replied in an awkward handwriting, legible, but somewhat juvenile. Against my advice, she joined the WAC, with the same heart and the same desire to help that made her buy war bonds, give blood, and fall for every sucker trick invented by the Office of War Information, like the aluminum drive and the rubber drive. She had pestered me until I gave her a perfectly good aluminum pan, which she took with other things to the Drive Depot. I had to replace the pan.

The Army sent Jackie to Des Moines to do some recruiting and to neutralize the image of the WAC that the overseas soldiers were creating in the minds of their families and girlfriends, the image of what the French call *le repos du guerrier* – the warrior's rest and recreation.

When Ike organized SHAPE – Supreme Headquarters Allied Powers Europe – the Army discovered that Jackie was fluent in French, and she was ordered to London. She was placed in an office that catalogued French collaborators and prepared teams of Americans, British, and French for parachuting into occupied France in order to help with Overlord, the planned invasion of the continent by Allied troops. These were the famed 'Jedburghs'.

And now, on this Saturday morning of my pass to London, Jackie was due at my hotel around 11.00a.m. We met downstairs, of course, in the lobby. This time, when we met, our embrace – no lip kissing, but kissing on the cheeks, *à la française* – was different in the gestures and the warmth. A year and a half had gone by. Opulently built and nearly as tall as I, she filled her WAC uniform to her advantage. She could even carry off her military hat, which reminded me of the French *képi* carried by French policemen and officers.

I was very fond of her, and I had much respect for her. I think she was fond of me too. It was a very nice encounter; much of the tension I was carrying drained out of me when we embraced. It was as if a cloth that had been compressed and squeezed out of shape suddenly unraveled to recover its body and its sheen.

We took the slow hydraulic elevator to my room. Jackie had a leather bag hanging on her shoulders, which contained her toothbrush and various sundries. She did not ask me to get her a room of her own, nor did she inquire at the desk. It seemed to be assured that she would spend the night in my room. As soon as we were settled in the room, Jackie asked me if she could take a bath. The WAC only provided showers, she said, and she was longing for a nice warm bath.

'Will an hour be enough?' I inquired.

'An hour will be heaven,' she replied.

I went downstairs to look for some magazines or books. When I came back to the room, now our room, I asked, 'Do you want me to get a cot for myself?'

'With a bed this wide, there's no need.'

She was refreshed and raring to go. It was cold outside, so I put on my British greatcoat and my white silk scarf for warmth around my neck. Jackie and I left the hotel and began walking side by side, as we used to do in Central Park. I was back in the mood of desiring her, but this time the feeling would not be going through another brother-sister act. I began humming a popular tune, 'I Can't Get Started with You', hoping that this time I could.

My greatcoat covered my uniform. For insignia of rank I had only one gold bar showing on each shoulder of the coat; I had not had time to get my Eighth Air Force patch sewn on, and the scarf covered the wings on my shirt collar.

As Jackie and I passed a crowd, me singing, 'I went around the world on a plane', a figure detached itself and headed our way – a colonel from the Quartermaster Corps whose staff loitered nearby, waiting to see how this execution of a second lieutenant would go. I had enough time to whisper to Jackie, 'Enemy fighter at one o'clock low.'

Jackie whispered back, 'I see him, I see him.'

The colonel stopped. 'Lieutenant' he said. 'Don't you salute your superiors?'

'Sorry, Colonel' I replied. 'I had not noticed you.'

'A poor excuse.'

Jackie and I came to attention, and we both saluted the colonel who then inquired, 'Lieutenant, are you also not aware of the regulations against dating between officers and enlisted personnel?'

'Sir, I have known Corporal Remington since our college days,' I answered. 'It is hard for me to think of her as enlisted personnel.'

'Give me your name.'

'Lt. Jesse R. Pitts, 0685214, pilot, 524th Squadron, 379th Bomb Group, Kimbolton.'

At this, the colonel began to get embarrassed.

'Cpl. Jacqueline Remington, 17157596. SHAPE Headquarters. I am one of the secretaries to General Eisenhower.'

Listening to Jackie's cultured voice, the colonel knew he was out-pointed. 'All right,' he managed to retort. 'I won't report you this time. But don't do it again.'

'Sir,' Jackie asked, 'could I have your name and unit?'

The colonel regarded her. 'Why?'

'I would like to transmit to General Eisenhower the name of a colonel of the Quartermaster Corps who is so very diligent about his duty.' Jackie replied solemnly. 'I know the General is very interested in getting good Quartermaster Corps officers in crucial positions for the coming invasion. Sir.'

'Well, never mind that.' The colonel turned around and took off while Jackie and I saluted him. And then we burst out laughing.

I said, 'You know, there is a name for officers like that. He needed his ration of blood today.'

'Yes, I know,' Jackie agreed. As we continued our walk, a captain from the colonel's retinue passed alongside.

'Well done, Lieutenant,' he grinned.

'I'm sorry for you guys working under such a character,' I sympathized.

'It's all in a day's work. Good luck, Lieutenant.'

I wished him the same and turned to Jackie. 'We have just been complimented on how we handled the incident. The compliment should really go to you. That was some nerve, claiming to be secretary to General Eisenhower!'

'But it did the trick, didn't it?' She took my arm and we walked on.

'Sure. But what if he had asked for your identification?'

She said, 'I saw he was somewhat bothered to find out you were a heavy bombardment pilot. You guys are the only Americans fighting the Germans in this theater. Difficult for a Quartermaster Colonel to report a combat flyer for failure to salute and dating an enlisted woman. Furthermore I have a friend who has a friendly acquaintance with the British gal who drives him around. They went to school together, and in England this means a lot.'

'I don't think I'm cleared for that.' We both laughed.

'I was asked to be a driver for some big-time general.'

'With your looks, no wonder.'

'I turned it down.'

'Good girl.'

We strolled past the shops and cafés as Jackie told me about her work in London. 'My job here is more interesting than at American Airlines. I use my French all the time. They even ask my opinion sometimes. I am developing files of French collaborators that will be helpful to our forces when the invasion gets moving. They've offered to send me to OTS so that I would have a commission.'

'For heaven's sake, take it,' I urged.

She shook her head. 'No, I don't feel like it. You know me, I want to stay with the toiling masses. I've made a couple of very good friends here, and I don't want to leave them.'

'I can understand that. That's one of the things I like about you.' Jackie's generous heart and loyalty were two of the things I admired most about her.

She gave me a smile. 'What else do you like about me?' she asked.

'If I start on that, we shall not have the time for lunch.' I teased. We were passing Lyon's, and I suggest we have a quick bite there. 'And tonight, we'll go to Maria la Belge and splurge.'

'And after that,' Jackie added mischievously, as I opened the door for her 'we can finish that bottle of Sauterne I saw in your room.'

'I love you, sweetheart. You don't miss a thing, do you?' We laughed and went in.

The tea room served among other things, pork fritters and brussels sprouts. The 'pork fritters' turned out to be fried Spam, which made us laugh. We ordered big mugs of tea served with milk, something I had not seen before and I found that I liked.

Over lunch, Jackie and I spoke of our admiration for the British people, for the way they bore up with the stiff rationing and with having their men overseas – with having to sleep in the subways to protect themselves from the German bombings, or because they had nowhere else to go … with their ability to keep the black market to a minimum. We speculated that it was easier for Britain to control the flow of food stuffs since most of it was imported, and also because shopkeepers here considered themselves, above all, to be Englishmen; they identified with their customers and would not take advantage of the position of power in which the war and rationing had placed them. We also admired the way they bore up with all the Americans. How would Americans, we wondered, have reacted if the situation had been reversed?

Our meal finished, we went for a walk in the theater district. I spotted a theater marquee advertising a matinee for a play in which Wendy Hiller was the star. I told Jackie that Wendy Hiller was one of my favorite actresses, along with Simone Simon, the pug-nosed French actress.

So we crossed the street, bought two tickets, and went in. The play had already begun. I don't remember the action; all I remember is Wendy Hiller in the flesh, and she lived up to all my expectations. At intermission, Jackie insisted we go backstage to say hello to her. I was not too keen on the idea, but before long, Jackie had succeeded in dragging me to the actress's dressing room, which was full of British officers and their well-coiffed wives. The officers were from various arms: RAF; Coldstream Guards; Scottish Highlanders, in kilts and ruddy knees; Navy men, all with their chests discreetly marked by DFCs, DSOs, and even one, I thought, by the Victoria Cross. Luckily enough I was in my Class A uniform with wings and Eighth Air Force insignia on my left arm. No medals as yet, although I was entitled to an Air Medal, but it would have been ridiculous to wear it in this group where heroism and high deeds of valor seemed the standard.

Now then, what to do? We had just passed the door of Wendy Hiller's dressing room, and we were being politely ignored with a mixture of surprise and condescension. I could feel the glass wall between us and the rest of the party. I signalled to Jackie that we should go, especially since I saw some of the RAF guys making moves to approach her, as she was younger and better looking than practically all of the other women there. They were each looking at Jackie's *belle poitrine* with the greedy eye of a fighter pilot who has found a lone German plane in an otherwise empty sky. We were about to turn on our heels and go back to our seats, when Wendy Hiller came to us. I introduced myself and presented Jackie. By that time I was blushing and tongue-tied. How does it feel to have the dream woman of your adolescence – I was a mature twenty and a half by then – facing you in the flesh? I did manage to stumble out my admiration for her roles in *Pygmalion* and *Major Barbara*, the two films that had given her stardom.

She used the opening to speak of poor Leslie Howard, who had died in a crash in Canada some months before. *Terrible terrible*. We spoke a little more, and then the bell announcing the third act rang to interrupt the pleasant and embarrassing moment. In her cultured accent, very important in England, Jackie thanked her for her hospitality and I remember Wendy Hiller saying, 'Be sure to come backstage next time you are in London. We must talk some more.' We went back to our seats, charmed and relieved, and sat quietly for the rest of the play.

When we came out of the theater, it was getting dark. Jackie and I returned to the tea room, where we ordered the original watercress and cucumber sandwiches, the likes of which I had first had served to me back in Cambridge by Margaret. The tea was not of the exotic nature that Margaret's mother had bought, but it was quite adequate. I remembered how in 1935 I had vacationed in Bournemouth, a bourgeois summer resort that doubled as a quiet place of retirement for aged professors and colonels, a sort of pre-war Camden. At the age of fourteen, I had walked alone in a tea room by the boardwalk and they served me as if I were an adult. Eight and a half years ago, I thought, and here I was already lost in nostalgia.

'Uh oh, where are you?' Jackie was saying.

I told her. She understood.

I paid and we left. I think we were on Regent Street, and we stopped at the window of Asprey, the old silver shop. I spotted a miniature silver tea set, which I thought my goddaughter would appreciate when she was older (she was only eight months old at the time), and Jackie told me, 'It's nice that you should think of your goddaughter that way.'

We walked and window shopped some more, and on the way to the underground restaurant of Maria la Belge, I told Jackie about a place I knew of in New York, an old speakeasy left over from Prohibition days that had been converted into an underground *pension de famille* restaurant. By being underground, the owner, a Frenchman who had come to America in 1913 to escape the three-year military service and the 'Great War' avoided all sorts of taxes (he certainly had to pay off somebody now) and served first-rate meals at reasonable prices. To 'join', you had to speak French fluently and be brought in by a well-known customer, presenting yourself to a spy piece from which you would be examined.

The French customers who were there were rather gamy. Some were smugglers of diamonds or had little rackets on the side. Sometimes clients would go to a small adjacent room to discuss 'private business'. Others owned pastry shops in town or were hairdressers, barbers, maître d's. One was an ex-banker who had run away in 1931 to avoid prison and made a living now by private tutoring in French; he would regale the table d'hôte by telling us the stories of the pupils he had taken to bed. He did not charge them for the time during the lesson spent in bed, he told us, although he might have. He seemed, from his stories, to be a superior *professeur d'amour*.

The clients were all fierce French patriots, of course. There were the Vichyssois (the majority, I thought, in 1942) and the Gaullists. Politics was a taboo subject at the table, otherwise they would have been at each other's throats.

The few women they brought had gamy pasts as well, but nobody would talk about that, although the men were not as discreet about their own pasts. The women were usually middle-aged and had, as the French say, *de beaux restes* – beautiful leftovers.

I had never thought of bringing Jackie to this place before, but now, telling her of its existence, I had to promise to take her when next we would meet in New York.

Now she would take me to Maria la Belge. It was the same scenario as in New York, with the same underground setting, but the 'spy glass' here was a latticed opening covered by a cast-iron shutter. A woman opened this shutter, and Jackie introduced herself in French and then her guest, me, *l'Américain*. No problem, the door was immediately opened.

In New York, there had been only one table, large enough for fifty people. In London, we had a regular restaurant with menus, waitresses, bright lights, and a crowd of perhaps fifty people, half of whom were Free French, Navy, and Air Force. The rest were British, with a good sprinkling of military, mostly RAF and Navy who probably owed their presence there to their Free French connection.

Maria, the Belgian woman, came to greet us at our table. I asked if she knew Mr Paul in New York, the owner of the speakeasy. With wonderment and pleasure in her voice she revealed that Monsieur Paul was her brother. With that connection, she regarded us right away as old customers entitled to dip into the quota of steaks she had about twice a week.

We ordered steaks and a little red burgundy. The meal was delicious. The steaks were enormous, illegal, and tender as only American steaks are tender, and came, I suspected, from some French-speaking tech ser-geant serving in the American Quartermaster Corps. The French fries were pommes soufflées, French-fried potatoes that had been fried twice in order to get them to balloon; the peas were early peas, very likely from a French can, supplied by the boats that also carried the French prostitutes. The only people always at peace are tradesmen.

While we were eating, we were visited by a Free French Air Force lieutenant, who said to us, 'Excuse me, but it is rather rare to meet two Americans in here who not only speak fluent French, but are also entitled to steaks.'

'To whom,' I answered in the French manner, 'do we have the honor of speaking?'

He introduced himself as Lt. François de la Bassée of the Free French Air Force. I introduced Jackie and myself and invited him to sit down.

'I don't want to disturb you,' he protested.

'You already have,' I returned 'but it does not matter. What drew you to us, the Corporal or the meat?'

'A little bit of both,' the French lieutenant acknowledged laughing, 'but mostly curiosity. I fly Spits V, and sometimes we accompany you on your way to Germany or on your way back. I wave at the pilots sometimes and they wave back. You are the first American flyer I have had the chance to talk to.'

Jackie asked, 'How many are in your party?'

'We are three,' he replied 'A paratrooper and his fiancée, and myself.'

Jackie turned to me and said, 'Don't you think we could invite them to our table for coffee?'

I agreed. 'Excellent idea. What do you say to that, Lieutenant?'

'It's very kind of you. We'll join you for coffee. *Bon appétit.*' He left us and went back to his table. After telling his companions of our invitation, he gave us the 'okay' sign.

'You were a bit provocative,' Jackie accused me, 'asking him whether it was "the Corporal or the meat" that drew him to our table.'

'But you saw he took it well?' I grinned and back to the steaks we went.

Jackie was chewing thoughtfully. 'You know' she said, 'I don't think it's quite right for us to be here. This is a black-market restaurant; in a way, we are helping the enemy when we contribute to breaking down the rationing system here.'

'Your scruples honor you, my dear.' I grinned at her. 'Though you might have expressed them earlier.'

'I know' she admitted. 'I've been here before. But still, we should have gone to a legitimate restaurant.'

'All you had to do was speak up.' I speared another piece of steak. 'The French side of me has no remorse whatsoever. This is the best meat I have eaten since I joined the Army, and I feel I deserve it. Furthermore, I bet it comes from the US Army stores. I sure intend to take us here on my next pass.'

'Speaking of the future, can't you give me more notice when you are coming in so I can organize my free time better? My lieutenant doesn't like me, and she will use any opportunity to mess things up for me.'

'I'll do my best,' I said. 'First I have to go through approximately seven missions to get here. It depends also whether my operations officer can spare our crew from his preparations for readiness. If one crew is grounded because of sickness, or because it's being sent to rest home – we call it "flak home" – then our forty-eight-hour passes will be postponed. But I'll try. I'll do my best. Meanwhile let's eat and make merry. You look splendid tonight. And I notice many men keep stealing glances at you. I am sure that Lt. François de la Bassée would like to attach himself to us for the evening. What can one do?'

'We could take in a show or go to a night club' Jackie suggested. 'Or go dancing?'

'You know' I protested, 'that dancing is not my strong suit.'

'It's time you should practice.'

When it was time for our coffee, the French group came over and la Bassée made introductions. The paratrooper had been training in Camberlay and was now, with his regiment being prepared for the invasion with hard training in hand-to-hand combat and in maneuvers. He was from Paris, where he had been an apprentice to the best *ferronnier d'art* in France; they made gates, big locks, decorative friezes on top of walls, and the metal worker's art had been displayed on the ocean liner *Normandie*. His fiancée, a cute brunette, was originally from Nice and had been working at the French Embassy, where the war and the debacle of 1940 caught her. When the Free French organized the BCRA or Bureau Central de Renseignement et d'Action, which was the Secret Service of the Free French in London and was, among other things, the office that organized the sending and repatriation of French agents in France, she was offered the chance to work for them and took it.

La Bassée came from Brittany; his father was a notary in Paimpol. He had taken pilot training during the lull of the 'phony war' and had escaped from France through the Pyrénées. He had been interned at the camp of Miranda, a transit station between France and England, and later between France and North Africa. In this camp the Spaniards held the escapees from France – the pilots, air crews, volunteers – and made them cool their heels for several months, thereby satisfying the Germans. Then they liberated them and put them in the care of English, American, and Free French authorities, thus satisfying the Allies.

From Miranda, la Bassée had gone on to Gibraltar, and from there to London and training on Spitfires. He had been operational for about six months now and had shot down two Germans. He had been nearly shot down himself a couple of times. He was now an element leader in his squadron and had his own wing man.

I don't remember where we went after we left the restaurant; we might have gone down to the Petit Club Francais. François and I discussed flying, while Jackie, the paratrooper, and his fiancée danced on the small dance floor. La Bassée introduced me to Schloesing, a French Spitfire pilot who had been seriously burnt in a crash. His face was 'tolerably' disfigured because the scars were white. Along with his hands and his eyelids, they had had to rebuild his mouth and lips. But his speech was still coherent and clear, as it needed to be given the importance of radio communications to a pilot. Schloesing was the French equivalent of Hillary. He was an ace, with six victories, and spoke with great eloquence of combat. At the end of the evening, we all exchanged phone numbers and addresses, and Jackie and I made our way back to our hotel, pleased with our new acquaintances.

Once in our room, we undressed, me to my undershirt and underpants and Jackie to her slip, which I discovered to be khaki, like the rest of her underwear. I kidded her about it, but she said, 'You know, many enlisted girls never had as many changes of underwear as they have now, and I don't think that many ate as well as they do now.' She grinned. 'But I don't think I could have used those arguments in my recruiting in Iowa. She slid into bed on the opposite side, but we soon found ourselves hugging and kissing and …

Zounds!

The following morning, we lingered in bed, reminiscing about New York. Jackie took a bath, and then I showered, feeling full of pep. We went down to breakfast. This being the last day of my pass, I checked out of my room (they did not jack up the price due to the double occupancy). I put the now half-consumed bottle of Sauterne in my kit bag, and we started walking toward Hyde Park.

Hyde Park was incredible. It was the great love park of London, with couples in each other's arms all over the place and others picnicking. And there was the speech-making. Anybody could take a soapbox, stand on it, and start talking about anything – you could talk about the war, preach pacifism or a new concept of God, attack the government. It was the equivalent to Columbus Circle in New York, although most of the speakers there were political, often splinter groups to the left of the Communist Party. There was not a bobby in sight.

There were also children in the park, moving between the intertwined couples without paying attention to the necking, and even heavy petting, that was going on in front of everyone's eyes. No doubt the war and the shortage of 'love space' had other privacy at high noon in the park. If you stared, you were improper.

I saw a little boy, perhaps around four or five years of age, running toward us and asking, 'Are you a pilot, or are you a soldier?'

'I am both,' I replied, 'A pilot and a soldier. You want to play with my wings?' I raised him up to the level of my chest, and I felt his body wiggling in my hands like a fish out of the water, quivering so full of life that I was overawed as if for a moment I held the mysterious essence itself.

The child started to play with my wings. 'Be careful now, it has a point. These are wings to fly with. You like them? Well, I like them too.'

His mother, a well-dressed civilian, came over to retrieve her son, in case he was being a nuisance. 'No, ma'am, he's not bothering us at all,' I assured her. 'A cute child you have there. Say, feller,' I asked him, 'what do you want to be when you grow up?'

'A cowboy.'

'A cowboy, huh? Good job that, long hours and no pay. Oh, you want to be a soldier, too? Not bad either. Not so free as a cowboy, though.'

He asked me if I had killed any Germans? I told him, 'Sure, about two or three hundred,' and he announced that he too would like to kill Germans.

'You're a bit young,' I said. 'Wait about twenty years, you'll make it. Here, you want to fly? OK, here is a loop. I grabbed his hands between his legs, and I pulled and lifted at the same time. 'Hop-la! How do you like that? Oh, you want some more? OK – hop-la! Now here is a slow roll.'

I grabbed his left hand and his left foot, and I turned quickly on my heels. He flew, making little squeals of delight as I made him climb or dive, like the flying ride at a county fair. 'What! You want some more? Here is your mother, though, I think she wants you now. Maybe you can come back later – yes, I will still be here. So long, kid.'

'Say goodbye to the nice man, George,' his mother told him. 'And say thank you.'

'Goodbye, thank you.' George rejoined the world of his mother from which I had allowed him to escape for a couple of minutes.

'You will make a good father,' Jackie said.

'You think so? But I lied to him; we are not going to stay here. It's gooey with love making.'

'You are not the first or the last who will lie to him. Or lied for his own good.'

'Of course,' I shoved my hands into my pockets. 'You know, when he asked me if I had killed any Germans I thought of the kids his age that I have killed. But I checked myself.'

'Good for you.'

'I wish I could check my mouth more often,' I told her. 'You know, these kids I have killed – it remains completely intellectual. I have no guilt. I sleep soundly. I have dehumanized the enemy; he is like a bug I have to squash.'

'You have never seen the people you have killed:' said Jackie quietly.

'That's true. At the base, there are devoutly religious airmen, but I have never heard any beefs from them either. The killing of civilians we do is "collateral". We aim at factories. Of course, ninety percent of our bombs fall outside of a 1,000-foot perimeter. What can I do about it? Nothing. But I don't lose sleep over it. After all, I do not intend to kill them. It makes sense that by destroying productive capability we hamper the German war effort, even if destroying that productive capability means that I am killing women and children.'

'I see you still think about it, though,' Jackie observed.

'Yes. I marvel that I can think about it, and that it doesn't trouble me. I heard a Brit civilian say that actually it was the Brits who began the bombing of civilians.' (He was right. The Brits began it.)

'The Nazis have a contempt for human life that we do not have.'

'That's true,' I agreed, 'I think, though, that the question of who began it is immaterial. We are engaged in total war, and we are going to win it.'

'It may be total war, but we have checked each other on gas warfare.'

'I hear it is because gas warfare is very dramatic but very inefficient.'

We walked and listened to the orators on their soapboxes. We heard some violent attacks against Mr Churchill, but many English women at Le Petit Club Français were anti-Churchill as well. The left and the right still existed in England, although without the fierceness of French politics.

Between lunch and the end of the afternoon, Jackie and I managed to talk a blue streak to one another. But we finally ran down, our minds beginning to think about the duties that awaited us. We separated at a subway station, she going to her WAC barracks and I to Victoria Station to catch my train to Bedford. We kissed on the mouth as we parted and held each other, and she did not give me the customary taps on the back that signal that the greeting is friendly but not loving. When it is loving, the arms just linger there around your shoulders, and they don't want to let go.

The trouble started when Jackie began to fall in love with me. At that point I was no more interested in love. Bed, yes, love, no. It already made things more complicated to have a date with her for a definite day, several missions would have to be accomplished first, and it made it just a little more important to return; it implied just a little more contempt for fate. It jarred the delicate edifice of resignation and lack of plans upon which depended a lot of our courage, and when, here in London, Jackie had finally offered me her love, I had rebuffed her. Knowing she would be waiting for me made missions become more foreboding. I would have much more to lose if a fighter got on our tail or flak connected with our plane.

So, one evening, while the Germans were bombing close to our hotel room, and Jackie was a bit frightened and too tender, I cut her short by joking, 'Hey! You wouldn't be falling in love with me, would you?'

She hesitated and said, 'Of course not. What made you think of that?'

'Just an idea.' I smiled. 'Because I couldn't afford it right now.'

So Jackie loved me, and worried about me, and wrote me once in a while, letters that I never answered. I kept on sleeping with her, sharing the two nights of my forty-eight-hour passes between her and whoever I could pick up freelancing. All I could stand from women right now was the deep hollow of their flesh – to wrap my body in the folds of their bodies and have it return me to the primeval peace.

O'Neil had described it well. For a man in combat it had to be that way.

22

PASS TO LONDON

A TASTE OF MY OWN MEDICINE

I have a disconnected memory of a pass to London in early February 1944, when the Germans were pounding the British with what they called 'The Little Blitz'. All I remember now is getting lost on the London subway after taking Jackie home and emerging in the East End during an air raid aimed at the docks.

Here I was, a Yank flyer in the midst of a bunch of Air Raid Wardens who were taking a break after the all-clear signal, before returning with daylight to the ruins to search for the living and the dead. Some were rolling up the hoses they had used on the major fires. Here and there, a few multicolored flames fluttered out of incendiaries, which were burning themselves out. A dresser, askew in the wreckage of a house, was still smoldering.

The Air Raid Wardens had with them some members of the Bomb Disposal Squad, who would check for duds and time bombs set to explode several hours, or sometimes days, after the air raid. These men bore cross wreaths on their sleeves and had been trained for the complicated procedure of getting to the fuses to disarm them, usually by removal. They would report each step they took by portable telephone so that, if they unwittingly triggered the fuse, the next person dealing with a similar bomb and fuse might not repeat the same mistake.

An armament officer in one of our own squadrons had these wreaths on his sleeve. He had been to the school, run by the British, but he had never encountered a dud or a delayed-action bomb that required his special skills. Nevertheless, he spoke as if he were the real thing, just like mail clerks on

leave would try to pass themselves off as air gunners. In 1944, those graduates of the school who had survived the raids of 1940 to 1941, or those on
Tobruk or Malta, were put to work again. Their job took guts, super-guts.
Even the Brits treated them as something special, but in the British way, as
if it were 'nothing at all'.

When the Bomb Disposal Squad spotted an unexploded bomb, they
cleared the area to give their men a safe field, free from any unnecessary
noise or shock. They also cleared the public, including the inhabitants, who
wanted to recover as many of their belongings as possible before looters
or groups of roving kids combed through them for valuables or toys or
clothing, or simply for trophies, which they could trade for money or
other trophies. It was a big deal for the kids when they found a box of
condoms, or 'French letters' as they were then called; they would decorate
the ruins with condoms blown into small balloons, while their elders 'tut-
tutted' in smothered indignation. Clearing the crowd meant that the Air
Raid Wardens had to suspend their rescue work in the same area, and I
wondered how they settled their conflicting priorities.

Everybody was drinking from mugs of hot tea with milk. There was an
ambulatory merchant who sold fish and chips for a shilling. One of the
Air Raid Wardens explained to me that the concussions from the German
bombs brought up to the surface many stunned fish, and for the local
merchants it had been an unexpected bounty. The merchant, in his crimson stand lighted by a few 'carbure' lamps, was pumping his hand-driven
machine to slice potatoes, into French-style chips and then shoving them
into cauldrons of boiling oil to fry them. A cauldron of boiling water was
reserved for the fish. I don't remember, when I got my plate of fish and
chips, if I got a fork. They certainly did not have the American plastic ones.
Did I use my fingers? Anyway, the fish was delicious. I only wish I could
get the same dish today.

I remembered that in Northern France, and in Dunkirk in particular,
before the war there were lots of similar stands, selling French fries wrapped
in old newspapers folded into a cone, *un cornet*. On the windswept beaches
where I built sandcastles or dug for comestible shell fish, I would meet
women with black scarves on their heads and navy blue aprons upon
their black dresses and black cotton stockings. They would have big straw
hoppers on their backs, from which they would sell in town cylindrical
measures, *pintes*, of small shrimps. Others would be fishing for live shrimp
by wading into the water up to their knees and pushing with a long pole
into the sand the nets held by a four-foot board. When they had finished
with fishing, they went home to cook their shrimp and change into dry
clothes before taking the trolley into town to do their selling. They called
out, '*Crevettes grises à vendre!*' – 'Gray shrimps for sale!' Many of these

women had vegetable gardens, and in June they would sell fresh shelled peas, letting their grown daughters do the fishing.

The small shrimps were very tasty. With a cornet of French fries, they made a fine meal for a child who had been running around all morning long on the beach, picking mussels on the rocks or on the planks left by old wrecks, sticking out like ribs in the desert. My French mother would give me one franc, and it would cover my expenses for the day.

And here I was ten years later in England, and I found the same ambulatory merchants, except that the English carts were smaller. The French and Belgian ones often were drawn by horses. The English cart was pulled by the owner, helped by a large dog. But they were all the same crimson color, the same acetylene lamps, the same slicing machines for the potatoes. The Brits used kraft paper for their cornets, which was cleaner than newspaper and strong enough to hold the wet fish as well as the chips.

As dawn broke, I saw more clearly the destruction around. Some houses had been sliced down the middle with only one half left standing. You could see the wallpaper and the furniture as if it were a gigantic doll's house, open to prying eyes; clothing was hung in open closets. Mirrors on the wall would be intact while toilet bowls had been uprooted. Well-made beds stuck out over half floors, ready to topple onto the floor below.

The wardens were organizing the crews to look for people buried in the debris. Luckily most of the inhabitants made it a habit to sleep in the bunk beds provided by the subway authorities rather than take a chance at home. I volunteered to help, but the Air Raid Wardens courteously turned me down. They did not want to be responsible for an airman breaking a leg or receiving a bunch of bricks on the head. They said they had no helmets to spare.

As I lifted my eyes up to one of the disemboweled flats, I saw a young woman, stark naked, fall down into the rubble underneath, arms outstretched as if she had just been released from a crucifixion. She was covered with white dust, probably from the pulverized plaster of the partitions, and she fell a couple of stories into the bricks, the broken planks, the torn blankets, the wash stands, the upside-down tables. We all heard the soft noise her body made when it hit on the ground floor.

A group of wardens rushed to where she had fallen with stretchers, levers and hooks, and a first-aid box. I was left alone next to the fish-and-chips stand, which moved somewhere else to sell its merchandise. A few people started to come out of the buildings and congregate in small groups, discussing the events of the night and how they had escaped the worst damage. Others had come out of the subway shelters to find their apartments burnt out, and they were rushing to see if there was anything left worth salvaging, before the authorities decided to cordon off the ruins.

Suddenly I vomited, right there on the street. Somebody patted me on the back and brought me a cup of tea. I drank and vomited again. Then I heard a voice yelling, 'Hey, Yank! You can dish it out, but you can't take it, right?' Someone else yelled back, 'That's not the way it is and you know it!'

I may have vomited, but I felt no guilt. War is war, we dished it to them, they dished it to us. I killed babies. They killed babies. I did it from 21,000 feet. And it is not the same thing as doing it face to face. I probably, I thought, could not do it face to face, could not even bomb an orphanage knowingly. We did bomb hospitals by mistake, in Brussels, in Lorient, and in other places our people never let us know about.

Someone brought me a wet rag with which I cleaned my face, my uniform, and even my shoes. I was steered to the nearest underground station and somehow found my way back to my hotel. I gave my uniform to an old groom to be cleaned and pressed, and I slept soundly until 2.00p.m., when my uniform was ready. Refreshed, guiltless, I called Jackie and made a date for the evening.

But I did not tell her of the episode. In fact I never told anyone.

20. Standing, left, Walter Bzibziak, next to William Barrett, February 29, 1944.

Above left: 21. William Barrett (left) and Ralston, February 4, 1944.

Above right: 22. Pilot Harry R. Simons (right) with Bombardier William Bonin Jr.

23. Harry Simons (standing, second right) and John 'Tex' Robins (second left). Crew and ground crew.

24. *Penny Ante*'s crew and ground crew. Standing, left to right: Chruby, Streit, Pitts, Marcott, Kundin, Finicle, Williams, Snell. First row: -?-, -?-, Boyovitch, -?-, -?-, Lopez, Owens.

Right and below: 25 and
26. B-17 formations.

27. Schweinfurt.

Above and below: 28 and 29. Russian generals, February 11, 1944.

30. *Penny Ante*'s crew, March 5, 1944. Standing, left to right: Streit, Pitts, Marcott, Kundin, Finicle. First row: Boyovitch, Chruby, Williams, Owens, Snell.

31 and 32. Identification insignias of the 379th Bombardment Group. The insignia on the left, the 'Triangle K', was painted on the aircraft's wing and vertical stabilizer. The triangle was assigned to the First Division, and the 'K' was assigned to the 379th.

33. 'Who did we find on the ground waiting for our arrival? General Doolittle' (bottom right), March 8, 1944.

34. It's over! *Penny Ante*'s crew returned to base for good! Left to right: Owens, Boyovitch, Chruby, -?-, -?-, Streit, Vicars, Pitts, Snell, Finicle, Williams.

35. Orly, France, 1945. The plane is delivered, a gift from the American government to General de Gaulle. Jesse Pitts, fourth from the right.

36. Jesse Pitts is awarded the *Croix de Guerre* by General de Gaulle (Orly, France, September 1945).

Above left: 37. 'What do you mean we've been called up again?' Hershell Streit (left) and Jesse Pitts, Tucson, Arizona. Fourteenth reunion of the 379th, September 1999.

Above right: 38. Navigator Larry Kundin, 2002.

39. Jesse Pitts and *Censored* Pilot Walter Bzibziak.

23

WHISTLING IN THE DARK

THE BAND OF BROTHERS

February 22, 1944. The 379th was alerted. Barring bad weather there would be a raid on Germany tomorrow. Outside my room, I heard the noise of the auxiliary motors charging the batteries, the muffled sound of voices. Ground crews were going out to the planes. I went outside and stopped a mechanic.

'What's the gas load?' I inquired.

'Full Tokyos.'

That meant a deep penetration, bound to be rough, and we were low diamond again. Still, I was alive.

By now the Eighth Air Force was in full swing; we could put up the equivalent of two groups on any one mission. We found out from *Stars and Stripes* that we were out on a series of missions to destroy the German fighter production capacity. *Stars and Stripes* discovered such information from the shot-down colonels, or sometimes even shot-down generals, who talked too much to their German interrogators, who spread it to Swiss and Spanish journalists. The staff of *Stars and Stripes* picked it up from the Swiss papers, or perhaps from Axis Sally or Lord Haw Haw, the British commentator on German radio who delivered much-listened to daily expositions in an upper-class accent, and who after the war was tried and hanged by the English.

Not that we read the paper every day, nor did we listen to Lord Haw Haw regularly. We were not very interested in high strategy. We just did our job. Simply we saw that there were more planes, which now were all silvery because they had discovered that the camouflage paint that covered the older ships like ours was not worth the 300 pounds of additional weight. More planes, more spare parts, and if the gunners wanted more ammunition than the 7,500 rounds usually allocated, there were no problems in getting it. There was the problem of loading this excess ammunition properly. For instance, if we gave too much of it to the tail gunner, let's say 4,000 additional rounds, we might not get the ship off the ground before we ran out of runway. I saw a ship with an overload of ammunition take off, disappear behind a curtain of trees where it had hopped after the initial take-off, reappear, and finally bounce back into the air, but with a precarious hold on its airspeed. The whole crew must have had their hearts in their mouths until their plane straightened out and started climbing again. It was better, we all found out, to store the surplus of ammunition in the radio room. (That's how we learned about center of gravity and proper weight distribution, not through ground school!)

To help prepare for the assault of the land troops against the continent, we had to do the maximum in clobbering the Luftwaffe. German fighters had, on the average, about thirty hours of experience in the FW-190 or the Me-109, compared with our P-47 fighters who had at least one hundred hours. We also were replacing the P-38s and the P-47s with P-51s; we needed a fighter that could go anywhere the heavy bombers would be going and still have enough gas left to both cause trouble for the German interceptors and fight its own way out of trouble.

Indeed, we were on our way to having a fighter that could outclass the FW-190 A-1, conceived in 1940, and the Me-109, which had first operated in 1936 to 1939, during the Spanish Civil War. The North American P-51 Mustang had been built to British specifications in 1940; when the Brits received their first Mustang MK1 in November 1941, they knew they had a remarkable airplane, especially for low-altitude performance, since the 1,200-horsepower Allison engine, with no supercharger, lost power above 12,000 feet. The Allison-powered Mustang's 'top speed of 382 miles an hour was superior to anything the British had,' because of the qualities of the North American wing.

The British had had the Rolls-Royce Merlin engine well tested and debugged; it produced 1,380 horsepower on take-off, and they used it for their Spitfire IXs. It seemed a natural thing for someone to get the idea of sticking the British Rolls-Royce Merlin 61 in the fuselage of the Mustang, but it took five months for it to happen. '… [A] British test pilot first suggested it in April of 1942, and Major Thomas Hitchcock,' an Air Force attaché at the US Embassy in London, 'prodded Washington to attempt the experiments.'

Of course, some modifications were needed to strengthen the body of the Mustang and to fit the heavier and more powerful British engine in its fuselage. 'Rolls did the job in six weeks. The first Merlin-engined Mustang took flight on October 13, 1942 .... On both sides of the ocean, the verdict was the same fifty to sixty miles-per-hour increase in speed to more than 440 miles per hour, at combat altitude. And after that North America couldn't build the things fast enough ... Testing and tooling took roughly ten months. By August of 1943, they were crating the first aircraft for shipment. The first P-51Bs reached England the following month.'[1] A year and a half after the commitment to the program.

Another crucial improvement in the performance of our fighters was the development of external and disposable fuel tanks; some of these were aluminum and others manufactured by the British, were pressed paper. With two 109-gallon disposable drop tanks, a Mustang could fly an additional 850 miles. This meant that it could reach Berlin, cruise around the target, wait fifteen minutes to meet a wing coming late in the bomber stream fight, and come back home without problems. (In October 1943, could we not have put these external fuel tanks on P-47s or P-38s, which were our main escorts then? We could probably have cut down our losses at Schweinfurt by half if not three quarters.)

If we wanted to break the back of the German Air Force before the coming invasion we sent out the bombers as bait, and we clobbered, with American fighters, the German fighters who came out to defend the fatherland. After 'Big Week,' that was essentially the strategy our Eighth Air Force generals followed.

(One of our veterans flew on a mission with General Travis as copilot after 'Big Week' and was indignant when over the radio the General, implementing that policy, challenged the Luftwaffe to come and fight. The joke was that the General shut up after a guttural voice asked in English for the number of the General's aircraft, which was apocryphal embroidery, as the numbers were too small to be read by a fighter moving at 350 miles per hour. What they would have used was the group letter, 'Triangle K', the lead ship's position and identification letter, unique to each ship in a squadron – and very visible. We were K for King, leaders of the second element, lead squadron, lead group. The general should have been E for Eager.)

This policy of using the B-17s as 'bait' for the German fighters was something we knew in the back of our minds but preferred to ignore. Again, we learned it from *Stars and Stripes*, who gleaned it from the blabbings of high Brass to German interrogators. That was one of the prices we paid for having generals who led us from the front instead of some bunker in the rear. At any rate, it did not prevent the Germans from continuing to fly into the lion's mouth, instead of husbanding their planes and, even more, their pilots for the coming invasion.

So, today, full Tokyos. And I thought again, 'Still, I'm alive.' I was perhaps eternal. *What was there to worry about? Let's go and say hello to the crew.*

While the officers had been given separate rooms, rooms for one, rooms for two, our enlisted men had remained in barracks. There were lots of empty beds in my crew's barrack. Where there had been five crews, there remained only two, McCall's and ours.

I found them huddled around the stove, and I was glad to have come, for my arrival seemed to create a welcome diversion. Boyovitch started a somewhat heroic monologue about Hollywood Boulevard with McCall's engineer giving him retorts, both flexing verbal muscles about their knowledge of the world, women and race tracks.

Boyovitch had been in the Army longer than any of us, but he did not have much luck; he had taken cadet training and washed out. He was sent to mechanic's school, made engineer, and worked in airfields before being sent to our group as first engineer. Then he went out on a binge between two trains and was a couple days late reporting from leave. The commanding officer of our training group had had enough of his delinquencies – reporting late from pass, giving lip to master-sergeants and even to the officers in engineering – and since Finicle was also a rated engineer, the commanding officer busted Boyovitch down to sergeant and tail gunner and made Finicle the official engineer for our ship. When Boyovitch showed up at the base sleeping his binge off in a downtown hotel, he found that he had lost his job and one stripe and was now assistant under Finicle, who had been in the Army only six months and had little practical experience. Finicle learned fast though, and Boyovitch resigned himself to a secondary position taking his punishment with good grace.

Though he was often full of wind he would stand up to a good fight anytime he had to. Once in a bar in New York (we all had sneaked out before we embarked overseas) he got into a fight with several sailors, and ten stitches had to be applied to his face. We decided to put him in the tail gun, which was a very responsible position and had also a good publicity rating. Just the same, it was rough on Boyovitch, smart as he was, to be but a staff sergeant destined not to go any higher, and so at times I used to let him fly copilot, coaxing him along and patting him on the back. He'd call out airspeed on final approach, adjust the throttles, raise the wheels, check instruments, and even sometimes fly the ship by watching the artificial horizon. These few times he had the wheel made him feel pretty good, and I really liked Boyovitch a lot. He sported a mustache plus a good belly, and really looked like a Balkan chief – a Balkan chief in exile, dressed in olive drab.

On the other hand, Williams, our right waist gunner, often had me wondering whether he was just dumb, or if that beatific smile was meant to be winsome. For Williams had wit that never ceased to amaze me. He came from the hills of Kentucky and the way he could wisecrack with that vacant look on his face – I couldn't believe the words that came from his mouth. At first glance, you'd write Williams off as a moron, which just proves that you must not judge people too fast.

Williams would lie down on the floor next to the post that held his machine gun, because he thought there was armor plate there and on the side, so he felt more secure He also didn't have to look at the flak. The radio man and the other waist gunner, Snell, would stare at Williams in amazement but never said anything to him, or to me, their pilot, sitting in the 'front office' of the cockpit and acting also as personnel manager. Snell was displeased, yet he didn't know what to say to Williams. Once the surprise was gone, however he looked upon Williams patronizingly, having decided that he was Williams's special protector, and he insisted on taking care of him. In fact Snell insisted on care of everybody. Snell treated Williams as a problem child, and before long he had us believing Williams indeed was one. So Boyovitch, who had discernment for all his big mouth, had come to me before we left for Emden on our first mission and had said, 'Lieutenant, I think it would be a good idea if you said a few words to Williams. Snell has the poor kid believing he's no good. Now, I know Williams has got the stuff. I think if you said something to him to that effect, he would feel better.'

I didn't know Williams any too well, but if Boyovitch said so, he would know. So I went and told Williams we all counted on him, that he was a good man, and that we would all try to do a good job and so forth. And damn it all, as I was talking, I got so wound up that I realized my speech wasn't going to do any good whatsoever – that I might get the kid to feel self-conscious and make it sound that my speech was more put up for my own reassurance than for his. But Williams must have felt that I meant what I was trying to say, though I was so embarrassed I couldn't stop talking. Anyway, Williams went through it all, taking the scares with the rest of us, and he stopped lying down at the foot of his gun unless directed.

The Army does not sanction merit or handle incompetence with infallible wisdom. Someone works hard and competently, keeps a clean uniform, and is present at all formations, yet he stays in the ranks. Another one is always goldbricking and doesn't know a gun stud from an ordinary bolt, but he gets promoted and sent to a good job. By and by, the Army succeeds in getting the right man in the right place, in the same way that when you throw a nickel in the air, eventually the heads and tails coming down will even out. However, you may also have streaks when tails come out ten times in a row.

From this failure to reward with implacable efficiency, the Army curiously enough draws much of its strength, for a failure to be promoted, or being sent into a 'hole' are not infallible signs that the individual is incompetent. Exceptions are so numerous, in fact, that the soldier stuck in an inferior position does not feel it is a just retribution for his lack of skill. And those around him do not draw the inference that he was sent to a particular place because he was no good elsewhere, even though it might be precisely the case. The soldier's self respect is safeguarded, and he can start anew without the handicap of a disparaging judgment against him. Often he will then turn out a good performance, which may not be rewarded but will confirm the feeling in himself and his buddies that he had merely been the victim of bad luck or favoritism. Few men can face their mistakes or, even less, their limitations. The Army can often succeed in placing people where they belong, pushing this one, relegating another, without creating a feeling of merciless competition, which is so contrary to its needs and traditions, and the individual's resentment can be diverted against the Army. The Army has a broad back, and meanwhile the men cooperate and that is the desired goal.

Snell was twenty-eight, the only married man on our crew. He was also a man who felt wounded in his self-esteem by being a waist gunner. While he was the oldest, he had a post of few responsibilities, and he could not hope to make tech sergeant. Like Boyovitch, he felt he had been put in a position beneath his capacity. Boyovitch countered the feeling by an epochal civilian life, Marcott by trying to become lead bombardier and Snell by playing Mother Hubbard to the enlisted crew. Snell however, couldn't take combat quite as well as the others, and it made him ashamed, since it contradicted so much his efforts at leadership. One time over Frankfurt, one of our P-51s turned away from the formation, and at the distance, which often makes it hard to tell whether a plane is coming or going, Snell mistook it for a German turning for a run into us and yelled, 'Jump it, Pilot, jump it!'

So I said, 'Keep your pants on!' But he repeated, 'Jump it, jump it!'

'God damn it! Don't you see he's turning away? Keep your mouth shut!'

Snell apologized profusely when we got to the ground. Too profusely – the crew had judged. Snell kept quiet from then on, but the vertical wrinkles on each side of his mouth grew deeper.

Now, in their barracks, I stayed a little while with my crew, registering their eternal complaints about food.

'It's kind of lonely here, Lieutenant with all those empty cots,' someone remarked.

'You'll get some replacements soon.'

'They don't replace all the good men we lost.'

'Give them time, and they'll become good men.'

'Remember the engineer? He and I used to be good buddies. He missed going down with his own crew, only to get killed two days later with another crew.'

'What's going to get you will get you.'

'Yes and no,' I countered. 'If everyone is on the ball, you've got fewer chances of getting it than if you don't pay any attention to what's going on around you.'

'Hope you're not still mad at me, Lieutenant,' Snell ventured, 'for that mistake over Frankfurt?'

'Listen, Snell, I'd rather have you make a hundred mistakes like that than have you miss a Jerry ship. In this business it's what you don't see that will kill you.'

'Hey, Lieutenant,' Boyovitch grinned, changing the subject. 'I found a steak joint in Bedford where you can actually get steak!'

'No kidding! Real steak?'

'Real steak. Not States' size, but steak.'

'We'll have to visit that place sometime. When we finish our missions we'll have to have a dinner altogether.'

'Ground crew too,' said Boyovitch.

'I think so; they work hard.'

'They sure do, and they sweat out our missions just like we do. Remember, Lieutenant, when we were late from Kiel? Link told me Pat had asked everybody about us and was practically bawling.'

'Where is Chruby?'

'Over at the club, drinking beer.'

'And Williams?'

'Here, Lieutenant. Just grabbing some sack time.'

'That's all he knows;' joked Snell. 'Sleep, drink, or eat.'

'Don't forget the women;' Williams added.

I laughed. 'Say, that's right! I heard you boys had quite a time in London on our last pass.'

'That's right,' replied Boyovitch. 'That was the night the Germans pulled that dawn raid on London. We were somewhere in the West End with some women, and here come the German bombers hedge-hopping over the roofs. Some night! And the women weeping in our manly arms.'

'"Weeping in our manly arms?" Where did you get that one?'

'I don't know. Shakespeare or somebody.'

'Manly arms? So the women were scared?'

'Sure thing,' said Boyovitch. 'Those Londoners don't take the "Little Blitz" so good. They say they're not used to it anymore.'

I asked. 'Snell, were you with them?'

'I'm a married man, sir,' Snell answered righteously. 'I just went to a show and slept at the Red Cross. I saw the raid though. A couple of incendiaries fell right back on our building. I thought the raid was very pretty.'

'What do you mean, "pretty"?' Boyovitch wanted to know.

'I don't know. The planes, the lights, and all. Don't you think it's pretty, Lieutenant? Snell turned to me. 'It's funny right in the middle of a mission, I sometimes stop and look at the fighters going back and forth, and I think it's pretty.'

'Look, you're not there to watch pretty pictures,' said Boyovitch. 'You're up there to shoot.'

'I still say it's pretty,' Snell insisted. 'Mostly when they do acrobatics. Isn't it, Lieutenant?'

'Perhaps.' I rose. 'Okay, boys, don't stay up too late. Goodnight.'

'Goodnight, Lieutenant.'

I didn't really know these men, not even Streit, who flew right next to me. I knew them superficially in relation to our job but we were not real friends. One day we would part; we would promise to keep in touch with each other, and we would never see each other again.

And it was perhaps better that way. Life was too precarious out here. If you made a real friend, that was so much more you lost if he died, and so you had to protect yourself against the possible sorrow. You refused to invest your friendship your love, upon what could be torn away from you so quickly.

Even so, it was possible you cared already more than you would tell yourself, more than you would have wanted to. The group you felt as a part of you, because it was eternal. But you would not acknowledge McCall or Gurney, or Barrett, or Ralston, or Tex because they were mortal. But what would the group be without McCall, without Barrett, without Tex? And we who were the pilots were sworn to protect their lives with our own, if need be. We didn't hear lectures on that, but it was understood, and we never discussed it among ourselves.

My room was cold when I reached it. I had started to write in big gothic letters the names of my missions: EMDEN, BREMEN, BEAUVOIR, LUD … KIEL, KIEL, but I never finished Ludwigshafen. I got as far as L-U-D and gave up. I had drawn a map with lines radiating from our base to the heart of Germany, but we went further than the map allowed, and so I stopped my accounting.

The bed was damp; it was hard to sleep. Every time someone came in the barracks I could hear through the thin partitions the door squeal and grate – *The Inner Sanctum*, all right. Images of combat went through my mind. I rehearsed what I would do if I were attacked from three o'clock. Our #3 engine had a tendency lately to detonate at high manifold pressure.

Might have to check the metering valve on the mixture control – mixture might be too lean. Snell was getting tired; we should get him to flak home. No mail that day. Fowler had a bunch of letters from his sweetheart in the Bronx, but Fowler was missing. Curious how the guys who were missing got all the mail.

The squeal of our *Inner Sanctum* door woke me before Brownlow's assistant Bledmoor did. 'Get your ass out,' he said. 'Breakfast at 3.30, briefing at 4.00.'

Shivering, I got clothed hastily. I cleaned my face and my teeth; that was all the cleaning we had time to do that morning. And the eyes sticky with sleep, the flavor of toothpaste in our mouths, we ran in the dark to the trucks. We piled in, not saying a word, and went to breakfast. Flapjacks. Balls of lead in the stomach. We ate by duty; this would have to last until five o'clock this night. It was not maple syrup they served us, but sugared water, stuff that was not fit for a dog.

Briefing was a ritual. It had suspense and dramatic moments. The room was filled; the map of our route through Europe was covered with a screen. The blackboard where the target was reproduced in colored chalk was draped with a GI blanket, as was the blackboard giving our various positions in the formation. We just sat there, exchanging rumors, trying to guess whether that blue chalk running off the cover on the target chart meant a lake or the sea. If it was the sea, it couldn't be too bad: Emden, Bremen, Kiel. If it was a lake or a river, it might be Schweinfurt.

Finally at four o'clock sharp, the Colonel came in. We all snapped to attention. He gave a quick look then uttered, 'Rest.' His executive officer, Lieutenant Colonel Rohr, knew how we felt. He had once taken Stilts, our communications officer, famed for his stuttering, to Schweinfurt. Stilts normally was a paddlefoot, but he had wanted to see what it was like. He saw plenty. Rohr swore he didn't stutter once the whole of the trip. But once back on the ground, when asked how he liked it, he replied, 'R-r-rough. N-n-ne-never again.' And never again it was.

Positions were revealed. Colonel Preston was the wing leader, and our wing was to lead the division – we would be first over the target. To complete the 41st Combat Wing, the 384th Bomb Group, Triangle P, was to have contributed to the high group but somehow had not shown up that day. It might be rough, all right.

Our own 524th Squadron had filled most of the lead squadron and all of the low squadron of the lead group. I knew all of the commissioned crews by sight, some from playing cards, others from conversation in a chow line, bitching together about the fact that the combat crews were not getting their bacon and fresh eggs as promised. They were the band of brothers. Among them, McCall and his copilot Gurney, and copilots Barrett and Tex were my closest friends, although I did not know whether they considered

me that way. But it was good to know they were all going to be within
100 to 500 feet from Streit and me, who were, as usual, the low diamond,
low squadron of this happy conclave. Two other consolations: McCall and
Gurney would be leading the second element of our low squadron and we
would have the protection of their tail gunner, who had proven himself a
sharp shooter. As low diamond had some flexibility as to where exactly he
chose to fly, I was not going to let more than a hundred yards intervene
between him and our own tail gunner, and we would stay a bit to the left
in order to give him a clear field of fire.

One surprise in all this was the presence of Holt on the left wing
of McCall. I remembered Holt as having been broken to copilot and
transferred to another squadron, his crew dissolved due to the many
aborts on his part and the unruliness of his enlisted men, including
sabotaging the oxygen supply on *Penny Ante* when they were assigned
to fly her once when we were stood down. Here he was, back again
as first lieutenant like all our first pilots, proving that though Colonel
Preston was a tough disciplinarian, he knew how to give a man a second
chance if he showed signs of having straightened up. For my own part, I
never spoke to Holt and was indifferent to his rehabilitation, but on this
mission he did his work.

No two briefings were alike. The boys might come in a mood of anger
because their last mission had been a bad show where lots of mistakes were
made, or they might be jubilant on the strength of a rumor that gave today's
mission as a milk run on the French coast. If there were lots of new boys,
they would sit there with heart flutters and quivering fingertips, as if this
was their first love affair or their first class in high school.

Some would sit during briefing bitching about the target and how rough
it was going to be; others would sit around and show off their unconcern.
A few would sit tense, paying strict attention, determined to do a good
job, faithfully, regardless of the outcome. And some would just belch a few
times and sleep right through it all. Of course, most of us did all these
things: belched, bitched, whistled, resolved to go through with it, wished
it was scrubbed, and didn't think at all.

Finally the screen covering the map did rise, slowly, with all eyes watching intently where the lines of red and blue wool were going to take us
that day. And everybody let out a little gasp, a few curses; some half got
up. And leaning forward, we heard Colonel Rohr say, 'The target for today
is Halberstadt.'

Airplane factories. Not exactly a milk run. We sat down, taking it in.
Some were still whistling; you'd have figured they were going to Berlin or
something, I thought. Self-pity. Those guys would bitch regardless of what
the target was. It was not so much worry as exhibitionism.

When the curtain rose and uncovered a raid to France, everybody would laugh and rub hands, unless it was their first mission. They would say, 'Good deal' or 'Milk run!' If it was a raid to Bremen or Emden, well, that was all right; that wasn't too bad. But the closer it got to Berlin, the more apprehensive we got. Those raids usually turned out to be rough, not exactly 'normal routine'. When the curtain went up on these, the whistling would begin – sounds of 'too-hot potato in the mouth.' Unless you were a screwball, a whistle was a vague protest, a gesture of independence. And 'Rough, rough' we would say. 'Who dreamed that one up?' 'Oh, I wish I was back on the farm.' You know, that kind of reaction.

And a couple of times the curtain would rise, and the colored wool would describe a geometric monster. A dead quiet would settle upon the room. Nobody would have any breath left for whistling, or coughing, or barking, 'Rough, rough' like a dog after a bone. We would think of our wives, of our mothers, of our friends. We would feel ourselves, to see if we were ready to die. Normally we were, in a resigned sort of way willing to take the chance. Sometimes the visiting General will get up and say a few well-meant words in the heroic tradition, which would go over with the American flyers like a lead balloon, lowering our morale a bit more and making those damned buckwheat cakes heavier still in paralyzed stomachs. For a while we would be completely alone. We would have to get ourselves together, get our bitching, our despair, our anger over with quickly. What was the use; we were going. Remember, we were not eager heroes, just plow boys willing to do a job if we were given a fifty-fifty chance to come back.

At the planes, we'd go about the routine of making ready, at peace with ourselves if not exactly cheerful. Perhaps we'd even try to bluff the gunners so they would feel better. We didn't fool them, though they appreciated the effort. Or perhaps we all wanted to fool ourselves, concluding in hurried whispers, 'It won't be so bad!'

Sometimes, then, the red flares would go up. Scrubbed! Not going! Were we happy? I guess we ought to have been, though we would suddenly be too tired to care one way or the other. This body, with its desire to live, too goldbrick to be 'back home on the farm,' which we had fought to a standstill would reassert itself and rejoice. Saved by the bell! And we would lie down like limp rags and sleep in the bunks in the ground crew's tent.

This time the whistling subsided quickly enough. There was no need to get excited. It might be rough, but most likely it wouldn't 'be so bad.' Colonel Rohr explained the details of our fighter escort and gave his diagnosis of the raid as a pretty good set up. And we all had confidence in his judgment. He could call a raid better than anyone else. If Rohr said it was not going to be so bad, it wouldn't be.

Briefing broke up. The copilots went to get their escape kits and candy bars. Normally our ration was one bar of chocolate and one candy bar a week, but on each raid we were allowed an extra bar of candy, which bore the very military name of Mars. Usually we waited until we were back over England to eat it; sometimes we preferred to eat on the way out. It depended upon our hunger and the nature of the target. In a crew there always were those who preferred to eat theirs now and those who preferred to wait.

The truck took us to the planes, dropping us off at each dispersal area. I jumped off, got my gear out, and walked toward our tent. Dawn was beginning to break. The wings and the tail of the ship, definite as day's work and the danger, stood against the flaming horizon. The 'putt-putts' were in action, coughing hesitating, and purring with vigor until the next cough. An engine being run up would whine and then settle to a rhythmic beat. The ground crunched under boots. Stars shone a last moment in the dissolving darkness.

The ground crew was cleaning the frost off our wings. The boys were rather silent this morning. Boyovitch went out with a long machine gun on his shoulder. Finicle was trying his turret. They all knew what the score was and were taking it in their stride. Pat, our crew chief, and I went over the matter of the #3 engine. Kundin came back from the navigators' briefing and gave us his miniature maps. We waited until all the guns were in their positions, checked the time, and the officers swung feet first into the plane. The first plane was due off at 8.00. At 7.50 we began to taxi out with long cries of the brakes. We took our position in line and waited. The Colonel didn't get off until 8.55, and he started to circle the field at 1,500 feet. The others got off at intervals of thirty seconds and more and joined the leader. At 9.15 we took off, the last ones off the field.

24

HALBERSTADT

The Colonel took the whole group formation through a thick cloud bank. For once we were in tight formation so, regardless of the reduced visibility, we could see the ship on whose wing we were flying. The risk of collision had to be taken; when it came down to it, twenty men were not worth twenty minutes' delay. We came out of the cloud bank as tight as we went in.

We flew on McCall's right wing. I rammed our left wing by his cockpit window and started waving at Gurney. During the whole crossing of the Channel we waved and thumbed our noses at each other. We only stopped when I did my 'battle stations' routine.

The visibility was perfect. We entered Holland without the usual flak. Our escort of P-47s was milling around with no work to do, and we entered Germany proper. Soon our escort had to turn around and go home. They were to be relieved by other fighter groups who would carry us further to the target. However, the reliefs were nowhere in sight. Twenty minutes inside Germany and no escort. We spread out a bit so we could have room for evasive action against flak if it should prove necessary, at the same time still keeping a tight formation reference so we could be a tight fighting unit within ten to twelve seconds.

A few minutes went by, rather tense, and at 12.35 a flight of FW 190s attacked us from eleven o'clock, firing cannon and rockets. The low squadron jumped as one, and the formation as we sprang up like a gaggle of geese from a lake, surprised by a hunter, with no one getting in the way of another. Colonel Preston, riding some 300 feet above and to our right, must have been pleased – what an ensemble! A rocket burst about twenty yards in front of McCall's ship. As we jumped, I noticed a large tear in the cowling of our #3 engine. I glanced at the instruments, watching the oil pressure with one eye, waiting for smoke to pour out of the engine. Nothing happened. We settled back to our normal position and surveyed the damage. The cowling on our #3 engine showed an unnatural twist and curl on its bottom, but the bombardier, after taking a look, saw nothing else to report, and the instruments did not budge.

McCall kept on flying without apparent problems, although he had been more exposed to the rocket than we had been. But he had been hit; we could see plumes of gasoline set afire by exhaust fumes starting to eat the trailing edge of his right wing. McCall was done for, due to explode any minute, though explosions in airplane wings obey strange laws. There are planes that blow up within thirty seconds, but there are also planes that land at a British base after having endured a fire for one or two hours.

I called McCall over the command set and told him what I saw. It violated the instructions for radio silence, especially since I called out his name instead of using the number of his ship. I guess I wanted so much to do something for him that I had to warn him. He did not reply but wagged his wings as a way of acknowledging my call. Meanwhile Streit and I decided to get out of his way in case he should explode. I felt cowardly to leave my friend like that. Here his wing was burning and I was leaving him as if he had leprosy. Our leaving him could only mean that he was condemned, and I was ashamed. Later he might reproach me for it, but what could I do? If he exploded in our faces we were done for.

Shortly afterward, his copilot Gurney shot a flare to indicate they were leaving the formation. Our gunners and our bombardier saw them take a course that placed them under the bomber stream and would take them back to England. Meanwhile the crew started to bail out. the distance between their ship and ours increased rapidly, the last I saw or heard of McCall and Gurney was that the ship was under pilot control, the right wing still afire; the reports on the chutes coming out the plane varied, from three to five. If they got out, I was sure that McCall and Gurney would be the last ones to bail out. No one was reporting their ship blowing up. It wouldn't be until much later that we would be able to learn that all bailed out safely and made it to prison camp.

The group was supposed to avoid the Ruhr, and the navigation had seemed quite good given the fact that the cloud cover underneath our planes was so amply thick. So when the flak started bursting in our formation, we assumed that the Ruhr had expanded, not that we were off course. For five solid minutes we went through the stuff, dark and deadly seahorses uncoiling and soon frozen white.

Streit pushed the throttles slowly forward while I gave him 2,300 RPM until we were in McCall's old position, leaders of the second element, no more low diamond. We signaled to our new wing men to close up. Colonel Preston had his wing men tight around him; he would be our model. It was the best protection against fighter attacks, though not against flak or rocket attacks; there you wanted some spread between the ships. Sometimes the best solutions to our problems were contrary and quite incompatible.

Hemphill was not doing a good job of leading the squadron. This was his twenty-fifth mission and we were having a difficult time keeping up with him; his turns were not well controlled. Since he was normally a good pilot, we thought perhaps some of his controls had been shot off by the F-Ws, and he was steering by his trim tabs and his engines.

Coping with Hemphill's erratic lead, we had less leisure to worry about flak, which finally subsided. But then at 12.55 we received a volley of flak that was accurate and substantial. What had happened? A navigation error had placed us in range of some of the guns that defended Munster, and the gunners down there were 'post-graduate'. With a minute our left waist gunner, Snell, was hit by a shell fragment in his left arm, close to the shoulder. Our radio man and right waist gunner, Williams administered first aid and gave him a shot of morphine; they said they could see the substantial piece of flak that was embedded in his shoulder. It must have been nearly spent when it hit Snell, otherwise it could have torn off his arm. Snell insisted he was all right. He was not bleeding very much, at least the blood was not saturating the dressing they had applied to the wound. I asked him if he wanted to lie down in the radio room, but he refused and insisted on standing by his gun. I was impressed. Finally the war had given him the chance to be the man he wanted to be. Could he still move his arm? Could he cock his machine gun? Affirmative to both questions. I asked Williams to check once in a while on the dressing.

So far damage to our ship was minor. There were flak holes here and there; a couple of spare oxygen bottles had been holed through. But the main system was intact. About 300 feet above us, to our front and to our right, was the lead element of the lead squadron, the Colonel with Simons on his left wing and Warden on his right. A quick look to Simons's ship showed small tongues of fire flitting through the closed bomb bay doors; fire in the bomb bay with all the gas lines interconnecting there – that was bad! All those hose connections were not as tight as they should have been; there were small leaks, and the fire attached itself to these leaks like a blood sucker. I put my interphone jack on 'command' and heard some conversation between the Colonel and Simons, who thought he could control the fire. So I went back to monitoring the crew and told Streit of the situation. Streit, who had been monitoring the crew while I was on the command set, switched back to command and took the wheel. Things might get hairy from one moment to the next.

The flames in Simons's ship did not seem to go out. Simons opened his bomb bay doors and three 500-pound bombs fell out with some smoking debris. The crew must have been tripping the latches with screwdrivers while fighting the fire. Bzibziak and Barrett, who led the second element of the lead squadron, had slipped to the left and, like naughty boys, had been looking up into Simons's bomb bay. They backed up a bit, and three more bombs fell out. Then the tail gunner's escape hatch flew out, and we waited for him to bail out, but apparently he changed his mind. Simons and Tex ran a tight ship, and they must have reassured the crew. It was not yet time to take to the silk. I imagined that the radio man and the engineer, who was a good friend of our own engineer Finicle, must have been emptying fire extinguishers on the fire and trying to beat down the flames with empty B-4 bags, while trying to keep their hands from getting burned. One of them must have been on the narrow catwalk, with no parachute and the ground 21 feet below.

For a minute, it seemed that the fire was losing out to the efforts of the crew. But it was only for a minute. Bombs kept falling one by one. The fire grew, though still limited to the bomb bay. Time went by; how long before the final explosion?

Not all the bombs had fallen from the bomb bay. We had counted six; six were left. But the fire must have been getting too much for anybody to work in there. All hands were probably fighting the fire, emptying fire extinguishers, beating the flames with blankets and B-4 bags. Two more missions left to go out of their twenty-five; they would ride the ship as long as they could. Simons was a pretty hot pilot, unbending in his will to get through. Tex must have been praying. I guess we were all praying, even I, the agnostic, though my prayer was somewhat devoid of consecrated words and ran more like, 'My God, man, get that fire out; smother it; use your blankets –!'

The Colonel fishtailed his ship to signal his two wing men to loosen up formation. Streit, who heard on the command set the conversation between the Colonel and Simons, made a sign to me that the Colonel had ordered Simons to leave the formation.

My immediate reaction to the Colonel's order was that it amounted to deserting our friends in trouble. My second reaction was that it was probably the wisest course for Simon to take. Simons took a position to the right of the Colonel and 300 feet above him and held it for some thirty seconds while considering his options. Finally regretfully, he peeled off to the left in a shallow dive that put him ahead of our formation. Then he made a 180-degree turn and came back, facing us but well below us, and I could clearly see Simons and Tex sitting there at their posts in the cockpit to begin their escape from Germany. Nobody had bailed out as yet, and we were all waiting for the bodies to start tumbling down – 'Bail them out, Simons, while you still have time!' – waiting to see the chutes open. We saw them come back about 200 feet below us, and as they were on the verge of crossing our path, the plane blew up. The fuselage cracked open along its whole length in a cauldron of fire and smoke while the wings folded up.

A body was thrown up by the explosion to our level. Both legs were missing, and blood trailed from the empty trousers. Even so, I recognized the massiveness of the body; it was Tex. His chestpack parachute tumbled some ten feet beyond his reach. But he must have been dead already, and the lost parachute made no difference to him. I saw all of it flash because we were well beyond him in less than half a second, although everything seemed to be happening in slow motion.

A large splatter of flames, two engines falling idly, a wing tip. Smoke hanging mid-air; that was all. Simons and his crew had died. During ten minutes of their struggle and agony not a word was spoken on the radio. They fought the fire and died in utter silence. A ship moved up and took their place by the Colonel, and we went on.

Streit and I exchanged a brief, sad glance. We signaled our wing men to tighten up the formation, which had spontaneously loosened up not only in the lead squadron but in the low squadron as well; no one had wanted to risk getting caught in the explosion of Simons's ship. Now it was over; it was behind us. I felt drained, with an especial fatigue around my eyes. We still had about an hour to go before we could reach our target. Usually I ate my Mars bar when we were back over the Channel, as a sort of reward to myself for having been a good boy and done my job. This time I could not wait; I needed some nourishment in my system.

After I had gobbled down my candy bar – candy bar in one hand, oxygen mask in the other and alternating Mars bar and oxygen – I felt better and checked in on the crew.

'Sergeant Snell, how are we doing back there?'

'Okay, Lieutenant. It's really nothing to worry about.'

'Very good. You're going to get the Purple Heart for this, but don't try to tough it out too much. Lie down when you feel like it. We still have three hours to go before we land at the base. Over and out.'

We reached the initial point of the bomb run at 13.53 hours. The IP, the initial point of the bomb run, between two and ten minutes of straight, level flight where no evasive action was possible (or tolerated), which gave the bombardier the chance to line up his sight, was the most dangerous moment of the mission as far as flak was concerned. We were going at about 190 miles an hour, ground speed, and as we approached Halberstadt and the area where the aircraft factory was supposed to be, we saw a cloud right over it.

The group formation obliqued to the right of the target and they made a 180-degree turn to the left, but the target was still covered by a cloud. According to the bombardier, the winds aloft were traveling at about fifty miles an hour, and one minute, two at the most, was all we thought we needed for the bulk of the cloud to be out of our way.

We finished the turn, and the formation flew as if on parade; nobody got whiplashed out of position. But – the cloud still sat over the factory area, and we were moving much faster since the winds were with us now, instead of against us as they had been on our initial approach. We were now moving at about 300 miles an hour, ground speed, and we could see straight ahead a little town, Wernigerode, which circumstances now revealed as an alternate target of opportunity. And this in fact was where the bombardier in the Colonel's plane was taking us.

As we came close, we could see the red roofs, half covered with snow, and clumps of fir trees; it looked like a German Lake Placid. The group unloaded about 220 bombs of 500 pounds each on that little town, smack in the middle. No flak, no fighters to disturb us. Later, back at the base, they would tell us that the town of Wernigerode was a flak home for the Luftwaffe, so we might have taken out some experienced German pilots in what appeared to some of us as a senseless killing of civilians. We suspected, though, that this was a story put out by our PR officers to alleviate our guilt.

On our last few missions, many of us had lost our sensitivity about targets. As I had experienced on my last pass, when the Germans bombed London they made no pretense of going for strategic targets, so why should we? Nevertheless, I could not help thinking of the *Hausfrauen* cowering in their basements with children pressing themselves against their warm and quivering bodies. One good thing for the German civilians about our method of salvoing or toggling our bombs as soon as the first bombs came out of the lead ship, was that if they were the target of just one group, it was all over in a minute. If they were still alive after that minute, they would probably be safe; and we were never going back over Wernigerode. I saw all of this in my mind's eye; still it left me emotionally cold.

The bombardier of the low group, which was following us a couple of minutes or so behind, thought he saw a clearing over the town of Halberstadt so he decided to go after the factory that was the goal of this mission. I think he missed the factory.[1] Meanwhile, our Colonel was leading us into a series of 'S' turns to permit the low group to catch up with us. When they had, we resumed our exit from Germany, skirting the Ruhr all the way.

But we still came close enough to enable the German 88 guns to bear on us and give us a few accurate salvos. At 15.05, near Koln, the right wing man of the Colonel, Warden, was hit by flak and went down in a spin. When a ship went into a spin, it was very difficult for the crew to get out, because they were riveted to their ship by the centrifugal force; from Warden's plane, four chutes were seen. At about the same time, a ship from our high squadron suffered a direct hit from flak, which blew off most of his right wing; no chutes were seen. A while later, a fifth ship went down from the low group. His #3 engine had been feathered, and he had been straggling; he was attacked by a Me-210 and several FW-1 90s. The ship went down under pilot control, yet no chutes were spotted.

Were our P-5s is unable to give this ship protection? Although there were miscues and missed rendezvous, most crewmen saw the P-51s around the target. But they were not there when they were most needed, as happened frequently in war.

As we continued to skirt the Ruhr, there was more flak. Morse got hit, put his wheels down, and dropped out of sight. Sloane got his wing chopped up and went down in a crazy spin. We were wondering what had happened to the lead navigator, that he would take us over the Ruhr this way. Whose fault was it? The fault of the lead navigator? The fault of the Colonel for not getting the navigator on the ball? The fault of the crosswinds, unpredictable in their direction and intensity?

And our lead bombardier, who had been responsible for the pattern, at the second Schweinfurt, one of the best of the whole war − what had happened to him? Bad luck pursued the Halberstadt mission.

Fighters hit us again at the Dutch coast but very ineffectively. They were trying long-range deflection shots with the thumb holding the button down until they had no more ammo − a quick and relatively safe way to be done with their duty.

Back at the base at about 17.00 hours, we learned that in the Colonel's ship, the Colonel, his copilot and the lead bombardier had been wounded. The Colonel was taken to Diddington, as he had some pretty bad shell fragments in his foot. The boys were talking loudly about what a good job Simons had done getting out of our formation before he blew up.

The lead bombardier's bombsight had been broken by flak. He had dropped by estimating, and his estimate had not been so good. Hemphill, the pilot leading the squadron, had had his rudder shot away, hence his over-controlling. One ship had been lost from the low group. Our group had lost four.

We were all somewhat haggard that evening. Tex Robins was dead; never would he wake me at odd hours to celebrate with him, though I would then have willingly been roused up every night if that would have brought him back. There had been harder missions but rarely were we given to witness the agony of a crew, knowing their frantic efforts to escape their fate.

I walked back to my room.

Later, O'Neil, who had not gone on this raid, met me in McCall and Gurney's room. This time it was to get first dibs on scavenging the spoils. Frankly, I did not know what to take. I decided I could use a flashlight, so I packed it away in the large paper bag I had brought to this expedition. I added a can of shoe polish. A brand new tube of toothpaste went, without guilt on my part, into the bag. I imagined the families would want their leather jackets, and their tailored Eisenhower jackets as well. The latter I had tried, the last time I was in London, to buy. I was offered a nearly finished jacket whose owner had not called for his last fitting two months previously; very likely he had been shot down. Was I interested? The tailor would give me a good price on it. I told him no thanks; it had cooled me off once and for all on Eisenhower jackets.

Still I had to take something.

I knew that certain personal effects were the property of the missing man's family. Others were available for 'sharing'. The family probably was not interested in socks and shoes or shirts, though a wife or mother might be. Tomorrow, after it had been ascertained that the missing crew had not simply been marooned on some British base near the coast, the supply clerks would come to do their inventory of what could be sent back to the families, including wallets, letters, and photographs. (The latter two sometimes required some censorship especially if the 'missing in action' were married.) When the clerks had finished, they would roll the mattress up which signified that the bed was now available for assignment to a 'replacement'.

By pilfering, I was doing what I used to despise. But the presence of O'Neil reassured me as to the legitimacy of what I was doing. I opened a drawer and was confronted by a fat wallet and some bars of chocolate. I took all the chocolate and ignored the wallet. I didn't even have a fleeting temptation. O'Neil took a couple of bottles, but I was not interested. I took McCall's coal scuttle, for which I had no use since I had a paraffin stove rather than a coal one.

The morning after, I had recovered my senses and returned the coal scuttle. I wondered, why did I fiddle with this mild pilfering? What was I trying to do? Almost sixty years after the fact, I think I know. I was trying to desanctify my friends; this was a way to begin their burial and to separate my world and their world. Thus their ghosts would not haunt me and beckon me to join them at a moment when all my strength had to be devoted to my duty and to preserving my life as the means of accomplishing that duty.

By taking advantage of their physical absence to steal from them, I denied our friendships. I treated them as if they were just part of the crowd, and we had no obligations to one another.

There had been a couple of times when I had felt on the verge of surrendering to the call of ghosts. Oschersleben had been one of them. I was not one for whom the call of ghosts would mean great fear or 'bugging out'. Rather it would mean that I had become indifferent to the struggle and wanted to rest. My betrayal of my friends would render me less vulnerable to the call of their ghosts.

By now I had learned that, for me at least, the burial of the dead was a crucial condition for staying alive. Robbing the dead was a crude way to take my distance from past friendships; they had their world and I had mine, and it was imperative there should be no confusion between the two. I had eight more missions to go. All my friends, except for Barrett, had been killed or were missing in action. I had given up the love of Jackie because too much involvement in the relationship made it harder for me to fly my missions, and it was very important to me that I do my job well. Detaching myself from both the living and the dead left me with only the identification with the band of brothers. We had the same problems and needed few words to understand one another.

Better to put other relationships into the freezer and hope that we might find them when, once more, we needed them.

25

SCHWEINFURT REVISITED

Two days after the raid on Halberstadt we were briefed for another deep penetration mission. This time when the curtain over the operations map was lifted, the lines of red and blue wool converged right in the heart of Germany. It was Schweinfurt. This was the target where on August 17 and on October 14, the dates of the two previous US attempts on the town, the Eighth Air Force had suffered the highest losses it had ever endured. In both Schweinfurt I and Schweinfurt II, on each raid, sixty B-17s had failed to return.

After the various groans, sucked in breaths, and catcalls that greeted the disclosure, we were told by the Intelligence officer that this time we would have fighter escort all the way in and out of Schweinfurt. The P-47s and P-38s that would provide the bulk of our escort had received new external wing tanks, which gave them enough range to fly and fight over the target. So, we were told, it would be quite a different story from the first two Schweinfurts that the veterans of 1943 had faced.

I tried my best to convince the crew that the conditions of the mission had indeed radically changed, but I am not sure that my verbal exertions had much effect. The enlisted men had heard versions of my talk about other raids, and when they had come back from those raids, they had heard various stories about fighters having missed the rendezvous with the bombers, about the flak being thicker than expected, the lead navigator having mistaken one German town for another, about a group that was supposed to have joined our wing getting lost on the way to the meeting point. This time I felt I had convinced no one except myself and left them braced for the worst.

February 24, 1944. Schweinfurt III. Our crew was not the only one affected by the gloom. As we entered Germany from Holland, I observed that the number of aborts seemed larger than usual, until I remembered that this was the point of no return. For those in our wing and in our division who had discovered deficiencies in their ships that made the mission a losing gamble, this was the time to turn back home.

About this time also, Boyovitch and Snell came to the cockpit and complained to me that there were 'bad engine noises' in #2 and #3 engines. In spite of having been relegated to tail gunner, Boyovitch still knew how to read engine noises better than I could read Shakespeare. So when he showed up with Snell, I was worried that something serious was afoot.

Still, the instruments did not show any variation from normal, and I could not hear the noises that Snell reported. Boyovitch stayed silent while Snell was describing the pings and pangs that he heard from the two inboard engines. I looked at Streit and said that I would go to the waist section and listen to the engines from that area. Streit replied, with a wink for my benefit, 'Good idea.' I disengaged my oxygen mask from the main system and picked up one of the 'walk-around' oxygen bottles, available for emergencies and good for about ten minutes.

In the waist, I could still hear no suspicious noises, and I told Boyovitch and Snell that I could not hear what they heard. I offered them the chance to speak to the first pilot about it. They declined. Boyovitch returned to his post as tail gunner, morose but ready. Snell was trying hard, now that he saw that I was persisting in my refusal to entertain any thoughts of aborting, to show a belated eagerness for the mission. I ignored his conversion, but as I went back to my seat, I asked our right waist gunner Williams how he was feeling that day, and he replied, 'Fine.' And as I went by Snell, I tapped him on the shoulder and said, 'Don't worry; I think the engines will hold.' His face broke out into a big grin, and as I turned away, I thought that Snell would be all right for the rest of the trip. He was even claiming some hits on a Me-109. Since he had never made a similar claim before, I was inclined to second his report of a 'damaged' enemy fighter. He and Boyovitch might have had a case of jitters, but the chance to talk to me and have their diagnosis challenged without prejudice seemed to have dissipated their 'Schweinfurt blues.'

As I sat back down in my seat and reconnected my oxygen mask to the main system, I reported to Streit with a gesture of my hand that I had no confirmation of malfunction in the two engines. With a smile in his eyes, Streit told me to get on the command set and listen to the radio traffic, while he covered the intercom.

The intercom played a crucial role in making the band of brothers available to the crew. The chatter could be bothersome at times, especially when someone in serious trouble was trying to communicate it to the front office. So pilot and copilot would often ask, over the intercom, for more discipline less chatter, more 'short bursts' of gunfire. Was it effective? Not very. But to those who were isolated in the ship tail gunner, ball turret, radio man – the intercom was life itself. It was a good antidote to fear, because each one was expected to keep his voice down and controlled and to give a good account of himself. Only Kundin was immune to the social pressures of the intercom.

Taking over the controls and listening to the radio traffic, it took me a couple of minutes to reorient myself, but soon I realized that by some quirk of the airwaves I was listening to the B-24 of the Second Division, who on that day had been sent to Gotha, a town some fifty miles north of Schweinfurt. They were being clobbered by swarms of German fighters. Our wing had fighter escorts and they had none. They were asking us, over the radio, if we could spare some of our fighters. Once in a while I heard a mayday distress call from a bomber on fire underlining their anguished requests.

Poor B-24s! Their predicament was the counterpoint of our good luck. But I would not say we were very sorry, except out of politeness. In these messes you thought of your crew, of your squadron, at the most, of your group. The rest could go hang. If you and your buddies could get back, the world could crumble. It was their tough luck. The band of brothers had its geographic limits.

Our crew had never had a squadron of enemy fighters line up to shoot us down personally. We had never had a fire on board that could not be extinguished in less than ten seconds. We had never lost more than one engine to flak and fighters. Our ship *Penny Ante* had never come close to a stall or a fall off on one wing that heralded a deadly spin. That was our luck. We now knew that there were nasty events that no amount of skill could control. We had to remain lucky. Everybody in the squadron believed that we had a lucky ship. Crewmen who had one or two missions to finish after the rest of their crew had already done their twenty-five would ask Brownlow to schedule them on our ship, and Brownlow would oblige if at all possible.

We were slippery noodles, I thought, and I laughed in my oxygen mask, which reminded me to massage the tube leading to the oxygen tank to make sure it was not blocked by the ice condensing from my breath. No, all was well. Perhaps the noises heard by Snell and Boyovitch were due to anoxia rather than anxiety! I ran an oxygen check with the whole crew. Everybody was alive and well.

On this raid to Schweinfurt, Streit had been given the responsibility of leading the high squadron. The first half of the mission had been easy, with little flak and few fighter attacks, all from the rear. Our bombardier warned us now that we were coming upon the IP. Visibility was good; he could see well ahead and he had a Norden bombsight for a change. Normally he toggled his bombs on seeing the first bomb drop out of the squadron leader's bomb bay; today he would be the master of the high squadron's bombs.

As I was congratulating myself on leading the squadron over the famous target and having everything go smoothly so far, I felt a slight jar to our left. I saw right away the #3 engine was not pulling its weight anymore, and as my eyes scanned the instrument panel, I immediately concluded that the engine had run out of gas. I rushed to raise the RPM on all the propellers and shoved the throttles forward. I gave the order to Finicle to leave his turret and attend to the business at hand, but he had felt the jar also and knew instantly what the trouble was. He rushed to his fuel-transfer valves that were in the front section of the bomb bay and started to transfer gas to the dry #3 gas tank. I retarded the throttle on #3 engine until it kicked in and raised the manifold pressure on all engines to thirty-five inches.

By that time we were some 150 yards behind the group leader, and we had to catch up without overrunning him. Already, when our #3 had gone dry, our two wing men had nearly overrun us and had had to chop their throttles only to push them forward again, creating an accordion effect throughout the squadron. Our second element had the same problem, though a bit attenuated, and I could imagine the curses they were throwing at us.

As copilot, I should have checked the gasoline supply shortly before we reached the target, admonished Streit, and started transferring gas before we began the bomb run. But I had the controls, I was responsible for the flying. Streit should have been responsible for my job until he took over the controls. But he had probably been sleeping, although ready to take over at the slightest change in conditions and not worrying about the gas supply, since it was theoretically my function. I might not quite approve of his policy, but while Streit was acting as aircraft commander, and I was copilot, subordinate to him, I would nevertheless abide by it. And at Schweinfurt, our engineer was giving priority to his job in the turret rather than thinking of gas supplies, something I could understand in view of the reputation of our target. He was not responsible. Under Streit's supervision, I was.

So in the ambiguity of my role as copilot, and while I was acting as pilot without being pilot, the job of checking the gas supply was not discharged, and with no red light coming on the instrument panel to warn us, we fell through the cracks.

Should I have passed the lead of the squadron to the ship on our left, the designated deputy lead? I did not think of it at the time. We had a Norden bombsight; the four engines were purring smoothly. We would be back in our normal slot and at cruising speed within the next two or three minutes ahead of the 'bombs away' signal. We kept our position as lead.

Our group was seventh in line to bomb the target. After us, two more groups came through the smoke and the dust to drop their bombs, and ten to twelve hours later, the RAF blitzed the whole area with double our bomb load, concentrating especially on the fires we had left behind.

A couple of seconds after the group lead ship, our squadron had released its bombs. As revealed by the pictures we were taking automatically, our bomb pattern was a little behind and to the right of the main bomb pattern. Instead of the ball-bearing assembly plant, which was our designated target for the day, we clobbered a jam factory.

The morning after there was no critique, since we were scheduled for a mission that day, so I did not have to explain what happened. Nobody asked me except the pilot who would have had the lead had I surrendered it to him during the bomb run. I told him that it had not come to my mind, that our four engines had been working well and the run had probably been less disrupted by our keeping the lead than surrendering it, that we had had a bombsight whereas I was uncertain that they did. The fact is, almost sixty years later, I still feel guilty about the mission.

As it turned out, the Second Division, sent on an average mission to Gotha, wound up meeting a 'Schweinfurt' of its own. They had dispatched 239 ships on the mission. Of these, 169 reached the target; the great majority of the seventy missing had aborted, and the rest had been shot down reaching Gotha. The total losses, coming and going, had been thirty-three ships, nearly twenty percent of the effective force. On the other hand, the First Division had lost eleven ships out of 238 effective: 4.5 percent.

As we did not find out until later, the trouble with Schweinfurt III was that 'Schweinfurt was only about sixty percent as valuable a target in February 1944 as it had been in October 1943.'[1] The management of the plant had begun to disperse its manufacturing either into the woods or into underground workshops that were largely invulnerable to our 500- or even 1,000-pound bombs.

The 379th had lost only one crew member, a waist gunner hit in the heart by a flak splinter. The pilot had warned the tower that he had one 'seriously wounded' on board. The medics knew that this was frequently a code for a dead man. If a pilot had seriously wounded men on board, he would have landed at one of the first British bases he encountered on his way home. After all, on only two or three engines, Kimbolton was between thirty to sixty minutes from the coast, depending on where you crossed and your ground speed.

This did not, however, mean that a pilot would necessarily land early. The pilot of a plane that had been badly hit would sometimes run home as if the Germans were still after him, forgetting his crewman bleeding in the radio room, if his copilot did not remind him of his obligation to turn over a wounded crewman to the medics as soon as possible. Otherwise, few crew members, unless especially attached to the wounded, would dare break into the stream of consciousness that possessed some first pilots as they drove relentlessly toward Kimbolton. (A pilot who would eat his candy bar on the way home was more accessible.)

On this mission, the waist gunner had collapsed on his gun and died instantly, without agony. On the ground, the medics came to take his body. Our flight surgeon was with them and was quizzing the crew for details, which he could consign to his report. He unwrapped the bundle of blankets surrounding the dead man's body and saw for himself the entry wound, and then he flipped the blankets back, signaling the four corpsmen that they could take the body to the morgue. It had been his second mission.

26

THE NINETEENTH MISSION

STUTTGART

Our first and only abort was on our nineteenth mission. By that time we had become real professionals, but that morning, after the briefing to Stuttgart, we were tired, very. Our bodies were sweaty, with a queer tremor in the muscles. This would be our third raid in four days, a solid week of alerts.

Penny Ante was out of commission; the ground crew had discovered that there was damage to the main spar of the right wing. Instead of her we were to take an old crate, whose status was questionable. When Streit and I arrived at the airfield, the ground crew, who were not our own, were running her up, trying to get the oil pressure of the #1 engine up to par. For a while, it was a toss up whether the crew chief would release the plane to us. The target was Stuttgart – nine hours – and we were to assemble over an overcast. We told him, 'Take your time; do what you please.'

But Streit took me aside and told me, 'This is going to be rough. We expect lots of fighter attacks.' I was rather surprised, because Lieutenant Colonel Rohr had told us the set up was pretty good, and I couldn't imagine where Streit had found his pessimism. But I was in no mood to argue, so I took it in – *Okay, it might be rough*.

By the time the crew chief was finally satisfied, we were late taking off. After we had climbed above the overcast, we couldn't find the formation anywhere. We began hunting for it, tagging along different formations, trying to read the letters on their stabilizers. Shortly into our search, I noticed the oil temperature on the #1 engine was way up past normal and drew Streit's attention to it. As we continued our pursuit, the oil pressure started to oscillate, dropping to forty pounds and climbing back up again. Streit turned to me and said, 'What do you say, Pitts, we go home?'

'Well, I don't know,' I replied. 'You're the boss.'

'Sure, I know.'

'Well, let's wait a bit longer and see how it turns out.'

And we kept on.

Stuttgart. If we lost #1, it would be a hell of a long ride on three engines. This was quite a challenge. Our gas consumption would then climb to a point that would leave us no margin of safety. If it had been only the oil temperature, we might take the chance that it was merely an instrument failure, but the oil pressure too? What could that be? Broken or damaged oil pump?

I knew too well I wasn't very eager to go, but I was reluctant to give in to that feeling. If I had been alone, I might have taken a longer chance. But the boys and Streit were not too eager either. And if I showed myself too much in contradiction with the first pilot and the secret desire of the crew as well, I might lose much of my influence and thereby affect the unity of the crew, which is as essential to its survival as four engines and guns. Furthermore, this #1 engine was likely to burn up on us. Could we afford the chance?

We kept on chasing formations and finally found one that belonged to our wing. We were set. Things had seemed to stabilize a bit. The oil temperature had ceased climbing, though it kept way above normal.

And then the oil pressure started dropping again.

I threw up my hands in disgust and told Streit, 'Let's feather it.'

But the propeller wouldn't feather, creating an additional argument for aborting. A windmilling propeller was a drag on the plane and a potential danger if it spun off, as many of them did.

We turned around and went home. After we landed, Streit went to write his report, and we went to bed.

The inspector chewed out Streit for turning back. The ground crew, though, found that the oil radiator was not functioning. Streit did not go to critique, so I stood up and gave our explanation. Brownlow said that whatever we did was okay by him, because he trusted our judgment. It was our first abortion in nineteen missions.

Even though I felt a bit guilty about it, that #1 engine had done us a good turn by acting up and giving us an excuse to turn around and go home. We had been willing to go on the raid, but on that day, it wasn't just our plane. We ourselves were not functioning properly. Our hearts were just not in it. We were tired, and we were stale. As it happened, the mission to Stuttgart had turned out to be mostly a milk run, which alleviated my scruples. It would have been hard to bear, having left your friends go to a tough mission without you.

If a mission was of supreme importance, and if orders were to proceed at all costs, a usually understandable excuse for aborting could be seen instead as cowardice and refusal to obey. But it was rare that the situation was so clearly defined. The interpretation of a situation and final decision about it were left entirely up to the crew and its leader. If a pilot aborted, he stood up at critique and rendered to his superiors and his peers his account for his decision.

The Colonel, of course, was very vocal and usually less than indulgent. His remarks would range from 'Tough luck; that old crate needed an overhaul anyway,' to 'This is your third abortion isn't it?' to 'Your abortion showed poor determination to carry out the mission – your tour of duty will therefore be twenty-six missions.'

At critique, all the mistakes were discussed publicly. Well, relatively. It was pretty hard for a shavetail like a second lieutenant to ball out a lieutenant colonel in public. You might bitch in private, but a lieutenant Colonel? Better to take it easy and keep your comments to yourself. Or wait till you were both drunk. And so we would listen and pass silent judgment.

On the other hand, shavetails could expect little reticence from a captain on up. On one particular occasion Roach was on the carpet giving the reasons for his abort. 'My #3 propeller ran away, and I pulled out of formation to feather it.'

Here Captain Brown stood up. 'Why did you do that? You don't to pull out of formation!'

Well, if anybody had no right to talk, it was Brown. On one mission over Bremen, he had been leading a squadron when one of his props ran away. He had pulled out of formation without signaling to the deputy to take over, so the others just followed him on out as well. Roach had been one of them. It was his second mission and he hadn't known any better As a result, he was attacked by Me-109s and was pretty shot up that day, all because of Brown taking them out of formation.

And now Brown was opening his big mouth. I could see Roach getting mad. But Lieutenant Colonel Rohr bent over and whispered into his ear, and Roach settled back and just took it all in. When critique was done and we were dismissed, we went over and shook his hand and told him what an ass Brown was. Sure, we knew Roach had made a mistake, but anyone can, and it was not Brown's business to rub it in.

'You know what Lieutenant Colonel Rohr said to me?' Roach told us. 'He said to just ask Brown what he did over Bremen.' We all laughed and agreed that Rohr was sure a hell of a good guy. Although second in command after Colonel Preston, a rank that should normally have excluded him, he had remained still a marginal member of the band of brothers. And we liked flying behind him; he was as eager as General Travis, but he kept our friendship.

Brown was from the original cadre. Sooner or later he would get a chance to lead the entire group. Why should he get the break when among the replacements were pilots who were better than he was? I couldn't completely blame the old boys for helping each other out; after all, they stayed overseas longer than the replacements usually did, and it was not altogether a bad idea to make people feel that being part of a group entitled them to some privileges and a better chance to make good. In the long run, a person is more apt to give his best to an organization if he is removed from the constant strain of competition, and if he knows he may err once in a while without drastic consequences to his status. In addition, he might not be so reticent about showing initiative. Only those who never try don't make mistakes.

Which Brown certainly did. The time came when Brown had been group leader on a mission, and it had been lousy. At critique, we sat bitching silently to ourselves, and suddenly from the rear, a new guy stood up and demanded, 'Why in hell weren't we in formation yesterday? No one was in formation. The squadron had a hell of a time staying with the group leader, and we never even got into wing formation.'

Brown replied deprecatingly, 'Oh, him! Don't pay any attention. It's his first mission.'

This wasn't true, it was his third. All of us laughed and cheered – that kid was telling the truth, even if we didn't have the eagerness or innocence left to say so. The Colonel knew it anyway without telling him, although he didn't say a word, and I bet that Brown got his butt chewed plenty, especially for the remark he made about the kid being too green to know what he was talking about. The Colonel has a way of making you feel pretty small and stupid with just a few words.

Sometimes at critique you could get a couple of good laughs. The day we came back from Chateaudun, the Colonel was in the tower explaining things to a bunch of visiting Russian generals. We had been expected to put on a good show, but, of course everything went snafu. Luckily enough we had a good formation when we came back over the field, and our Brass was keeping their fingers crossed hoping our windup would be more impressive than our beginning.

The Colonel got a hold of the flare pistol and announced, 'I am going to shoot a red flare in front of a bomber, and instead of landing, he will go around.'

The interpreter explained and the Russian generals nodded their heads gravely: 'Yes, very interesting.'

So, at the first opportunity off goes a red flare.

But Duvall, who is the victim of this demonstration, instead of going around goes right ahead with his landing. He had been practically on the ground anyway, and he could see no obstructions, and *What the hell*, he thought, *let's land and get out of here*. The Russian generals were left grinning, wondering if they had understood correctly. And so at critique, Duvall got chewed out.

'Duvall!'

'Yes, sir.'

'Are you color blind?'

'No, sir.'

'Are you unaware what a red flare means?'

'No, sir.'

'Then why didn't you go around when I shot that red flare in front of you?'

'Well, sir, I was practically on the ground at that time and couldn't see any obstructions.'

'Well, Duvall you just never mind what you see or don't see. The time you see a red flare, you just go around. Understood?'

'Yes, sir.'

At this point, the Colonel had worked off his humiliation. He could even smile now. Hell, we all laughed, thinking about those Russian generals trying to understand what was going on. We just wished we could have seen the Colonel's face when Duvall landed!

On the Stuttgart mission, Larson, who flew a 'spare', had taken our place in the low diamond after we had aborted. On that day, Davis had vanished, and McCall had come back on two engines. Larson had barely missed being shot down and was late reporting in. I saw him at interrogation, where he was feverishly telling his story. His tail gunner had apparently been wounded and bailed out, perhaps out of panic, but perhaps also because he was afraid of bleeding to death before they got back to base. At high altitudes you bled much more profusely because of the reduced pressure of the atmosphere. Larson had had one engine shot up and had not been able to feather it; the prop fell off when he landed.

When we saw him at debriefing, we told him, 'Good job, boy, good job.' Someone from engineering came and told him they had found an unexploded 22mm in his gas tank. Larson went pale, and I thought he was going to faint. If that shell had exploded, it would have been curtains. Larson didn't say a word to anyone.

In subsequent missions, he kept drawing low diamond. I knew it got him mad; he thought Major Culpepper wanted to get rid of him. At Frankfurt, he got badly shot up again. This stuff was going too far. Larson was getting jittery. You might have thought they would have given him safer positions to fly, but Larson was a good flyer, and it might not have been a good idea. If you treat someone as if he's sick, he might get sicker. It might be better to ignore whatever trouble there is. And it was not so easy to determine what was just talk and what might really mean something. Larson bitched, but so did all of us.

The Russian generals came for another visit. That day we had a raid deep in France, and we were once again expected to do a bang-up show for the edification of our Russian allies. The Colonel took the generals up in his own plane to show them how we assembled in group formation, then in wing formation, and then how tightly US bombers flew in formation. As usually happens when you're trying to show off, we were more rotten that day than ever. It was the worst group formation we ever flew, and we never even got in wing formation until we had crossed the French coast and the Colonel and his distinguished guests had turned back.

Larson had been the last to take off, having been delayed by minor trouble. The Colonel took off thirty seconds after him. The Colonel found our group formation; Larson did not and aborted. The obvious conclusion was that Larson had not sought very hard for us. We felt sorry for him; the situation was getting somewhat out of hand for him. He was a good flyer, just not tough enough. I might have felt the same way if I had had his luck, but the Colonel could not afford to let this pass. I imagine he suspected the state of affairs, but he could not put his arm around Larson's shoulders and say, 'Too bad, Larson, take a week off to flak home.' Or perhaps, indeed, he did not know. And how could Brownlow, usually so perceptive, ignore or not see a situation of which most of us were aware?

Larson was not a coward, but he was tired. There were deep lines in his face. We felt towards him as you do towards a younger brother who has been severely punished by your father. And regarding him as younger brother was indication as well of us feeling rather superior. But we had not been tried so sorely, and our virtue might have depended more upon lack of temptation than upon strength.

Larson was no coward, and he was determined to prove it. On another mission, he was again delayed taking off. But he had resolved to find the formation, and he went deep into France all alone. He finally had to give up the chase and abort again. This time he got chewed out for going so deep into France without an escort. That was pretty dangerous stuff. He must have had a lousy navigator, but that was neither here nor there; he was responsible, even if he had to do his own navigating.

And finally, one day, Larson flew a mission over Berlin and disappeared. We were not surprised.

There were few laughs at the next morning's critique.

27

VOLUNTEERING FOR
A SECOND TOUR

After Halberstadt I thought I had it made. I only had seven missions to go, and a form of invulnerability, which had characterized my early days in combat, had reappeared in the form of an exaggerated evaluation of the worth of my combat experience. Being alerted for the next day did not create anymore the type of tension that would mount in the evening, accompanied by a certain melting of the insides. I was no more conscious of anticipatory fear; I repressed it well.

As I came even closer to the end of my twenty-five missions, only three or four remaining, I started to give some consideration to volunteering for a second tour. It was not patriotic fervor, nor a conviction that unless we gave our all to the Eighth Air Force we might be defeated, that prompted these thoughts. First and foremost it was the opportunity of getting a crew of my own and eventually a captaincy. I was tired of being the anonymous utility, the understudy of Streit. Not that the role did not have its satisfactions. I knew that I had the esteem of our gunners and of my first pilot, as well as the esteem of our operations officer. I had friends like Barrett, and there were some with whom I had exchanged only a few cordial words here and there, but I knew if we ever had the chance, these few words would blossom. Except that some of these potential friends were killed or shot down before we ever had the chance to let friendship grow between us.

There were certain traits that distinguished me from other flying officers in the squadron. I was half-French, I was a college boy (I didn't let them know the half of it, otherwise I would have been beyond the pale), and I was eager. And being eager was not something we discussed with our fellow airmen; eager guys would mostly smell each other out. We might argue more easily the depth of our cynicism, and even that was somewhat taboo, but we did not argue the depth of our commitment. Being eager was like being tall or plump or lean or blond, something beyond argument.

All my gunners were eager, more by followership, perhaps, than from inner conviction. Gunners were assigned to us by Operations; they came having had little independent experience and were assigned arbitrarily to crews where they usually knew no one, certainly not the officers. Yet they were sworn to obey the latter, to carry out an officer's will even when their own minds told them to do it differently. Officers knew more and had experience. It was better to believe in them than to worry about their competence. After some nineteen missions, my gunners and I, on the level of our profession, knew each other well.

A second tour would be safer if we could do it together. When we began our first tour, we had certain problems in common: the control of our fears, how to cooperate, how to forgive each other the sharpness of our voices when we gave orders that had the urgency of fear or emergency. The first missions were usually the most dangerous because of the crew's general inexperience with war, and the need to work out our combat roles among ourselves. By volunteering we would avoid the vulnerability of the first five to ten missions, thus increasing our collective chances of finishing a second tour.

Another tour of combat duty would give us a thirty-day furlough and then a non-combat assignment. The least we could expect was six months of duty in the training command. I would be training pilots and copilots and flying navigators and bombardiers in their practice missions. Our gunners would be teaching gunnery. After six months, depending upon the need for combat crews – high if the German jets had increased our losses, low if the decline in fighter interceptions persisted – we would be integrated into a group going through staging for overseas. If the seven of us stayed together, all we would need would be to pick up three flying officers: a copilot, a navigator, and a bombardier.

The prospect of another tour of combat had given me the idea that I would move from the right seat to the left seat – I would forsake the role of copilot and become a first pilot. A second tour of combat would very likely see me get my captain's bars. For me, a second tour was as much an opportunity as it was an exposure to further danger. No question, if I could do another tour of combat with my present enlisted men, my chances and theirs would be increased.

If they volunteered with me for a second tour, we would probably be the first on our base to do so, and it might entice others in the squadron, and perhaps even in other squadrons, to do the same. I knew that the percentage of volunteers among first pilots was a bare ten percent, not exactly a high number. Our group was going to lose to tour completions a fair number of experienced airmen, and two-tour volunteers might be welcomed by the Brass.

Remained for me to sell the idea to the crew.

I went to the non-commissioned officers' mess as I did once a month to check out the food and talk to our crewmen about their complaints. This time it was the food. The boys complained that their breakfast on the morning of missions was definitely insufficient. Rather than powdered eggs – since they took for granted that fresh eggs would not be theirs anyway – they wanted pancakes with syrup and butter. After all, it would be twelve, perhaps fourteen hours before they could eat again, except for the Mars bars they would get from me with their escape kit before take-off.

After the matter of food had been disposed of, I told the crew that I was going to volunteer for a second tour.

'No kidding!' Boyovitch exclaimed.

'Well, I figure a second tour two or three months from now is better than a second tour in six or seven months. To start with, the 524th will be practically another squadron when I come back. Our group commander will very likely have been promoted to the wing leadership and some of the Brass with whom we like to fly our missions will have been promoted out. There will be a lot of strangers on the base, and I'll be just another one. Brownlow will not be here anymore. *Penny Ante* will likely not be available; one of the squadron leaders will have put the arm on her. As a "lucky ship" she will not lack suitors.'

'She is a good ship all right,' Finicle agreed

'And I would be sorry to lose Link as a crew chief,' I added.

'You are quite right,' Boyovitch said. 'Do you think you could ask to get *Penny Ante* back?'

'I could try.'

Boyovitch went on, 'It might be difficult if a crew had had her for twenty missions and did not care to let her go.'

'On the other hand,' Snell reflected 'I would not mind if our next ship had the waist section enclosed instead of being open as it is now. It gets damned cold up there.'

'That's for sure,' agreed Williams. 'Especially since six or seven months from now will be winter.'

'I wonder how the newest B-17s cope with the problem of the radio hatch?' Chruby wanted to know. 'I don't think I've shot at many German fighters from my position except for a few that lingered above us.'

I asked, 'I take it you all won't complain too much if we cannot keep *Penny Ante* for a second tour?'

Finicle answered, 'The silver B-17s are lighter by about 300 pounds, and that's a good deal if you are coming back on two engines.'

'What about you, Owens?' I inquired. 'What do you say about all of this?'

'You know me. In my ball turret, I go wherever I am taken. If you guys put in for a second tour, I'll do it too. I like having my buddies watching over me. In my position, I have to trust that the guys in the fuselage won't leave without telling me or making some effort to get me out. I would prefer a second tour with people I can trust, and I can trust you guys.'

'That's the way I feel from my tail station,' said Boyovitch.

'So then:' I concluded, 'I guess you support my suggestion that all present here tell our Headquarters that the seven of us are interested in volunteering for a second tour on the condition that we fly and fight as a team, in the same crew.' I felt very pleased. 'I'll transmit the information to our operations officer and see what happens?'

As I reflect over these times, I realize that I had put the squeeze on my crew without giving them the chance to consolidate a private opinion that it was hard enough to finish a first tour without having to commit oneself to a second one. By confronting the enlisted men as a group, I had given little chance to an individual dissenter to speak out and find echoes among some of the others, reinforcing the discovery that they were not alone in their qualms.

In order to dissent, a gunner would have had to break the boundaries of the group of which I, the copilot, had become the spokesman. What I took for unanimous support was really a simple reluctance to rock the boat and challenge the authority of the copilot, the number two man in the crew, a position that neutralized the differences between the sergeants, the staff sergeants, and the tech sergeants. We never had a vote on this second tour issue – a consensus emerged for which Finicle and Boyovitch were at bottom responsible. If either had declined my proposition, I was pretty sure that it would have been useless to raise the issue with the crew. An unspoken negative vote would have entailed for me a loss of prestige. As it was, I had elbowed out not only the first pilot, who was not interested, but also the navigator and the bombardier. The latter had *de facto* left the crew to try and become a lead bombardier; he was in a pool of trainees and was psychologically detached from the crew.

I told Brownlow of my plans and of the crew's willingness to volunteer for a second tour. Brownlow seemed supportive, and in the forty-eight hours between Berlin I and Berlin II, called us together to make our report to the Colonel. We followed him into the administrative building where the Colonel took his meals with Lieutenant Colonels Kittle and Rohr and the major ground officers of his command. After Brownlow had reminded the Colonel of our visit, the seven of us stumbled forward. The silence that greeted us compelled me at last to speak. I said, 'Sir, the seven of us would like to volunteer for a second tour on the condition that we could fly together as a crew.'

The Colonel replied, 'Well, that's fine. That's very good. Sign a request along those lines. Have it approved by your operations officer and your squadron commander, and we'll take it from there.'

The seven of us saluted, the Colonel saluted us back, and we left the room.

I was a bit disappointed. What did I expect? Did I feel that he should have complimented us on our zeal? After all, crews that wanted to volunteer as a unit must have been rare.

But that was our Colonel, a man of few words who thought that devotion to duty went without saying and who expected us to feel the same. But I was not quite up to that level. My virtue required some support, some encouragement, some acknowledgement.

Lieutenant Colonel Rohr, who was present, had not said a word either, nor had Lieutenant Colonel Kittle. I could tell the gunners were a bit puzzled. So I told Boyovitch to organize a dinner for seven at a good local eatery, an Italian place in Bedford, with wine and ice-cream dessert, and I would pay for it. We would have it after our last mission.

28

ART AND REALITY

I had my head on Jackie's lap, and she was passing her nails through my hair. I felt so good I could have purred. I am sure, in fact, I must have made some noises to that effect.

We were in the country, on the banks of the Thames somewhere. It was March 1944. I still had a couple of missions to go, and I was preparing my exit from the group, beginning to detach myself from the place. As it was, most of the pilots and copilots I knew had been shot down, and it was as if the squadron was detaching itself from me.

On the Thames, pleasure boats, sculls, and paddleboats mixed together, the result of an early spring that is sometimes stimulated in England by the Gulf Stream. Barges loaded with coal or logs or steel beams were passing by, sometimes letting out an impatient toot at a row boat whose rower was a little too distracted by the passenger with an umbrella that he was entertaining. Sometimes we would wave at members of the barges' crews, and they would wave back.

'Look at that!' I pointed at an eight-oared scull, a jockey-type coxswain at the helm. We watched as it glided swiftly by, leaving the other boats behind. 'There will always be an England,' I remarked.

Jackie drew my attention to a nearby playing field. 'Look over here. There's a cricket match going on.'

'Cricket is beyond my ken,' I told her. 'But don't you like the distinguished way the people clap to congratulate the batter?'

She agreed. 'Quite different from our screaming and whistling, isn't?'

'Yes, it's only on the soccer field that I can recognize them as our cousins.'

A Spitfire V with clipped wings went over our heads at about 3,000 feet. The sky held cumulus clouds, which were beginning to grow, and the pilot decided to play. He put his plane into a sharp climb to the left and made a complete circle around the cloud. At about 5,000 feet, he felt cocky enough to fly upside down right through the cloud and completed his half roll as soon as he got out of the white mess.

A new graduate from flying school, I thought. Maybe putting in some time to familiarize himself with the Spit V before being put in a Spit IX. And perhaps showing off to his girlfriend. Back in the States, that was how most training accidents happened: a pilot buzzing his home or the girlfriend's home, or doing acrobatics too close to the ground, with only half his brain in the cockpit and the other half on the ground thinking of impressing everyone.

Jackie asked, 'When you are up there, doesn't it feel wonderful to be flying so high, to be so free, to see the earth with all its colors? To see the houses looking so little, with the women hanging the wash on strings in the yard?'

And I thought of Richard Hillary, who had written *The Last Enemy*, and of Antoine de Saint-Exupéry, author of *The Little Prince*, both of them fighter pilots and both of them writers who could squeeze art out of the banal, the mechanical, and the deadly. Hillary had been shot down and had his face and hands badly burnt; after they had fixed him up so that he looked half-human again, he had returned to fly combat. In 1943, he was shot down again; this time was the last. Saint-Exupéry had been allowed five missions by the French theater commander, who could not refuse anything to 'Saint Ex.' He had returned from the first four of those missions with his P-38 full of holes. In 1944, on the fifth, a reconnaissance mission over the Mediterranean coast, he was to be shot down, apparently by a pilot who became a minister. At forty-four years of age, he did not belong in the air war anymore. But why grieve? He died the way he wanted to. Flying so high …

And to Jackie now I replied, 'You're right, it's a wonderful feeling. It's certainly preferable to an infantryman's life, in the mud much of the time, with the smell of the dead lingering in the air you breathe, in the air wherever you eat or sleep. I only smelled it once, smelled burnt human flesh when I went to the scene of Schuenemann's crash.'

Jackie stopped scratching my head and was silent.

'I'm sorry,' I said. 'I didn't mean to upset you.'

But I wondered, did I? What demon had pushed me? After all, there was no need for me to remind her of my combatant's status right then, and it wouldn't have changed anything between us. Why did I have to bring Schuenemann body into this?

'If it could end the war tomorrow' Jackie said, 'I would accept death right now.'

'That is a noble thought, and I mean that,' I told her. 'You are *Jackie-la-poire*, Jackie the sucker, and I love you for it. It must take a lot of good openness to be able to stand a quick badly brought-up boy like me.'

She laughed, 'Well, sometimes you are a bit sarcastic and unbearable.'

'I know. Sometimes I can hardly stand myself. You'd think my remorse would stimulate me to better behavior, but no. It's really an alibi, permission to do it again.'

She asked, 'What can we do about that?'

'Scratch my head some more.'

She resumed. I said, 'Remember the Aztecs? Every year they sacrificed large numbers of their youths to their gods. If you were climbing the steps to the executioner's altar, I could not let you go by yourself. I would come with you. That is, if I thought that your heart and my heart would satiate the hunger of the gods.'

'Could they convince you?' she asked.

'That's just it, Jackie. You see, you don't have to be convinced you believe. You trust. It is part of your maternal instinct. You believe if you are needed, it is your duty to help.'

'What do you believe?'

'I guess I believe also. Although I have a left-handed conviction. But when I buckle my parachute, grabbing the right strap between my legs to connect it to the clip lying on my stomach, doing the same with the left strap, I am giving my agreement. They need my heart? Well, here it is. Up to now, the high priest has not asked for my heart; he has been satisfied with the heart of someone else, flying in the next element or the next squadron.'

I thought for a moment and went on. 'What is sacred is what you are willing to die for. Every society needs the sacrifice of youth to attest to its own sacred character. America is worth dying for.'

'Even if Roosevelt tricked us into war,' Jackie asked, 'by placing the Japanese in an impossible situation by embargoing oil and scrap iron?'

'Yes, even though we shall not know for decades whether his policy was the correct one. Even our inevitable victory will not settle that. But meanwhile, my country, right or wrong.'

Jackie stared at me. 'I'm not sure I agree with that attitude.'

'Perhaps it is because you don't realize that you already have that attitude. It is like my child, right or wrong, or my father, right or wrong. What's important is the relationship. Everything else is secondary, including 'right' or 'wrong.' I agree it has its dangers. Ancient Judaism, for example, always placed the prophet above the king, although I imagine most prophets made it to the scaffold before they made it to the Bible. But 'right' is above 'might'. Right is more important than the tribe, which determines the sacred. Right is God's command, although God is the incarnation of the tribe. I argue about that with Barrett, another copilot who is my best friend at the base.'

'Is that what they taught you in college?' demanded Jackie.

'They taught me to bear with the contradictions,' I replied, 'and to climb the steps to the altar where the high priest is waiting, without running away, without flinching. And let me confess that I have felt like running away a couple of times. But I did not flinch, and that is what counts.'

'Where did you get the idea that the Aztec sacrifice of youth was an equivalent of war?'

'I don't know. Perhaps in listening to a guest lecture by the great California anthropologist Kroeber. He thought that the growing demands of the gods for more blood was upsetting the upper classes, from which most of the young victims were taken. By the time of the Spanish invasion, they were up to 20,000 a year; it made them welcome the Christians who put an end to the practice. But I think he was projecting a Western viewpoint upon the Aztec upper class. They were a warlike tribe who for two centuries had been deprived of war, due to their crushing defeat of the local population. They found a way to make up for that, to make it up to the gods, by the sacrifice of their young.'

'It makes me shudder.' Jackie said. 'It means that we shall always have wars or some form of human sacrifice.'

'But you remember, Jackie,' I argued, 'that it was a common view that the coming war, our war, would wipe out civilization. It has not done that. In fact, the French peasantry and those working directly or indirectly for the German war machine are earning more than before the war, and eating better, which is how a European worker measures his welfare. In the US and the UK, a ten-year depression was eliminated by the war. Criminality has probably diminished or taken forms that come less to the attention of the authorities. Burglars and armed robbers have probably gone into black marketing, and a few may even have gone straight.'

'Well, if that is the case, is there nothing bad about the war?'

'Of course,' I said, 'it kills, and worse, it brutalizes people. If I had been told when I entered the Air Corps that my job would be to kill civilians – men, women, and children – I would have shuddered. I might have gone into the Navy. The truth is that I wanted to fly, so I did not look too closely into the fine print of the contract. I was seduced into the butchery of civilians by the myth of precision bombing. I don't aim at civilians. I carry a bombardier to the target where on a good day when he can directly see our target, an armament factory, most of our bombs will still land outside of the factory area. But from 21,000 feet, I can't see those I kill, accidentally or otherwise. So now I don't care, I don't even think of it.'

'You are thinking of it now!'

'Yes, but in a very detached way. It doesn't trouble my sleep. It's an intellectual construction. But we are inventing better cannons, better bombers, better bombs, and indeed Kroeber is probably right, there will come a time when the gods of war will demand too many youths from the colleges and the football teams. Though we are still pretty far from what the French lost at Verdun, or the Brits at Ypres, and the Somme lost during the First World War. But one of these days it is going to be true that we could destroy civilization. Which means that we'll need trust, and cooperation and sacrifice, even though many people may be hungry and bleeding.'

'Do you ever discuss these things with your fellow flyers?'

'Very rarely. My fellow flyers, as you put it, are not interested. They are there to do a job, and they do it. Basically they trust their leaders. They are fully aware that there are many lies, cover-ups, favoritism and profiteering, and above all, many mistakes. They don't like it very much when I try to steer conversation to these iffy subjects. They are trying to stay alive in a world full of goofs – their goofs, the goofs of the wing commanders, the group commanders, the squadron leaders, the goofs of the fighters who don't meet us at the rendezvous point.

'Mind you, if we were told to aim at German orphanages and hospitals, I think there would be massive refusal to fly the mission. I have no illusions about my fellow flyers, but I have a good deal of respect for them. I would prefer to die rather than let them down or do something they would despise.'

'That's what they call high morale, I guess,' Jackie remarked.

'Kiss me for my high morale,' I said. She bent over and gave me a chaste kiss on the lips.

I suppose many people think that flying gives plentiful opportunities for beautiful feelings. 'Doesn't it feel wonderful to be flying so high, to be so free, to see the earth with all its colors?'

But they forget, a flyer is a worker. The sky is to him what the land is to the farmer. While a passenger is admiring the landscape, imagining holding in his hand the small houses of men, the pilot is calculating ground speed, estimating the time of his arrival over the next town, gauging the wind, watching his instruments, embracing the ground with that instinctive look for long, flat fields into the wind should he be forced to land due to the failure of an engine. That beautiful cloud, boiling in the sky, so powerful in its implacable whiteness, is to him but a sign of dangerous turbulence, something to be carefully avoided – unless he, like us, was flying combat, when that cloud might offer protection from a German fighter.

A flight at night. The stars, the moon, the smoothness of the air, yes. But the flyer's ears are listening to the radio beam; his eyes are searching for these winking beacons, for the possible ship straying in his path; his mind is analyzing the weather just reported by the last station; his muscles are keeping the course straight, the altitude steady. While his passengers watch the glow of a position light in a cloud that has just engulfed the plane, he is turning on the de-icing equipment, readying the microphone for a position report to the ground station, preparing for a request for permission to lose altitude.

True enough, one is sometimes allowed a moment, when the routine is handled by a minor portion of consciousness and the purple of a cloud illuminated by the position light on the wing, or the reflection of the moon in a river running after your ship, will suddenly permit a moment of freedom, of enjoyment, a moment useless and soon denied. That night, so inviting to others, is darkness to us, where one flies as carefully as the blind walk. His passengers are absorbed in the enjoyment of the moment, appreciating the kaleidoscope of sky and land and stars. To the pilot, these elements are figures in an equation, meaningless by themselves. They are the elements of a problem, and his beauty is in the solving of that problem. It is the beauty of the mathematician, cracking neatly a tough puzzle of numbers. It is a beauty of good muscle control, of good flight planning, of danger foreseen and avoided, or of danger unavoidable and surmounted.

Even in combat there was something beautiful in the flight of a Me-109 going through a formation in a vertical slow roll, the orange flame of his cannons shooting at the next group, of course – the way the plane would arch back like a fish returning to the water. Sometimes that beauty sliced through all your concerns like a knife and for a moment paralyzed your will to live, disarmed that tireless energy of defense.

And there were some, perhaps, who died in an ecstasy of speed against a cloud, in the vertigo of ground and stars, in a ship exploding against the hard wall of the sky.

Defenseless against a single-minded enemy, whose lone beauty lay in our destruction.

29

BERLIN: THE LAST MISSIONS

LETTING GO OF THE ROCK

On March 3, we were briefed for a raid to Berlin. More specifically, a raid to the industrial suburb of Erkner, where the still untouched ball-bearing plant waited our visit.

I don't remember it making a big commotion among the crews when the curtain was raised at the beginning of briefing. There were some of the usual hoots and barks, but we understood quite well that a fighter escort both on coming and going made a big difference. All we had to do was have our formation leaders fly with precision and connect at the right time and the right place with our escort. Along with the weather, the failures of our lead were now the main enemies. They were the reasons whole groups missed assembly into the wing formation and aborted the mission.

By this time the Germans were fully aware of our bait policy. We were now about to spring on them a combination of both bait and target they were not likely to resist: Berlin.

But on that day, we never got to Erkner. Bad weather and the thick contrails, which we ourselves generated, reduced visibility, and the mission was recalled.

On the missions I had flown thus far, the one thing I had missed was 'unexpected terror.' I had had a taste of it on the return from Kiel, when flak had pursued our solitary ship from 700 to 100 feet with a salvo every five seconds. But it had been only a taste, since Streit had soon had us 'on the deck' and out of range, while my knees – not my teeth – were still quivering from the experience.

As we turned around to go home, the leader of the wing that led the First Division made a fast 180-degree turn that whipped around the second elements and the low squadrons of the groups and came down a couple of thousand feet on the reciprocal of our course. At first, because of the distance of about five or six miles, and the difference in altitude between our wing and the lead wing, I did not react. But within twenty seconds, the lead wing continued to lose altitude and came smack in line with our formation. Collisions were imminent unless some action was taken by the leadership of the wings about to collide – immediately, if not sooner!

For about five to ten seconds I must have been frozen in fear, although I was not experiencing the feeling of fear, while by some 2,000 yards we came closer to collision. I had not foreseen that the division leader, who on the reciprocal of his course was trying to avoid the other wings that had not yet finished their 180-degree turn, would lose altitude so fast. We were hemmed in by our formation, where we led the second element of the low squadron. Our wing was going down about 1,000 feet per minute, while the lead wing did not budge from its collision course.

I looked for a hole and could not see any. I let some distance spread between the first element and us, and I saw a space on the left and below. I looked to the right and saw a wing of the Third Division come barreling in over the ships of the First Division. I pressed the wheel downward and to the left; at least two collisions took place about 150 to 200 feet above us.

As usual, the sudden shift in our controls wakened Streit instantly. He followed my eyes upward, saw the remnants of the collisions fluttering down, and at once pushed on the controls with me. He took them over until we were back over the Channel.

Nobody in the 379th was involved in a collision. But Streit told me, 'You looked green,' and stronger than the memory of fear was the bite of guilt. For five to ten seconds I had been out of it while our two formations hurtled toward one another at 230 yards per second. Luck, and the fact that our wing leader had lost sufficient altitude to be out of the way, had saved us.

The two colliding wings had disintegrated into squadrons and elements of three, which were looking for their group leaders, who were shooting flares to guide them. Since we had avoided the worst, we suffered relatively little disorganization. It was easy to reassemble into groups and finally into a wing formation, and we returned to base.

On the way back, a wing of the First Division managed to drop on Wilhelmshaven; fourteen ships from the Third Division and four from the Second Division dropped on targets of opportunity. Of the 748 bombers that had been dispatched, a mere eleven percent had been effective, and for once our fighters, mainly P-51s, had lost as many as they had shot down. One ship from the 100th group had landed on a German airfield thinking it was Sweden.

Apparently, it had not occurred to the leaders at Wycombe Abbey to send ahead of our squadrons any reconnaissance ships, who could have radioed back the height of the cloud barrier before we got there. The mission could have been called off before we had gone through the perils of take-off and assembly and the expenditure of so much gasoline. As it was, we did not discover the full state of the weather until we had crossed the coast of Europe at 26,000 feet and found a barrier of clouds surging in front of us that reached probably 10,000 feet above us. After consulting the air commander in the lead ship of the First Bomb Division, a recall order was issued by Wycombe Abbey, leaving each wing free to find a target of opportunity which would give it credit for the mission and would camouflage somewhat the collapse of this second briefing to Berlin.

An atmosphere of confusion and error pervaded the whole mission from the beginning. When I tried later to get the mission reports from the 379th archives, there were only two or three pages there, no comments or reports whatsoever, impossible to know what leaders had presided over this mess. (If it had been General Travis, we could be sure it was not for lack of determination that we failed to get to our target.)

Anyway, we got credit for the mission, so we did not ask too many questions. Except for the collisions, a waste of eleven B-17s, it had been a milk run.

As a result of the aborted raid to Erkner, we were briefed once again for Berlin on March 6. This would be a *maximum effort*, meaning that all available ships and all available pilots would fly, regardless of whether they had flown the day before. My friend and fellow copilot, Barrett, who had one more mission to go, arranged with Brownlow to take the navigator's slot on *Penny Ante*.

The Eighth Air Force was about to sustain the highest losses of its whole existence.

On this day, 730 bombers were dispatched; the bomber stream was some ninety miles long. If a wing leader was late in joining the procession, his ships would not connect with their fighter escort, and to catch up, he would increase the speed from 150 to 155 or even 160 miles per hour, creating an accordion effect within the group and also opening gaps in the formation. Groups of German fighters, spotting those gaps, would dive on the formation where it looked ragged and loose. Pilots trying to cope with the accordion effect were distracted from coping with the fighters. And although some 800 fighters of our own, mainly

P-38s and P-47s, had been dispatched to cover us, they could not be every place at once.

On this raid, it occurred several times. In the First Division it happened to the first two wings, resulting in eighteen losses out of 248 ships. In the Second Division, the 198 B-24s that had been split between three targets – Genshagen, Berlin, and Potsdam – lost sixteen ships. The Third Division, searching for targets of opportunity, split between six targets – Templin, Verden, Kalkeberge, Potsdam, Oranienbourg, Wittemberg – lost thirty-five out of 226, with the 100th Group alone losing fifteen out of twenty ships.

The 384th, our 'sister group' in the 41st Combat Wing, aborted. 'The leader had simply failed, through poor navigation and worse pilotage, to join the wing formation. Instead of joining another wing and going to war, he elected to return home.'[1]

Lieutenant Colonel Kittle, his command reduced to two groups, could have aborted his wing, but he went on, a true student of Colonel Preston.

At about 13.21, we entered a bomb run of some five minutes. When I raised my eyes, I could see all the silver B-17s of the high group above us, flying close to the lead group and looking like a school of silver fish. Intermingled among them were the older B- 17s, dark green in their old camouflage paint.

As we came closer to Berlin, the fighter attacks and the rocket attacks by the German twin-engine Me-110s and Me-210s became more numerous and determined. When a rocket with its preset fuse exploded on or very near a B-17, it blew it out of the sky, but that didn't happen very often. The fuses for the rockets were not terribly reliable, and time and again the rockets blew up behind our squadron or hopelessly in front of them. The electronic 'proximity' fuses, which would respond to the presence of a target, were still nine months in the future, and neither the Germans nor the Americans had yet mastered the problems of miniaturization.

Our wing, though, was largely ignored by the German fighters, and even though our wing had been reduced to some thirty-five or forty planes due to the defection of the 384th, the only bomber we lost in this raid was Hendrickson's.

We experienced three or four flak attacks. One was at Diepholtz with ten guns to our right, another at Branghe, to our left but light, and another at Brandenburg, again off to our left. At the target, the flak was more accurate, but not very dense. We sustained six to eight flak holes and a large rupture on the wing caused by an 88 shell, which had gone through our wing and then exploded harmlessly above us.

We had one fighter attack from the front, which did no damage. All the enemy fighter attacks were aimed at the group ahead of us. We saw one ship shot down, no chutes, and one ship falling in a forty-five-degree dive, trailing one chute that had been sucked in by the open bomb bay, the crewman having pulled his ripcord too soon. I saw him trailing the ship in his parachute harness and wondered how many minutes it would take the ship to hit the ground. Mercifully it would probably explode before then, and perhaps the chute would be blown out of the bomb bay before plane and crewman reached the ground.

We had been assigned the position of leader of the second element of the low squadron of the lead group. After the bomb run, what did I see? Ahead of us a B-17, with one engine feathered, had the bomb bay doors cracked open around the booted leg of one of the crewmen. That leg was now hanging limp in the slipstream. The bomb bay doors should have opened under his weight; perhaps the pilot had activated the electric mechanism in order to prevent the crewman from being dumped without a parachute.

We learned later that the crewman, the engineer, had got his leg caught outside the doors as they closed, and the pilot had not been able order action to extricate the engineer before he died. Normally, over the target, the 10,000 pounds of bombs should have been released, and the body allowed to fall with it. But the dead man's leg and the felt boot enveloping it remained in the slip stream until the end of the mission, like some macabre aiming point to keep position that I did not need. I was angry.

The bomber crews claimed a total of forty-seven fighters shot down, and our escort claimed thirty-one. If we do the usual reduction to account for the realm of pleasant self-deceptions, I figure we probably actually shot down about thirty German fighters. This had been one of the heaviest concentrations of enemy fighters. Against the loss of eleven American fighters, these were excellent figures for the attrition policy, if we disregard the loss of over sixty B-17s, also shot down. (Four B-17s went to Sweden.)

The bombing results were mediocre. We lost the pathfinder lead of the Third Bomb Division, from which only three crewmen survived, including 'Red' Morgan, the Medal of Honor winner who succeeded in clipping his chest-pack to his harness as he fell at ninety miles an hour. He flew as copilot to Gen. Russ Wilson, who led the 4th Combat Wing that day. 'As an attempt to curtail production at the three primary targets [Erkner, Genshagen, and Klein Machnow plants] the attack was a failure ... The most serious effect on production was the two working hours lost at all plants while the work force went to and returned from shelter.'[2]

On our return to Kimbolton, after nearly nine hours, who did we find on the ground waiting for our arrival? General Doolittle. I believe our formation was tight as we came over the field, but one B-17's landing was nearly catastrophic. Until the pilot was able to get it back on course and go around for a better try at landing, his ship, veering off the runway, had been aiming straight for the official party.

On the morning of March 9, 1944, when Brownlow came to wake us, he congratulated us on finishing our tour of combat missions. I felt somewhat at loose ends, alternatively hopeful and apprehensive. I remembered the occasions of those who had been shot down on their last missions. One would have thought with their experience that they would have been spared the ironies of fate, but the fact was nobody took for granted that his twenty-fifth mission would be a milk run.

At our mess hall, I discovered that they were giving us eggs and bacon for breakfast. At last. They must have received enough eggs for all the ground officers in order for the aircrews to get some. After breakfast, the trucks took us to briefing.

It was Berlin again!

I passed out the escape kits and Mars bars to the crew. Kundin would not be with us this time, having already completed his twenty-five missions by volunteering for the raid with McCall, while the rest of the crew was on pass. The line was mainly silent. When I came abreast of Streit, he asked if I wanted to do the take-off this morning. I respectfully declined, telling him, 'Streit, the twenty-fifth mission is your mission. You're the best pilot in the squadron, and this is no time for courtesies. It is prudent and fair that you should fly the plane and put all the chances on our side. But thanks anyway.'

Over Berlin once again. Over Berlin and ready to drop. I don't remember why at this point I had left my copilot's seat, but I was soon very glad that I had, because I became suddenly and acutely aware of the danger to our ship. Not from the enemy but from the high squadron and, worse, from all the ships in the high group. All we had to do was lift up our nose to see all the bombs on their attachments ready to let go within a few minutes. The trouble was that between the bomb bays of the high squadron and the German factory on the ground 25,000 feet below, lay our combat wing. We tried to contact the ships of the high squadron by the VHF radio, but without success. Our engineer Finicle was told of the situation, and Streit and I decided that when the bombs started falling, we would slide to the left. Finicle was stationed behind Streit. When I signaled to Finicle that the bombing had begun, he immediately tapped Streit's left shoulder, and we slid out of danger.

A ship to our right was not so lucky. 'Bombs away' resulted in its losing its tail, sliced off by bombs falling on it. We saw no chutes come out. Other than that, and at least two collisions that I saw, the raid went off without incident for us, and we flew back home.

Except for some comments by those members of the crew who thought they could make out the features of our parking lot as we came closer and closer to it, we were all silent as we taxied back to our squadron's dispersal area. We all recognized the rhythm of the end of a mission, as the pilot made smaller course corrections and finally pivoted around the left wheel to take the ship to its appointed position. It was a position that, like the others, was always revised by the luck of the draw, by the blank spaces left by the missing.

Once in place, the crew jumped out, some kissing the ground as they reached it, and the others followed with jokes and snickers. Some left the plane as they had entered it eight and a half hours before, and others just exited through the doors of the fuselage by a pull-up, no heroics.

Later, the squadron photographer would arrive and the boys would line up for pictures. Could we send copies of our last picture taken together to our families? Nobody knew, though everyone understood that permission could be withheld if the pictures involved material still not declassified.

In different buildings we returned our equipment: oxygen masks, flak suits, parachutes, guns, all the rest. We hung around the barracks, waiting for orders to return home. Some felt elated, others, like me, felt let down.

In the following days, I got involved in a poker game, the one in which I took Major Culpepper for $250, practically a month's pay – for me at least, not for him. He finally quit, and that broke up the game. The other players had not lost much, but they declared that no one was going to win against a player who had just finished his twenty-fifth mission. Since they all quit the game, I did not have to go on playing half the night and was able to keep my early winnings.

The crew and I also had our 'Italian dinner'. The fare was simple but quite good, and the wine was ample. We reminisced about some phases of our training in the States and about recent incidents. The boys asked me if our raids to Berlin would become our habitual fare. My answer was that the presence of our P-51s had changed the situation, and that a raid to Berlin today was less dangerous than a raid to Bremen the previous fall or to Kiel that past January.

Mentioning the first raid to Kiel started the gunners reminiscing about our night assembly. I reminded them that it was the last time we had a night assembly; after all, our leadership learned from its mistakes, so the collisions in the take-off pattern were a thing of the past. Several of the crew commented that this was one of the times when they were scared the most, and I agreed with them.

And on this I confided that I had lost my enthusiasm for a second tour, several things having combined to knock that enthusiasm out of me, one being that I had become aware that I had manipulated the crew's adoption of my policy. Perhaps that's always the way a consensus develops, people more or less bulldozed into a policy that has morality on its side. I did not feel that I had a right to involve them in my volunteering or not volunteering. It was their business whether they did or not, and they should not feel any obligation to follow their copilot in a venture from which I had more to gain than they had. I would not want their families ever to reproach me for leading them into perils from which they had not returned.

Perhaps more than participation in a second tour, what I really had wanted was a vote of confidence, and I had received that.

We continued waiting for several days, going downtown, playing cards, talking, waiting. As planes returned at the end of their missions, I felt one foot in the past, the other foot in the future. But what future?

Finally, a typewritten note was handed to me. My orders: to be ready to embark on the *New Amsterdam*. Events happened quickly after that; within two or three days we were sailing across the Atlantic. My combat days were over, six months in all. I had changed, but at the time I did not know how.

(Back in the States, I did recruiting for Air Force personnel in the 6th Service Command, then was Advanced Instructor. I was a pilot for the Air Transport Command when I was discharged in October 1945.)

EPILOGUE

I did not then know how I had changed; that was something that time and looking back and perhaps the wisdom of older years would bring. But I did know that there had been moments that had affected me profoundly.

On February 20, we had flown a raid to Leipzig. One of the ships on this mission was piloted by a friend of mine, Paul Breeding. It had been a hard fight, a tough mission, and at some point I saw Breeding's plane lag behind, and enemy fighters began to tear at him. But he somehow kept flying, and soon I forgot about him, for I had to stay alive myself, and the fight was hard and the temptations to surrender many.

We finally landed, and I was driven to the tower because I wanted to wait for him. But he and his crew were to land elsewhere, the decision having been taken to put down at the first air base they could make it to. Their copilot, Jerome Bowers, was dead, and Breeding was badly wounded. The bombardier, Tony Zaldonis, could fly the plane back, but he could not land it. Zaldonis had suggested that the rest of the crew jump and save themselves, but they refused to do so, for men who have fought together will often prefer to die together rather than survive alone. They were going to try to make it back to England; once there, they would parachute Breeding out with one of the gunners, who would take care of him when they reached the ground. Then they would bail out together.

When they told Breeding of the plan, he refused. At his insistence, they brought him back from the radio room where he had been lying, back to the pilot's seat, and to do this they had to drag him with all the pain and the bleeding through the catwalk, so narrow, with the buckles catching as they carried him. They put him in his seat, with Zaldonis in the dead copilot's seat. And Breeding, half conscious, brought the ship down. Against all procedure, he landed downwind without flaps, and with Zaldonis standing on the brakes, he brought the ship to a screeching halt at the end of the runway, where he passed out. The engines turned idly on the immobile ship, as ambulances and jeeps converged upon it.

The morning afterwards, I took a jeep and went to the hospital to find out how he was doing. They led me to his room where he lay thin and unshaven with tubes tied to him, giving him plasma and draining his wounds. The nurse said that he was not fully conscious. Every so often in his agony, he would utter a command, always the same, 'Flaps down! Flaps down!' – the procedure that had not been done when he landed his ship. His hand would move as he said it. And I sat astride on a chair, a powerless witness to this man's fight with death, still trying to do his duty, obsessed with what he had forgotten, or the command not obeyed, oblivious of his pain, all of his life aiming at doing his job well.

I sat there watching him, remembering times we had spent together in the dayroom, listening to the radio or exchanging thoughts on flying. I liked Breeding; he was someone with whom I could talk – about fear, about love, about my crew. And now he was perhaps leaving us, in a last obsession with duty left undone.

I got up awkwardly, grieving, yet trying to preserve my distance from his agony. For how could I go on if I saw that my flesh also was vulnerable? I walked out into the fog, which had settled around the hospital. It was cold and damp, and I was alone.

It is the American ideal that our work should express our love, our tenderness, our longing, and when death comes, it should find us at that work, creating for others the world of tomorrow. My friends who fought and lived, and the friends who died and were buried without ceremony – departing discreetly so as not to upset the living by reminding them how fragile an assembly of cells the human body is – I have never buried. They come back to haunt me when the day has been sterile, the duty not done, or when I have tried to escape in the comfort of love from the work I am committed to do.

And so many years later, reflecting back on that short time in my life, that brief six months, I came to understand how it changed me. It was on that day outside the hospital where my friend Breeding lay that I decided that he and the others were my people – that I, born of an American father and a French mother, I, who had lived in both countries enough to know them, but not enough to cease being a stranger, would live with these lonely men who fought and died in the obsession of duty done. These were the people I chose as mine, these men, this band of brothers.

On the day our wing leader had taken us over the Ruhr, even when the flak cracked our windows, I had been at peace with myself. If I got scragged on this mission, I wouldn't complain. I'd be satisfied I was doing my duty. Here, death was not a failure, an accident, an illness, a withdrawal. Here, death was the highest level of accomplishment I could reach. It wiped out whatever mistakes I had made in my short life. I thought, 'If I die now, it will be all right. I've been fully paid.' It was a marvelous feeling. I had it a couple more times in later raids, in lulls between fighter attacks. I have never had it since, though romantic love comes closest.

War does bring moments like this because it is a great simplifier. I don't recall when being a father, a husband, a professor, ever brought on such untrammeled satisfaction, when ego and superego were fused. In these civilian roles, I could never be sure that I had done the right thing, or that I couldn't have done it earlier or better, or that I hadn't forgotten something important.

Now, in the evening of my life, I will remember – while opening a door, picking up a shoe, eating a radish – something mean or foolish that I did or, more likely, said forty years ago, twenty years ago, ten years ago – try yesterday – and it bites, literally. Perhaps that's why I take refuge in my memories of the war, when I know I did it right and it mattered. I'm glad I've been through it.

At 21,000 feet, duty was clear, simple, and glorious: follow the orders to fly tight formation on your immediate leader, and charge the enemy.

ANTE UP

On May 24, 1944, target Berlin,
the *Penny Ante*'s new crew, flying their sixteenth mission,
were apparently hit by fighters after bombs away.
The plane appeared to explode, and six chutes were seen.
It is said that the crew had not continued the custom
of taking the penny and returning it.

NOTES

4 THE FIRST MISSION: EMDEN

1 Anti-aircraft fire. From the German abbreviation FL(ieger) + A(bwehr) + K(anone): aircraft defence gun. In the First World War the common expression was ack-ack, a British expression.

5 THE SECOND MISSION

1 And there was a next time. The mission was Oschersleben, on January 11, when we lost the same percentage as at Schweinfurt. The General, who was leading our three-group formation, had already lost his right and left wing men to enemy fighters when he received from Wycombe Abbey the order to return to base. He disregarded the order. Our group won the Distinguished Unit Citation that day and we lost the appellation 'Junior Birdmen'. All that thanks to the disobedience of 'Iron Ass' Travis.

6 OUR LEADER, COLONEL PRESTON

1 Although the characters were comical and thus safely condescended to, *Amos 'n' Andy* did a lot to teach rank-and-file Americans that the 'colored' were also human, all in all good preparation to accepting their equality. My father loved the show, and he was definitely less prejudiced than his friends.

2   In France, most milk came from small farms with five cows or less. The loss of a
    tubercular cow to the veterinary services was a serious blow to a small operation,
    and often enough the veterinarians would cooperate in the deceptions used by
    the farmers. In 1952 there were only two major milk cooperatives that could
    meet the sanitary standards of the US Army stationed in France. As a result, the
    Army bought its milk from Holland. TB control would become a reality only
    in the 1960s. Since then, of course, the French dairy industry has made great
    progress and has given the global market some of its finest cheeses.

3   Foreword to *Shades of Kimbolton: A Narrative of the 379th Bombardment Group* (*H*)
    (San Angelo, Texas: Newsphoto Publishing Co., 1981). A book about the 379th
    put together by officers and men of the ground personnel; first published in
    the late 1970s.

4   Ray Carré, *Maximum Effort* (Burbank: National Literary Guild, 1984), p.77.

9 MANAGING THE GROUND TROOPS

1   A supercharger was a small horizontal turbine, large like a soup plate, activated
    by the exhaust gases of our engines, which compressed air at high altitudes to
    increase manifold pressure and give more power. We had a supercharger for
    each of our engines. You lost a supercharger and you could not stay with the
    formation at high altitude.

11 ELEMENTS OF SURVIVAL

1   Elmer Bendiner, *The Fall of Fortresses* (New York: G.P. Putnam's Sons, 1980),
    p.124.

13 COPING WITH FAILURES

1   I have adopted the name given to the Major by Elmer Bendiner in *The Fall of
    Fortresses*, pp.113–114.

2   Developments in radar technology, made by the British and MIT, made this
    possible. But it was only a palliative, not a guarantee of precision. It worked well
    on harbors and river towns because of the contrast between land and water on
    the radar screen.

16 MISSION ABORTED

1 Mark K. Wells, *Courage and Air Warfare* (London: Frank Cass, 1995), p. 107.
2 *Courage and Air Warfare*, p.105; pp.113–114. Picture of Urban L. Drew, American fighter ace, with commentary, is number 13 after p. 80.

19 GOOD LUCK, GOOD SHOOTING, AND GOOD BOMBING

1 *The Fall of Fortress*, p.161.
2 Ibid., p. 227.
3 During the Battle of the Bulge, General McAuliffe tried to imitate the reply at Waterloo of General Cambronne to the British suggestion that he surrender the Imperial Guard. 'Merde,' replied the general. Our American general replied 'NUTS,' which he knew would make the evening news. But it does not have the zing of General Cambronne's reply (which was translated, for the non-military public into: 'The Guard will die but will not surrender').
4 *The Fall of Fortresses*, p.225.

21 LOVE AND WAR, AND ALL THAT'S FAIR

1 WRENs were members of the WRNS, the Women's Royal Naval Service.

23 WHISTLING IN THE DARK

1 Clarence E. 'Bud' Anderson, *To Fly and Fight* (New York: St Martin's Press, 1990), pp.63–64. Most of my information about the Merlin Mustang and the quotations can be found in these 'Memoirs of a Triple Ace'.

24 HALBERSTADT

1 The group navigator reported: 'It is felt that the bombs hit a bit past the target in the southwest corner of the target area.' *The Official Account of the Army Air Forces in World War II*, edited by W.F. Craven and J.L. Cate (Washington D.C.: Office of Air Force History, 1983). Vol.III, p.37, is more blunt: 'Bombing was poor at Halberstadt.' Yet our lead bombardier had been responsible for the pattern at the second Schweinfurt, and it had been one of the best of the whole year.

25 SCHWEINFURT REVISITED

1   W.F. Craven and J.L. Cate, *The Army Air Forces in World War II* (University of Chicago Press, 1949), p.40.

29 BERLIN: THE LAST MISSIONS

1   Dale O. Smith, *Screaming Eagle: Memoirs of a B-17 Group Commander* (North Carolina: Algonquin Books of Chapel Hill, 1990), p.118.
2   Jeffrey Ethell and Alfred Price, *Target Berlin: Mission 250, 6 March 1944* (London: Arms and Armour Press, 1989), p.143, 144. (First published by Jane's publishing Company Ltd. in 1981.)

APPENDIX

Photostated from original copies in 379th Mission Folder, National Archives Military Records Facility.

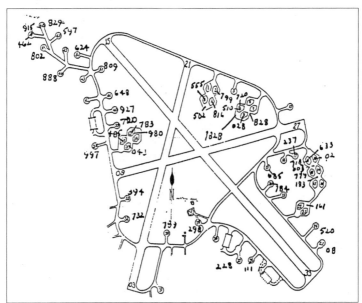

40. This illustrated map of Kimbolton Airbase shows the positions of each aircraft in the 379th prior to take-off for the Halberstadt mission, February 22, 1944. *Penny Ante* was number 828 and would be positioned in the upper right of the map.

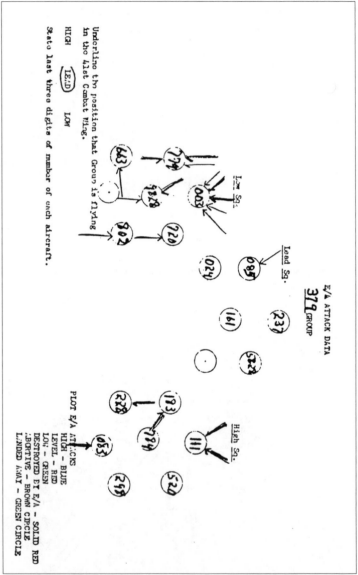

Above and opposite: 41 and 42. A diagram (top) of the 379th formation for the Halberstadt mission. The 379th is the lead group in the 41st Combat Wing. The *Peny Anie* is in the low squadron. The check form illustrates the attacks on the low group by FW-190s.

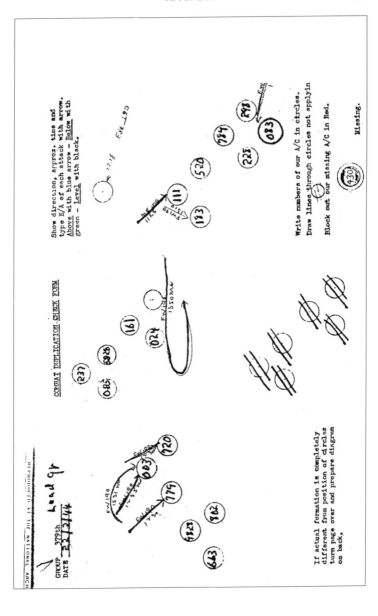

INTERROGATION FORM   DATE _22 February 1944_

1. GROUP _379_ SQUADRON _526_ A/C NO. _9829_ LETTER _B_

2. POSITION BRIEFED _L4-Lo-2-_ OVER TARGET _L6-2-1_

3. TIME TAKEOFF _0155_ TIME LANDED _1649_

4. ROUTE: AS BRIEFED, YES _NO_ (If NO describe) _as briefed on way in_

	TIME	PLACE
5. ENG. COAST-OUT		
ENEMY COAST-IN		
ENEMY COAST-OUT		
ENG. COAST-IN		

9. TIME OVER TARGET _1404_ HEADING _270_
HEIGHT _20,000_ LENGTH ST. & LEVEL RUN :

PILOT _1st Hershell E. J. Streit_
CO.P. _2nd Jesse R. Pitts_
NAVIG _2nd Lawrence (NMI) Kuchi..._ ✓
BOMB. _2nd John A. Magro_
RADIO _T/Sgt. Leo A. Cosby_
TOP T _T/Sgt. Raymond W. Winkle_
BALL _S/Sgt. Stanley R. Owens_
R.W. _S/Sgt. John M. Snell_
L.W. _S/Sgt. James A. Williams_
TAIL _S/Sgt. Mike R. Bovenich_

7. Bomb Load _12 X 500_

8. Disposal: _Salvoed_
Osterweck or
Wernigerode

10. OBSERVED RESULTS OF BOMBING: (Circle One) GOOD (FAIR) POOR NIL

11. FLAK:

TIME	PLACE	ALTITUDE	Intense	Moderate	Meager	COLOR	LOCATION BURSTS IN RELATION TO A/C
	Ruhr Valley			1	1		
	Liege				1		

12. WEATHER OVER TARGET _7/10 cover over Primary._

13. DAMAGE TO OUR A/C _Oxygen system, No. 3 gas tank,_
Elevator damaged - 20 flak holes.
Major damage. Radio compass ru...

14. FLYING EQUIPMENT
Not enough gloves to go around.

15. TECHNICAL FAILURES _No_

DE........... ...ER EXECUTIVE ORDER 12356, Sect.
By _____, _____ NARA, Date _____   745005

STAND REC GR 18 BOX N39 T-962 379ᵗʰ BOMB GP FO 288, HALBERSTADT/WERNIGERODE 22 FEB 44
#9828 STREIT

16. CREW OBSERVATIONS AND UNUSUAL TACTICS (Aerial Bombs, Rockets, etc.)
Rockets

TIME____PLACE_____HEIGHT_____COMMENTS___
shot as us from FW190 or ME109. This ship
shot both rocket and about 20 rounds
of 20 mm. They shot a continuous burst
An individual formation without aiming at an
TIME____PLACE_____HEIGHT_____COMMENTS___
individual ship. They sprayed the
formation. Mass deflection shot attack.

TIME 122 PLACE STLS- 0600E HIGHT_____ COMMENTS a/c 41510
Lt McCall. Hit by fighter. Wing fire on #3
engine. Plane under control.
a/c 028 Capt Simons ship. Bombay on fire and
plane beat up. -   6 to 8 B-17s down.

17. CREW SUGGESTIONS
Do not want to be taken over
flak in Ruhr Valley.

18. CASUALTIES: (Give name, position in A/C, type of injury and cause)_____
S/Sgt Snell wounded in left shoulder.

Time 1815   Interrogating Officer B H. Fuler

DO X 1550 379th ☒G

CONFIDENTIAL

GROUP 379th
SQUADRON 524th

MISSING: DATE February 22, 1944
PLACE Wernigerode, Germany
CIRCUMSTANCES Halberstadt-Wernigerode

A/C 42-31028 COMBAT CROSS MISSING IN ACTION

STATUS	NAME	RANK	A.S.N.	POSITION	HOME ADDRESS	REMARKS
Pilot	Harry M. Slevca	1st Lt.	O-795641	Pilot	Long Island, New York	
Co-Pilot	John H. McKim	1st Lt.	O-680736	Co-Pilot	Newburgh, Texas	
Navigator	Robert W. Jones	2nd Lt.	O-687855	Navigator	Norfolk, Virginia	
Bombardier	William (NMI) Bogin, Jr.	1st Lt.	O-676050	Bombardier	Cranbury, New Jersey	
Radio Gunner	Olin F. A. Malone	T/Sgt.	10540881	Radio Gun	Dorsey, Pennsylvania	
Aerial Gunner	James F. Falling	T/Sgt.	33335824	Top Turret	Denby, Pennsylvania	
Aerial Gunner	Robert W. Till	S/Sgt.	14018440	Ball Turret		
Aerial Gunner	Leo S. Barnowski	S/Sgt.	32501635	Left Waist	Floral Park, New York	
Aerial Gunner	Raymond K. Walder, Jr.	S/Sgt.	32390949	Tail Gun	Buffalo, New York	

At about 1255 hrs at 5145-0521 E/P this was apparently hit by flak and the bombay section caught on fire. The pilot turned away from the formation.

379th ☒G

GROUP 379th
SQUADRON 524th

MISSING: DATE 22 February, 1944
PLACE Wernigerode, Germany
CIRCUMSTANCES Halberstadt-Wernigerode

A/C 42-31510 COMBAT CROSS MISSING IN ACTION

STATUS	NAME	RANK	A.S.M.	POSITION	HOME ADDRESS	REMARKS
Pilot	Donald P. McCall	1st Lt.	O-802872	Pilot	Johnstown, Pennsylvania	
Co-Pilot	Charles L. Guncy	2nd Lt.	O-748512	Co-Pilot	Buffalo, New York	
Bombardier	Leo (NMI) Williams	2nd Lt.	O-682035	Bombardier	Houston, Texas	
Aerial Gunner	Thomas S. Geary	Sgt.	32472082	Nose Gun	Woodhaven, New York	
Radio Gunner	John P. Dutskirch	T/Sgt.	19117913	Radio Gun	Seattle, Washington	
Aerial Gunner	Fisk, James E.	S/Sgt.	35174107	Top Turret	Indianapolis, Indiana	
Aerial Gunner	Eugene F. Blevly	S/Sgt.	36902913	Ball Turret	Kort Park, Montana	
Aerial Gunner	George (NMI) Falling	S/Sgt.	13097185	Right Waist	Chico, California	
Aerial Gunner	Joseph F. Janelos	S/Sgt.	34035547	Left Waist	Wallington, New York	

At 1237 hrs at 5145-0600N E/P the right wing and the #1 engine were on fire. The plane left the formation and went down under control. No chutes were seen. Pilot L. W. Williams S. W. Wms (B/3E3) Lt. Co/Pil-Geo. Wickly

DECLASSIFIED PER EXF "IVL ~~~~~ ~~~~, Section J..,
By VSW/WL _____ NARA, Date 03-03-86

FRC   GP 18   Box 1540   379ᵗᴴ BG

6 MAR 44
FO 296
#1 To BERLIN

HEADQUARTERS   (D-A-1)
379TH BOMBARDMENT GROUP (H) AAF
Office of the Intelligence Officer

A.A.F. Station #117,
6 March 1944.

SUBJECT: Crews' Tactical Suggestions.

TO   :

1. Lt. Col. Robert S. Kittel, leader of the 41st Combat Wing states,
"The Pff ship with the equipment in place of the ball turret makes an
excellent lead ship. Visual run was not made on the Primary Target because
of four things. Could not fly over the briefed IP because of the two Combat
Wings ahead of us. The weather was questionable for a visual run but had
there been a lead bombardier who was used to working with the lead navigator and lead pilot in the leading ship, it is this Officer's belief that
a successful visual run could have been made on the Primary Target. There
was a cloud bank approximately three miles east of our target on right
angles to the course on which we approached the IP. East of this cloud
bank the cloud coverage was five to seven/tenths. Because we were forced
to over-shoot the IP, we could not see the target until it was too late to
bomb it."

2. T/Sgt. Leo A. Chruby, radio-gunner, "Take radio hatch out. You
can't see out."

N. N. NORGREN,
Major, Air Corps,
Group S-2 Officer.

Above: 45. A report from the 379th, concerning the first mission to Berlin, March 6,
1944, includes a tactical suggestion from *Penny Ante*'s radio-gunner, Chruby.

Opposite: 46. These documents list the missing in action from the Halberstadt
mission. The top form lists the crew members of *Mojo*, which include pilot Harry
Simons and copilot John 'Tex' Robins. The bottom form lists McCall and Gurney as
prisoners of war.

All Combat Missions Flown By

Pitts, Jesse R

Show Personal Profile

Crew Photo

Date:	Saturday, December 11, 1943	City:	Emden	Country:	Germany
Group Mission No:	47		Target: Port Area		

Date:	Monday, December 13, 1943	City:	Bremen	Country:	Germany
Group Mission No:	48		Target: Port Area		

Date:	Friday, December 24, 1943	City:	Cueschart / Beauvoir	Country:	France
Group Mission No:	52		Target: Fly-bomb Sites		

Date:	Thursday, December 30, 1943	City:	Ludwigshafen	Country:	Germany
Group Mission No:	53		Target: Chemical Works		

Date:	Tuesday, January 04, 1944	City:	Kiel	Country:	Germany
Group Mission No:	55		Target: Port Facilities		

Date:	Wednesday, January 05, 1944	City:	Kiel	Country:	Germany
Group Mission No:	56		Target: Port Facilities		

Date:	Tuesday, January 11, 1944	City:	Oschersleben	Country:	Germany
Group Mission No:	58		Target: Fighter Aircraft Assembly Plant		

Date:	Friday, January 14, 1944	City:	Cueschart	Country:	France
Group Mission No:	59		Target: Fly Bomb Site		

Date:	Saturday, January 29, 1944	City:	Frankfurt	Country:	Germany
Group Mission No:	61		Target: Engine Component Plant		

Date:	Sunday, January 30, 1944	City:	Brunswick	Country:	Germany
Group Mission No:	62		Target: Aircraft Parts - Steel Plant		

Date:	Thursday, February 03, 1944	City:	Wilhelmshaven	Country:	Germany
Group Mission No:	63		Target: Shipbuilding		

Date:	Friday, February 04, 1944	City:	Frankfurt	Country:	Germany
Group Mission No:	64		Target: Engine Component Plants		

Date:	Sunday, February 06, 1944	City:	Chateaudun	Country:	France
Group Mission No:	66		Target: Airdrome		

Date:	Friday, February 11, 1944	City:	Frankfurt	Country:	Germany
Group Mission No:	68	Target:	Engine Components Plant		

Date:	Sunday, February 20, 1944	City:	Leipzig / Bernburg	Country:	Germany
Group Mission No:	69	Target:	Aircraft Factory and Depot		

Date:	Monday, February 21, 1944	City:	Quakenbruck / Bramsche	Country:	Germany
Group Mission No:	70	Target:	Aircraft Factory		

Date:	Tuesday, February 22, 1944	City:	Halberstadt	Country:	Germany
Group Mission No:	71	Target:	Aircraft Factory		

Date:	Thursday, February 24, 1944	City:	Schweinfurt	Country:	Germany
Group Mission No:	72	Target:	Ball Bearing Plant		

Date:	Friday, February 25, 1944	City:	Augsburg / Stuttgart	Country:	Germany
Group Mission No:	73	Target:	Aircraft Engine Parts Plant		

Date:	Monday, February 28, 1944	City:	Vacqueriette	Country:	France
Group Mission No:	74	Target:	Fly-bomb Sites		

Date:	Thursday, March 02, 1944	City:	Frankfurt	Country:	Germany
Group Mission No:	75	Target:	Engine Component Plant		

Date:	Friday, March 03, 1944	City:	Erkner	Country:	Germany
Group Mission No:	76	Target:	Ball Bearing Plant		

Date:	Saturday, March 04, 1944	City:	Aachen	Country:	Germany
Group Mission No:	77	Target:	Military Storage		

Date:	Monday, March 06, 1944	City:	Berlin	Country:	Germany
Group Mission No:	78	Target:	Ball Bearing Plant		

Date:	Wednesday, March 08, 1944	City:	Erkner	Country:	Germany
Group Mission No:	79	Target:	Ball Bearing Plant		

Date:	Thursday, March 09, 1944	City:	Berlin	Country:	Germany
Group Mission No:	80	Target:	Ball Bearing Plant		

Show Crew | Audio Clip | Video Clip | Mission Map | View Printout | Close This Form

Opposite and above: 47 and 48. Courtesy of Arlo Bartsch, Military Heritage Database.

49. *Penny Ante*'s crew, 5 March 1944, the day before the Berlin raid. Standing, left to right: Streit, Pitts, Marcott, Kundin, Finicle. First row: Boyovitch, Chruby, Williams, Owens, Snell.

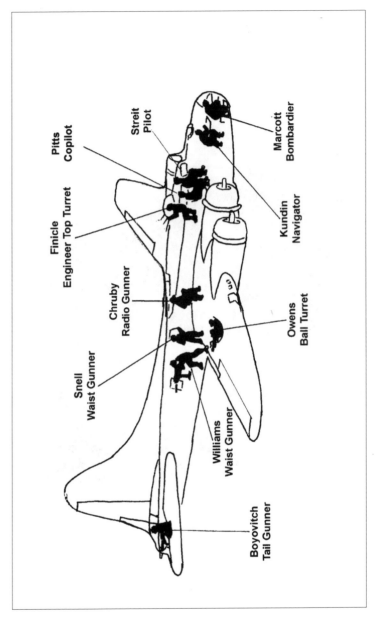

50. Respective positions of crew members inside *Penny Ante*, a B-17 F.

51. Jesse Pitts, Paris, 1986. (Allard, *Le Point*)

BIBLIOGRAPHY

Anderson, Clarence E. 'Bud', *To Fly and Fight* (New York: St Martin's Press, 1990).

Bendiner, Elmer, *The Fall of Fortresses* (New York: G.P. Putnam's Sons, 1980).

Caidin, Martin, *Black Thursday* (New York: E.P. Dutton, 1960).

Carré, Ray, *Maximum Effort* (Burbank, California: National Literary Guild, 1984).

Cassens, Kenneth H., *Screwball Express* (Paducah, Kentucky: Turner Publishing Co., 1992).

Chennault, Claire Lee, *Way of a Fighter* (New York: G.P. Putnam's Sons, 1949).

Corner, John, *Combat Crew* (New York: Pocket Book, 1989).

Cooper, Robert Floyd, *Serenade to the Blue Lady* (Fort Bragg, California: Cypress House, 1993).

Craven, Wesley Frank, and Cate, James Lea, *The Army Air Force in World War II* Volumes I and II (Chicago: The University of Chicago Press, 1949).

Doolittle, James H., *I Could Never Be So Lucky Again* (New York: Bantam Books, 1991).

Ethell, Jeffrey L., *Target: Berlin* (London: Jane's Publishing, 1981).

Frankhouser, Frank, *World War II Odyssey* (Bedford, Virginia: Hamilton's, 1997).

Freeman, Roger A., *The Mighty Eighth War Diary* (London: Arms and Armour Press, 1990).

Fussel, Paul, *Wartime* (New York: Oxford University Press, 1989).

Hillary, Richard, *Falling Through Space* (London: Reynal & Hitchcock, 1965).

Jablonski, Edward, *Flying Fortress* (New York: Doubleday & Company, 1965).

Kaplan, Philip, and Smith, Rex Alan, *One Last Look* (New York: Abbeville Press, 1983).

Keegan, John, *The Second World War* (New York: Viking, 1989).

Knoke, Heinz, *I Flew for the Führer* (England: Morley Books, 1972).

Kuhl, George C., *Wrong Place! Wrong Time!* (Atglen, Pennsylvania: Schiffer Publishing Ltd, 1993).

Levine, Alan J., *The Strategic Bombing of Germany, 1940-1945* (Wesport, Connecticut: Preager, 1992).

Lind, Les, *War in the Blue – A Remembrance* (Tallahassee, Florida: 1995).

Merrill, Sandra D., *Donald's Story* (Berlin, Maryland: Tebidine, 1996).

Novey, Jack, *The Cold Blue Sky: a B-17 Gunner in World War Two* (Charlottesville, Virginia: Howell Press, 1997).

Rudel, Hans Ulrich, *Stuka Pilot* (New York: Ballantine, 1958).

Schaffer, Ronald, *Wings of Judgment* (Oxford: Oxford University Press, 1985).

Shades of Kimbolton: A Narrative of the 379th Bombardment Group (H) (San Angelo, Texas: Newsfoto Publishing Co., 1982).

Smith, Dale O., *Screaming Eagle: The Memoirs of a B-17 Group Commander* (New York: Dell, 1990).

Thixton, Marshall J., Moffat, George E., and O'Neil, John J., *Bombs Away by Pathfinders of the Eighth Air Force* (Trumbull, Connecticut: FNP Military Division, 1998).

Townsend, Peter, *Duel of Eagles* (New York: Simon and Schuster, 1971).

Betz, Frank I. and Cassens, Kenneth H. ed., *379th Bombardment Group (H) Anthology*, Volumes I and II (Paducah, Kentucky: Turner Publishing Company, 2000).

Wells, Mark K. *Courage and Warfare* (London: Frank Cass, 1995).

Woolnough, John H. ed., *Stories of the Eighth* (Hollywood, Florida: The 8th AF News, 1983).

– *The 8th Air Force Album* (Hollywood, Florida: The 8th AF News, 1978).

INDEX

If you are interested in purchasing other books published by Tempus, or in case you have difficulty finding any Tempus books in your local bookshop, you can also place orders directly through our website.

www.tempus-publishing.com